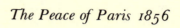

The Peace of Paris 1856

The Peace of Paris *1856*

Studies in War, Diplomacy, and Peacemaking

———◆———

Winfried Baumgart

Translated by

Ann Pottinger Saab

ABC-Clio

Santa Barbara, California   Oxford, England

Library of Congress Cataloging in Publication Data

Baumgart, Winfried.
    The Peace of Paris 1856.

    Translation of Der Friede von Paris 1856.
    Bibliography: p. 213.
    Includes index.
    1. Paris, Declaration of, 1856. 2. Crimean War,
1853–1856. I. Title.
DK215.B3513   947'.073   80–39532
ISBN 0–87436–309–8

*Copy edited by Paulette A. Wamego. Indexed by Sasha Newborn. Composed in VIP
Baskerville by McAdams Type of Santa Barbara. Printed and bound by BookCrafters of
Chelsea, Michigan. Cover and text designed by Tom Reeg.*

ABC-Clio, Inc.
Riviera Campus
2040 Alameda Padre Serra, Box 4397
Santa Barbara, California 93103

Clio Press Ltd.
Woodside House, Hinksey Hill
Oxford, OX1 5BE, England

Manufactured in the United States of America

To my teacher

Abbreviations

AGKK	Akten zur Geschichte des Krimkriegs
BGSA	Bayerisches Geheimes Staatsarchiv
f.	folio, page
GLA	Generallandesarchiv
HHSA	Haus-, Hof- und Staatsarchiv
PA	Politisches Archiv
v	verso, reverse side of a page

Contents

Translator's Preface

FOR MANY YEARS, the Crimean War has suffered the image of a "cute" little war. The layman, if he has heard of it at all, remembers the charge of the Light Brigade and the work of Florence Nightingale. Those whose historical grounding runs a little deeper may recall that it was the first war to be covered by news correspondents at the front, and the first war to be photographed. But this seeming modernity is belied by the scenes that emerge of heavily bearded generals, fantastically garbed başi-bozuks, and appalling equipment, especially in the sanitary services. The Crimean War appears as the last of the old-style cabinet wars, rather than the first war of modern times.

Serious scholarly interpretations of the origins and course of the war have tended to reinforce uninformed notions. A long tradition of historiographical writing, starting with contemporaries and reinforced by major twentieth-century surveys, such as J. A. R. Marriott's, has seen the Crimean War as the product of a long "chain of 'bluffs and blunders.' " The immediate source of the war, the Holy Places question, with its intricate disputes over keys and the silver star, rights of access to the churches and the altar furnishings to be displayed, is difficult for modern, secular, Western scholars to treat without a curl of the lip, unless some deeper significance is read into it. And there were so many occasions (most notably the Vienna Note negotiations of the summer of 1853 and the Vienna Conference of the spring of 1855) when it seemed likely that war could be averted or stopped in mid-course. Surely a little more effort, a little more urgency in the attempts to get everyone together, could have solved the problem. The many personal shortcomings which have been documented play into this: if only Brunnov had been a little more forthright, Buol a little more decisive, Stratford de Redcliffe a little less imperious! The "if onlys" are so numerous and so tantalizing that when they have all been expounded, an almost overwhelming impression emerges that the Crimean War after all was accidental and hence avoidable.

All of this makes it hard to justify studying the Crimean War at any length as a major field of historical concentration. "Bluffs and blunders," if elevated to a cosmic principle, may be an appropriate, indeed an ideal, subject for the tragedian or the moralist; they do not attract the historian, interested in examining trends more particular to, and hence more revealing of, a specific historical period.

Nonetheless, in the mid-twentieth century, a number of attempts have been made to reassess the Crimean War and to revive it as an object of serious scholarly study. Although similar ideas can be traced back to the war itself, and different interpretations often coexist in the same works, for the sake of clarity these efforts can be roughly classified into two broad categories. One approach, probably the earlier to achieve a major impact, emphasizes the importance of the Eastern Question and sees the war as part of a continuing Anglo-Russian confrontation with the goal of worldwide hegemony. England's political stakes are explored by Temperley and his followers; the economic issues are analyzed by Puryear. Another approach, prominent a little later, claims in A. J. P. Taylor's phrase, that "the real stake in the Crimean War . . . was central Europe." In this view, the Crimean War becomes locked into the sequence of power shifts in central Europe which began with the revolutions of 1848 and ended with the proclamation of the German Empire in 1871.

Winfried Baumgart's study builds on both these traditions in Crimean War revision and goes beyond them. With a comprehensiveness which is characteristic of his painstaking and thorough approach, he manages to deal in some depth with a wide range of problems, which have been treated more exhaustively in monographs and documentary collections in a variety of languages, including Swedish and Rumanian. Yet he does this with engaging modesty; despite or perhaps because of his own extensive researches into the archives most readily available to him (in Germany and Austria), he is always aware of the many documentary riches yet to be exploited and he never claims that his work is anything more than a progress report.

In a sense, a very good sense, this is true: *The Peace of Paris* is an excellent place for the student to go for a digest of the latest thinking and writing on almost all the major problems of mid-nineteenth-century European history, as they played into and were focused by the war and the peace. But Baumgart's study transcends the category of summary in that it is also an enormously suggestive invitation to further inquiry. Baumgart reevaluates the role of every major power and concludes with an important new assessment of the war as a whole.

Much of Baumgart's attention, and his most original research, is devoted to Austria. In contrast to earlier accounts, such as Friedjung's classic narrative, and in keeping with recent revisionist writing, Baumgart rates the policy of Buol, the Austrian foreign minister, very favorably. He argues that Buol did not follow an indecisive "seesaw diplomacy" but really intended to balance between the eastern and western blocks. This position was founded on a perception, which was generally shared in Vienna, of Austria's weakness in the aftermath of 1848, particularly in the financial sphere. Buol is given high marks for refusing to yield to the seductions of territorial annexations in Moldavia and Wallachia, which tempted the Austrian generals throughout the war; the chief fault attributed to him is his failure to oppose effectively the demand at the peace conference for the cession from Russia of a strip of land in Bessarabia. This ill-advised claim brought Austria no real military advantage and won her much bad feeling, particularly in St. Petersburg. But here Baumgart feels that Buol's mistake is to be attributed to his isolation in the imperial councils; not strong enough to defeat the proposal in Vienna, he at least refused to urge the conditions, in all their original stringency, at Paris. The episode contributed to Austria's increasing isolation in Europe, a result which is generally seen as the most disastrous outcome of Buol's diplomacy; but in Baumgart's evaluation, this negative aspect, which has been exaggerated in any case, recedes behind the positive accomplishment of ending the war.

This latter attainment assumes especially large proportions because Baumgart insists that the war, at least after the fall of Sevastopol, was about to assume new dimensions—those of a world war—which would have made it the crucible for all Europe's smoldering nationalisms. His assessment of French policy recapitulates much recent work on Napoleon III's aims and intentions: Baumgart emphasizes the ideological underpinning to the restless search for French hegemony through a redrawing of the boundaries laid down by the Vienna settlement. This objective, an unmistakable factor in Napoleon's twists and turns down to his forced abdication in 1870, is often interpreted in terms purely of power politics, a game which Napoleon is supposed to have played avidly, but badly. Baumgart follows the Guerard tradition, which has been amplified by later scholars, in believing that Napoleon III took his principle of nationalities seriously and was defeated not so much by lack of diplomatic finesse as by the inherent difficulty of the task.

But in contrast to most historians, Baumgart asserts that the real visionary among the European leaders of 1856 was not Napoleon III but Palmerston. Although he does not go as far as Paul Schroeder in reading back Whig ideology into the origins and early years of the war, he does maintain that after the fall of Sevastopol, when England's other war aims had been essentially won, the ideological factors which had always swayed the British public became paramount in the prime minister's mind also. Baumgart's standpoint leads him to a comparatively harsh judgment of English diplomacy in general and Palmerston in particular: although his comments are milder than some of Schroeder's barbs, he does offer a thorough-going critique of the interpretation current in many British sources, which sees the British government as selflessly engaged in performing the service to Europe of restraining Russian ambitions which threatened the continental equilibrium. Baumgart sees the confrontation between the two world powers as an imperial and essentially amoral conflict, rather than as a kind of moral crusade, in which right was clearly on the side of the British lion.

Yet despite the insistence on confrontation, it is Russia's weakness that emerges most sharply from Baumgart's account. To be sure, historians of Russia have stressed the connection between the wartime defeat and the later reform movement, particularly the abolition of serfdom. But diplomatic historians, whether they came down for Nicholas I or against him, have implied that he was a dominant figure. It matters relatively little whether Nicholas is seen as an evil genius or a European gentleman; in either case, he is by implication the arbiter of European international relations. Much of this distortion springs from the fact that the story of the war is usually written from the beginning forwards, working from the basis of Nicholas's seeming hegemony in the Europe of 1849. By telling the story in effect backwards, with an eye throughout for the collapse in 1856, Baumgart achieves a juster evaluation of Russia's position before and during the war, which was far less solid than it seemed. Since Baumgart wrote, John Curtiss's important new study, *Russia's Crimean War,* based on extensive research in Russian archives, has amplified this point.

In addition to these revisionary treatments of the policies of the European great powers most heavily involved in the war, Baumgart has much interesting light to shed on the diplomacy of states which were less important or less deeply affected. His discussion of the Ottoman Empire affords a masterly presentation of much neglected and technical, but highly significant material. He is one of the few to integrate into the picture of European politics the important finding of contemporary Ottomanists that the Ottoman Empire was engaged in a serious and by no means hopeless process of modernization. In so doing, he corrects the legend of irremediable barbarism and corruption which many European historians have borrowed uncritically from disgruntled late-nineteenth-century observers. By implication, he casts more blame than usual for the fall of the Ottoman Empire on European interference. And he shows persuasively that the question of the Russian protectorate over the Greek Orthodox inhabitants of the empire, far from resting on a mere verbal quibble or an inconvenient and controversial tradition, involved vital divergences of opinion on how the empire was to structure its reforms, on which people within the empire, as well as people outside, were divided.

Baumgart also produces fascinating short evaluations of the diplomacy of Sardinia and Prussia. In line with recent Italian scholarship, he discounts Cavour's contribution and denies that Cavour created the prerequisites for his later successful unification of Italy in 1859 to 1861./ Indeed, if the inevitable comparison between Sardinian and Prussian diplomacy must be made, Baumgart feels that the Prussians were in fact the more capable and forehanded. That the Prussians made such a success of a basically negative role, is further evidence to him of the general overestimation of the value of the Italians' participation.

/All these individual reassessments add up, in Baumgart's skillful hands, to a reevaluation of the place of the war and the peace, taken as a whole, in European history. Although Baumgart has a fine eye for irony, he has substantially modified the "bluffs and blunders" theme by demonstrating that the Crimean War sprang from causes which went to the roots of tension in nineteenth-century Europe./ From this vantage point, he is able to state convincingly that the accomplishment of the peace congress at Paris, in providing a compromise acceptable enough to postpone the holocaust for another sixty-odd years, was one of the most considerable achievements in the annals of international congresses, qualifying the Paris meeting to figure along with Westphalia or Utrecht in the annals of peacemaking and peacekeeping. The Crimean War is accordingly locked into the prehistory of 1914, and in the words of Fritz T. Epstein, the major question becomes not "Why did World War I break out in 1914?" but rather "Why did it not break out earlier?"

Important historical revisions usually depend on at least one of two prerequisites. In some instances, the stimulus has come from the discovery of unknown or unutilized primary source materials. Baumgart has benefitted by his exploitation of German and Austrian archival sources. But no one knows better than he how much documentary material still exists behind political or linguistic barriers that make broad access and informed discussion difficult in the foreseeable future. At least, a number of scholars in different countries are at work on pieces of the story, in line with their particular interests and competencies.

In the absence on a large scale of this kind of revisionist potential, Baumgart's work depends on another prerequisite for originality, namely a shift in philosophical point of view. Leopold von Ranke taught his disciples to write history "as it actually happened." Laying aside the many intellectual difficulties involved in determining "actuality," the assumption that certain facts are given can shade into a kind of determinism; when we emphasize that history happened this way and no other, we are not far from implying that history must happen this way and no other. The Marxists have made this philosophical jump and are prepared to support a deterministic view of history. It is not surprising that a young historian working on the frontier with the Marxist world should have produced a highly sophisticated antideterministic system. Baumgart tells us in his preface that it is the historian's job to relive history as potential and to present what might have happened as well as what in fact did happen. He is able to use this technique to supply an extraordinary richness to his narrative; it enables him to sketch in many plans, hopes, and aspirations which are too "iffy" to pass muster with many more conventional historians, but which form an indispensable part of the atmosphere of the time.

Baumgart reveals some leanings towards the "primacy of domestic policy" as it has been practiced by many diplomatic historians since A. J. Mayer's ground-breaking works on the First World War. This approach is implicit in the link Baumgart forges between the Crimean War and the First World War. In a strictly diplomatic sense, the Crimean War does not qualify as part of the prehistory of the First World War, as do the First and Second Moroccan crises, or even the war-in-sight crises of Bismarck's post-1870 diplomacy. The Crimean War, fought before the unification of Italy and the unification of Germany and before the acquisition of most of the Second British and French overseas empires, belongs to a significantly different diplomatic frame. What is similar, however, is the nature of the domestic problems, and particularly the related problems of popular sovereignty and ethnic identity.

Finally, Baumgart breaks new ground in his analytical and topical organization. Classical diplomatic historians have usually presented their material in terms of the exchange of diplomatic notes and despatches. Such a procedure was justifiable when politics was considered to be of primary importance and people were thought to be rational actors with a more or less clear conscious grasp of their own motives. As other factors—economic, military, psychological, cultural, to name only a few—have assumed more importance, this sort of two-dimensional narrative has come to seem less and less satisfactory. But it requires a virtuoso performance to reconcile a topical approach with at least the necessary minimum of forward narrative movement. This achievement Baumgart has brought off very well.

In short, *The Peace of Paris* is a deceptively simple little book. Purporting to be a monographic study of the peacemaking process, it deserves to be read for its broad insights into many problems, foreign and domestic, of mid-nineteenth-century history, for its comprehensive summaries of the latest research in many languages, for its suggestive new interpretations, which are certain to stimulate discussion and further research, and finally, as a paradigm for thinking and writing about diplomatic history.

Ann Pottinger Saab
University of North Carolina
at Greenboro

Author's Preface

THE CRIMEAN WAR cannot be explained by a neat formula. Like all the struggles for hegemony of sixteenth- to twentieth-century Europe, it contains no conspicuous feature dominating other traits. Only through comprehensive study can one adequately, though not exhaustively, examine and interpret it. It is legitimate to cut through the chaos of details by focusing on a single cause, event, or consequence. But this unavoidable stage in analysis should be only preliminary to an inclusive interpretation. Historians are far from that ideal, despite intense contemporary discussion, followed by decades of scholarly debate and many valuable revisionist insights. Indeed, interest in the Crimean War, from the moment the first Russian soldier crossed the Pruth until today, has its own history, now over a century old, which itself merits scholarly research.

The Crimean War is one of those periodic convulsions typical of Europe since Charles V in which one great power tried to dominate and was pushed back by the other powers. The Russian colossus, at once feared, admired, and relied upon by the rest of Europe because of its forty-year role as policeman, made a final bid for hegemony through acquiring the inheritance of the "sick man on the Bosporus" only to be frustrated by the interference of the western powers in the name of the "European balance of power." Such an interpretation must immediately be qualified and restricted. Did the autocrat Nicholas I, at the head of his awe-inspiring military machine, consciously strive to dominate the continent by breaching the strategic barrier at the Dardanelles? No interpretation could be farther from the truth. Nicholas, although sincerely committed to the rules of the game prescribed by the European Concert and the treaty system of Vienna, was forced to fight against his original intent.

The same is true of liberal Britain; a generation of British historians adopted Aberdeen and Clarendon's phrase "drift towards war"[1] to describe the role Britain played, or found herself playing, on the eve of war. This phrase reflects an interpretation of the actions of the British government (and the other European chancelleries) as a tragic chain of "bluffs and blunders."

Finally, contrary to a common impression, the same is true of France under Napoleon III's plebiscitary Caesarism. It would be deceptively simple to assert that Napoleon seized the opportunity provided by this international crisis to divert attention from difficulties at home. Intervention was neither a golden opportunity nor a masterly resolve. Napoleon hesitated for a long time and carefully calculated the dangers and potential sacrifices of war.

Searching the long chain of causes of the war yields as the crucial link that made war inevitable for the western powers the massacre of Sinope of 30 November 1853, in which in a few short hours, three thousand Ottoman sailors, shot by Russian cannon, found a watery grave in the Black Sea. For both western nations, the incident provided the excuse for war. As soon as this intrinsically legitimate act of war was reported, public opinion in western Europe (especially Britain), already at the flood, suddenly burst and spilled over all the dams laboriously contrived over a period of months by the European diplomats meeting at Vienna.

From another perspective, the Crimean War can be seen as a link in the long chain of Russo-Turkish wars starting under Peter the Great and ending only in our own century, and as a violent attack of the festering Eastern Question. In contrast to the Ottoman wars of the preceding century, this nineteenth-century struggle assumed a primarily international character; that is, the European Concert was called into play as soon as the first shot was fired in the Balkans. Related to this is the fact that in the nineteenth century after the French Revolution, national feeling among the ethnic groups of the Ottoman Balkans became a factor in the complex Eastern Question.

But despite the internationalization of the Eastern Question in the nineteenth century, and despite its "inflammation" by virulent nationalism, military conflict between the Russian colossus and the enfeebled Ottoman Empire did not automatically involve the other powers. The intensification of the Eastern Question does not in itself explain the Crimean War: the previous Russo-Turkish war during 1827 to 1828, and the subsequent one, in 1877, did not turn into European wars. The importance of public opinion, already mentioned, suggests another cause: a Russophobia reaching back to the 1830s which fed on the role of the Tsar as the policeman of Europe, an image reinforced by the suppression of the Polish Revolution, the warning of Unkiar-Skelessi, the stamping out of the Hungarian Revolution, and the rebuke to Prussia at Olmütz.

This hostility to Russia, highly influential in mid-century and paralleled to some extent by Slavophilism on the Russian side, implies that the previously accepted interpretation of the Crimean War as a cabinet war is one-sided. Although apparently justifiable on the basis of the purely external sequence of military events, occurring at first sight on the isolated periphery of the tsarist empire and ended by a seemingly well-timed diplomatic demarche, the Austrian ultimatum of December 1855, this perspective conceals the strategic planning of the two belligerents, who actively considered other fronts, and also discounts many strategems of later total war that were available to both, from use of economic weapons to arousal of foreign ethnic groups in the participating multinational empires. In the end, the Crimean War did not become a world war because, contrary to the hitherto accepted interpretation, the Austrian emperor and his foreign minister acted responsibly and successfully avoided entering the war, which would then have encompassed the whole of Europe and might have toppled the Hapsburg empire, and because Alexander II and his advisers wisely decided after the defeat at Sevastopol to break off a struggle which Russia had certainly not yet lost.

Significant work has been done in the last few years on the causes and diplomacy of the war, which busied even the smallest European chancelleries. But relatively little attention has been paid to the interplay between the war and the belligerents' domestic circumstances or to the peace negotiations and their many ramifications because historians have concentrated on searching, as with the First World War, farther and farther into the past for war origins. Furthermore, the publishing of sources, a lifetime's work, has hardly started. Finally, historians have seemed to agree on the consequences of the war, in contrast to the origins; but this consensus should be scrutinized more sharply.

The Crimean War and the Peace Treaty of Paris are usually regarded as a turning point in nineteenth-century international relations. They closed four decades of repose in Europe during which a multitude of international crises were dammed up in the name of legitimacy and the Holy Alliance. The Crimean War and the peace of Paris ended the defensive alliances of this period, prized by a consciously conformist generation of statesmen; instead of following a shared European idea of law and order, the new generation, Gorchakov, Cavour, and Bismarck, acted opportunistically according to national interests and infused their alliances with a corresponding aggressiveness. A system of order was demolished and a period of anarchy began.

Such a stark contrast between the periods before and after 1856 is seductive and can be backed up by the actual course of history, but it represents an interpretation based on the hindsight of a historian who orients himself solely to concrete events and refuses to allow the period under consideration to assume an existence of its own with all its "agonizing choices."[2]

Students of international law assess the peace of Paris more positively than do historians in general. The Crimean War and the Paris Peace

Congress are an important source of precedents, contributing decisively to classical international law in the nineteenth century and hence to the ordering of international relations. The Paris Congress ranks among the great peace congresses from Westphalia in 1648 to Berlin in 1878. Certainly there is a difference: in the beginning, it was not organized to resolve European conflicts in their entirety, but was simply dedicated to handling one overriding problem, the Eastern Question. But during the meeting itself, the gathering was transformed into an ambitious congress formulating binding international regulations. Thus it contributed to the evolution of plans for peacekeeping, whose milestones include Richelieu's proposal for collective security,[3] the Barrier system established at Utrecht, the theme of eternal peace running through the Enlightenment, and the international congresses of the nineteenth century.

The Crimean War apparently buried the Holy Alliance, that unique combination of European powers designed to preserve peace permanently after the cataclysm of the revolutionary and Napoleonic periods; its passage was signaled for contemporary statesmen by the December Treaty of 1854, which the French greeted with great joy and the Russians with genuine anxiety. But the alliance lived on, as its historian Bourquin has emphasized, in the European Concert of the second half of the nineteenth century. As late as 1914, the Concert of Europe remained intermittently active; although possessing no legal force, it commanded political respect and averted war on numerous occasions. The Paris Peace Congress of 1856, despite many characteristics destructive of European order, nonetheless demonstrated the shared goals and world view of its members. In the twentieth century, due to the division of the world into political and ideological blocks, we no longer have the prerequisites for a congress in the style of the nineteenth century. Versailles 1919, in contrast to Paris 1856, abdicated before the enormous task of restoring world harmony.

Using the relatively little-known Paris Peace Congress as an illustration, the following little study will examine the interactions between war-making, diplomacy, domestic developments, economic and commercial relations, and peacekeeping efforts in the mid-nineteenth century. The inquiry will be a reflective quest for motives rather than an analysis of events, and a preliminary study rather than the comprehensive treatment which is eventually desirable, since as yet, many of the sources remain to be discovered. The guiding methodological principle has been to understand the events which actually occurred as only one possible sequence among many, and to investigate history as an inner tension between freedom and necessity, in its pluralistic character.

While the book was in production, Paul W. Schroeder's manuscript *Austria, Great Britain and the Crimean War: The Destruction of the European Concert,* a work based on wide archival research, came into my hands. The final chapter treats the Paris Peace Congress. In spite of the different aim of Schroeder's research and his somewhat different source material, I essentially agree with his evaluation of British and Austrian policy—an evaluation which conflicts at various points with the interpretations hitherto accepted. The criticism of British policy during the Crimean War, seen by Schroeder as the product of the "Whig ideology" put forth by Palmerston and Clarendon, is somewhat harsher than that expressed here. The fact that, working independently on the same sources, we arrived at the same view of Austria's fundamental motives confirms my own view that we can say good-by to the prevailing interpretation of the Austrian "seesaw" policy, generally considered the worst possible choice Austria could have made, both in the way it was implemented and in the results it achieved. One or another of my questions may be answered, at least in part, by the information Schroeder has collected.

I dedicate this work to my teacher, Konrad Repgen, who gave me unusual freedom to pursue my scholarly development during a series of unforgettable formative years. No "reforms" in the "structure" of our German universities, no matter how well intentioned and well executed (and there is much more destructive than constructive in the present changes), could ever create the conditions for teaching and doing research that sprang naturally from the relations between me and my teacher—rigorously directed towards the subject, not towards dogmas, philosophies, or "reform models," disciplined and yet deeply happy. I wrote and finished this work knowing that, in the contemporary intellectual disorientation of our universities, I am one of the last who can be unreservedly proud of such a relationship, now impossible to restore.

Winfried Baumgart
Johannes Gutenberg University
Mainz

NOTES

Full citations appear in the bibliography.

1. Cf., e.g., J. B. Conacher, *The Aberdeen Coalition 1852–1855*, p. 277. For a new interpretation, based on Turkish documents, see Ann Pottinger Saab, *The Origins of the Crimean Alliance*.

2. Cf. Hans Freyer, *Soziologie als Wirklichkeitswissenschaft*, pp. 196–97.

3. For further reference see Winfried Baumgart, "Die grossen Friedensschlüsse der Neuzeit (1435–1945)," pp. 788–89.

I.   The Road to Peace

The Strategic Situation after the Fall of Sevastopol

THE FALL OF SEVASTOPOL on 8 September 1855 was perceived by contemporaries and later by historians as the turning point in the contest between the great powers. It finally opened the road to peace after previous efforts had failed. Sevastopol, developed since the early nineteenth century as a major sea fortress and powerful naval arsenal, seemed to the western powers to be the symbol of Russian resistance; it was also the jumping-off point for Constantinople, the Ottoman capital, equally vulnerable by sea or by land; and it was, after all, to defend Constantinople, in nineteenth-century Europe a question of the balance of power, that the war had broken out. Once the traditional theatre of Russo-Turkish wars on the lower Danube had been neutralized by an Austrian army of occupation in the summer of 1854, the sea powers' goal became the assault on the mighty Black Sea citadel. Britain was all the more attached to this goal because she could compensate for her weakness on land by exploitation of her naval potential. "Delenda est Sevastopol"—this phrase, used by the British First Lord of the Admiralty in March 1854,[1] expresses the core of Britain's original war aims, which Napoleon III shared.

Considered from a military standpoint, the fall of Sevastopol was not decisive. The fortress lay on the periphery of a peripheral province of the Russian empire. It was defended by a garrison of 130,000 men, a mere fraction of the Russian army, 2 million strong. The other parts were deployed on the offensive in the Caucasus; on observation duty along the long land front from Odessa through Warsaw to the Baltic, to counter possible Austrian intervention and to dampen the Poles' enthusiasm for revolt; on the defensive along the Baltic centered at Petersburg and at the naval fortress of Kronstadt, the Sevastopol of the north; and finally as reserves and militia in the interior. To reach the heart of the empire and force the enemy to his knees in open battle, a broad land invasion would have been necessary; for this the sea powers were inadequate as long as the other two great powers, Austria and Prussia, held themselves aloof. Given the existing military and political situation, there were only two alternatives: either war in the Baltic along the lines used since autumn 1854 in the Black Sea, that is, destruction of the Russian Baltic fleet, the siege of Kronstadt and subsequent capture of Petersburg, or—perhaps as a complement—an extended blockade of Russia's coasts. Either option was eminently favorable to Britain; either would effectively exploit Britain's maritime preponderance and her industrial and commercial superiority. An invasion by land, particularly suited to French interests, would have presupposed removal of certain political obstacles; it implied enlarging the western alliance, above all by Austria, since without Austria the necessary ground troops could not be put into the field.

The fall of Sevastopol did not unequivocally mean peace. Weeks passed before the first promising demarches were made, and months before the decision to negotiate was taken. Meanwhile on both sides planning continued for a new campaign in 1856. These plans give important insights into allied war aims. Since most military studies of the war do not go beyond the fall of Sevastopol and since the relevant military documents have hardly been assessed, one must depend on published sources which are widely scattered. They yield the following rough sketch, which of course will need revision as documents become available.

Thanks to British control of the seas, Russia was like a giant fortress under siege. The western powers had the advantage of being able to choose and change the theatre of war, knocking out important defenses by occupying or demolishing strong points and generally crippling Russian resistance through a strategy of attrition. The situation can be compared, in modern military history, to the position of the Central powers in the First World War or the Axis powers in the Second World War, when the enemies, ruling the seas, could choose which would be the major theatre of war and which would be important secondary theatres. In contrast to these twentieth-century world wars, the inner lines in the Crimean War offered Russia more disadvantages than advantages. The "infrastructure" was lacking: above all there were few railroads, so that Russian troops were condemned to a high degree of immobility. The consequence was that about three-quarters of the Russian army was obliged to stand idle guarding the frontiers with Austria, Prussia, and Sweden.[2] A military success by the sea powers could deal the enemy a crucial blow at any moment, while Russian successes could only temporarily eliminate the allies' bases.[3]

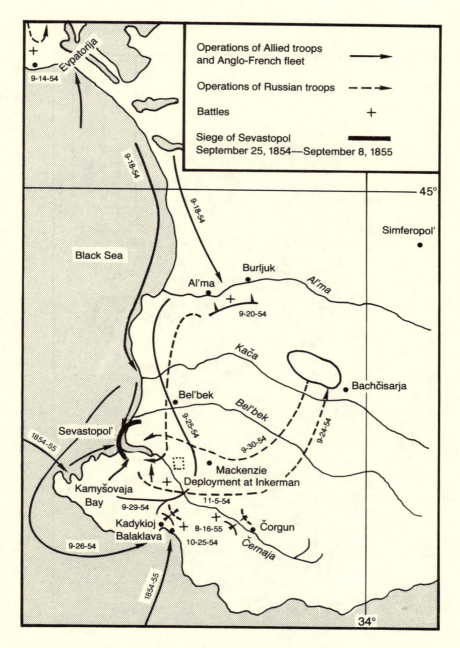

Operations of Allied troops
and Anglo-French fleet

Operations of Russian troops

Battles   +

Siege of Sevastopol
September 25, 1854—September 8, 1855

45°

9-14-54

Evpatorija

9-18-54

9-18-54

Simferopol'

Black Sea

Burljuk

Al'ma

Al'ma

+
9-20-54

Kača

Bachčisarja

Bel'bek

Bel'bek

9-25-54

9-30-54

9-24-54

1854-55

Sevastopol'

Mackenzie
Deployment at Inkerman

Kamyšovaja
Bay

+
9-29-54

11-5-54

Kadykioj
Balaklava

+   8-16-55   Čorgun

10-25-54

Černaja

9-26-54

1854-55

34°

1. The Crimean Campaign September 14, 1854 to September 8, 1855

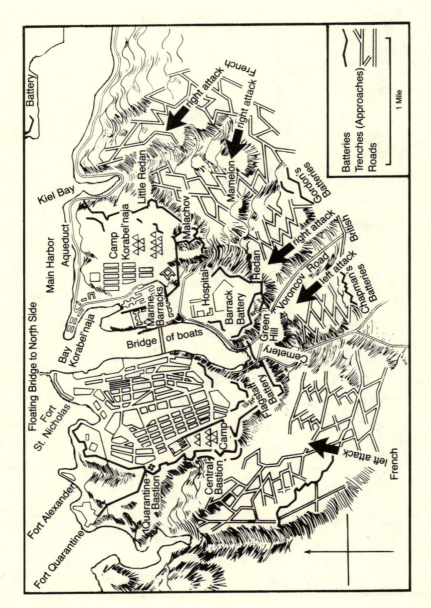

2. The Fall of Sevastopol on September 8, 1855

THE ALLIES' STRATEGIC PLANNING

The Caucasus front was the only area where this unfavorable situation could be reversed. On 26 November 1855, after a five-month siege, the Ottomans surrendered Kars, "the bulwark of Asia Minor,"[4] a city always hotly disputed because it was the gate to the Ottoman heartland. The Russian siege army (50,000 men) was no longer checked by regular Ottoman troops. The vital military road to Erzerum was free, and from there the way led into inner Anatolia. In Petersburg they demanded a march on Constantinople, followed by Mesopotamia and India.[5] The allies learned from the Russian camp before Kars that preparations were actually being made for an advance towards Erzerum and for establishment of a volunteer Greek legion to rally the Greeks of western Anatolia. To be sure, these were idle plans given contemporary technology, especially supply problems, and only the conquest of Erzerum and perhaps Trebizond could conceivably be accomplished; but the mere rumor was calculated to give the allies pause. Furthermore it had a demonstrable influence on their decisions.

So far as can be ascertained, contemporaries—not to mention historians—were not aware of the significant fact that after the fall of Kars the Russians controlled more square miles of enemy territory than did the sea powers. Paradoxically, the conquest of Kars disposed the Russians to listen to peace soundings since it redeemed the setback at Sevastopol, in accordance with contemporary notions of military honor, which seemed crucial to Alexander II and also to the Russian government.[6] Conversely, the allies perceived the loss of Kars as ignominious. Queen Victoria described it as "a disgrace to the Allies" and pointed out that they had remained idle in the Crimea with over 200,000 troops, busy building roads, without sending relief to Asia Minor.[7] For Napoleon and the French nation events in this theatre meant little, since its defense was tacitly left to the British;[8] for them, the honor of France, lost at Waterloo, had been restored by the capture of the dominant Malakov bastion[9] and so this victory removed an important obstacle to peace. These conceptions of military repute and disrepute, later increasingly outmoded with changes in fashion, were critical to political calculations on both sides in the Crimean War up to 1855 and must be considered.

But for the British Cabinet and military leadership in autumn 1855, the eastern theatre seemed more important than ever. It was not only that people wanted to compensate for the defeat at Kars and rescue the peoples "east of the Black Sea," the "Circassians" for example, from the Russian yoke by bestowing independence upon them; nor was it simply the idea that to safeguard Ottoman security a buffer ought to be established between Russia and Turkey. Much more important was

British concern for defense of the Indian Empire, a point hitherto neglected because of gaps in the sources and still in need of confirmation. In a general way, historians have related British interest in Ottoman integrity in the nineteenth century to the desire to secure access routes to India (the Isthmus of Suez, commercial routes through the Black Sea or through Anatolia and the Caucasus); but scholars have failed to make the connection with the plans for a Caucasus expedition in 1856, which were not implemented because peace was concluded. This historiographical neglect is analogous to the treatment of the similar, although differently directed, German plans for the Caucasus during the last year of the First World War, whose significance has only recently been appreciated.[10]

Britain naturally perceived Russia's occupation of the Caucasus during the Crimean War as a threat to her position in India, just as she later distrusted the extension of Russian influence to Bukhara and Khiva. Britain's war with Herat (west of Afghanistan), which began in 1856, and the Indian Mutiny of 1857 demonstrated the necessity of keeping the Russians away from this weak point. It is ironic that the Crimean War, a British victory, hurt Britain in the long run, since the attenuation of Russian influence in the Balkans and in Europe encouraged the Russians to drive for expansion in Asia and thus provided the occasion for the growth of new tensions between the two European fringe powers.

In 1855 these long-range results could only be guessed at.[11] However, this anxiety about India persuaded British leaders to open a special theatre of war in Asia Minor in 1856 without the French. The relevant proposals were discussed in the Cabinet during December 1855 and January 1856.[12] Of the 80,000 troops under British command in the Crimea,[13] a force which included Ottoman and Sardinian auxiliaries plus foreign legionaries, about half were to remain before Sevastopol; the rest would be transferred to Asia Minor. Obviously no final conclusion was reached about a landing place. Some Cabinet members advocated prompt despatch of troops to Trebizond to meet the anticipated Russian advance head on; others preferred Batum and Poti, so that the corps could operate in the rear of Russia's Caucasus army by moving inland towards Tiflis. A decision was postponed until the allied war council which was supposed to meet in mid-January 1856 with Napoleon presiding. The British representatives were instructed by the Cabinet to argue "that it would be good to separate the armies, and that the importance of clearing Georgia was great."[14]

Published accounts of the decisions of the war council on this and other points are contradictory;[15] they can only be verified by French, British, and Sardinian primary sources as yet unavailable, such as operational plans and protocols of meetings. For Napoleon, the war council's main purpose, announced in the press many weeks in advance, apparently was not making binding decisions but exerting pressure on the Russian government through demonstration of allied resolve. In fact, when the war council's first session was held, on 16 January 1856, Petersburg's decision for peace had just been communicated.

When examining British operational plans, one should remember that the British troops had suffered a body blow during the storming of Sevastopol: while waves of French attackers had thrown the seasoned Russian defenders out of the Malakov bastion, the British assault on the Redan, the second most important redoubt, had bogged down in the communication trenches. The Russians evacuated Sevastopol just because of the loss of the Malakov bastion. British leaders were outraged by the failure at the Redan, especially in comparison with French glory. The Queen's comment, that she could not endure the thought that " 'the failure on the Redan' should be our last fait d'Armes"[16] expresses the prevailing opinion in Britain and offers one explanation for British intransigeance.

Alongside the diversion in Asia Minor, British strategy called for intensification of the naval war in the Baltic. There Russian naval power should be reduced to zero; that is to say, the fleet should be sunk, as in the Black Sea. The 1856 war in the Baltic would be the counterpart to the Black Sea operations of 1855. Preparations for the naval war were started on a gigantic scale and were pursued into the spring of 1856. In a speech in the House of Lords,[17] Clarendon described them as unparalleled. In the dockyards, preparations were pushed so hard that in the spring of 1856, 150 modern steam-powered gunboats were commissioned.[18] The French too would go into their coordinating campaign with new weapons. They had successfully used armored ships for the first time at the bombardment of Kinburn on the Black Sea coast (17 October 1855). Besides this, they possessed new ships' gunnery with a range of up to five thousand metres.[19] The allies calculated that these floating batteries would prove irresistible and considered Kronstadt as good as conquered.[20] While the British navy would bear the brunt of reducing Kronstadt, France would provide the bulk of the landing troops. Napoleon felt that sixty thousand to eighty thousand men would be necessary for this purpose.[21] Preparations had already started in the French army of the north and in the camp at Boulogne.[22]

The experts had not yet agreed about details of the Baltic expedition, including the choice of landing points—these were to have been decided by the war council at Paris, and any action taken remains unknown. Nonetheless, complete success was anticipated. Whether things could have turned out as expected seems dubious in light of our knowledge about Russian defense measures. The fortress at Kronstadt was better constructed than Sevastopol. The Russians had transferred the great siege engineer Totleben from the Crimea and had given him the top command at Petersburg.[23] And they, too, had a new weapon for naval warfare, mines. Since they were not used extensively, Russian scholars disagree about their potential importance for warmaking at that time.[24] Later, this invention of the Crimean War was developed by the Russians into a highly effective defensive weapon, as its test in the First World War brilliantly demonstrated.

So this is how British strategic planning for 1856 shaped up: maintaining dominance on the Black Sea, consolidating Sevastopol as a base for further operations, despatching an expeditionary corps to Transcaucasia to win back Kars and dislodge the Russians, a naval expedition to the Baltic in cooperation with the French landing force to reduce Kronstadt and occupy Petersburg. Britain believed that she could accomplish these goals with the existing allies, France, Sardinia, and the Ottoman Empire.

There is a noteworthy gap here in historical scholarship on the Crimean War. What role did the Ottoman army play after the loss of Kars, and what role was assigned to it in the following year's campaign? We lack the most elementary facts: number of troops, figures for losses, equipment, morale of the troops, leadership, and so on. Serious Marxist historians have accepted the explanation which originated with Friedrich Engels that from the original Ottoman army of four hundred thousand men virtually nothing remained except the army of occupation on the Danube and a small expeditionary force at Suchum on the east coast of the Black Sea.[25] Supposedly, the soldiers had been ruined by battle or illness, reduced to invalids or demoralized into robber bands. Engels's reporting must be weighed, since he disposed of astonishingly rich sources for his commentary, but proving his version is a task as necessary as it is difficult.

In general, historical writing on the Crimean War has unjustly neglected the role of the Ottoman Empire, although its preservation was, after all, the real object of the war.[26] This phenomenon is related to the flatly humiliating way of handling the Ottomans employed by the allies politically. After the fall of Sevastopol, Ottoman statesmen must have longed for the end of tutelage to the allied ambassadors and must have regarded continuation of the war as a mockery of their independence, in flagrant violation of the cause for which the western powers ostensibly had gone to war.[27]

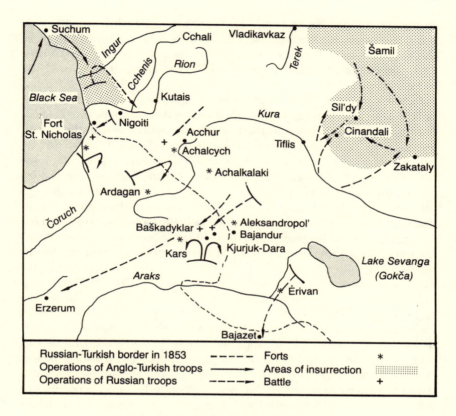

3. The War in the Caucasus

British War Aims

Protection of Ottoman independence and integrity, "the defence of Ottoman territory in Europe and in Asia against Russian aggression," was the original war aim laid down by the allies in the Treaty of Constantinople of 12 March 1854. Had this goal remained the same during the war or had it been "further developed" by Britain? How was it interpreted after the fall of Sevastopol?

The dominant political figure in Britain during these years, or more accurately between 1830 and 1865, was Palmerston. He appears with justice to the twentieth century as the symbol of that period of British history when Great Britain ruled the seas unchallenged and became the "workshop of the world" and the center of the international money market. In judging Palmerston and his foreign policy, one must remember that nineteenth-century Britain was not only a European power but had evolved into a world power. Palmerston's life coincided with the phase which has been somewhat inappropriately named the

Industrial Revolution and with the years when British free trade won out over continental protectionism. Palmerston's Britain saw itself as the defender of a Pax Britannica whose mainstay was the "European balance of power" and which implied British ascendancy outside the old continent.

Palmerston was a patriot for whom "England's interest" took precedence over everything; he was firmly convinced that "the English nation" was the greatest and the English climate the best in the world, and he believed that England's constitution offered a model for all Europe. His diplomatic methods resemble in many respects the gunboat diplomacy of William II, as is demonstrated by some episodes during the Crimean War. Yet it would be more correct to remain within the context of British history and call his activities jingoism. It is true that this does not do full justice to his qualities as a statesman. But it is a striking feature of his policy, and it made an unfavorable impression in Europe. One Palmerston scholar put it in a nutshell: "Palmerston did not have to play the part of John Bull; he lived it."[28] He held his Commons seat for forty-eight years, a span equalled by very few British politicians, such as Gladstone and Churchill. His time in office, fifty-eight years, has never been exceeded. It is typical of Palmerston that he insisted on dying at the office. In the *Daily Telegraph* obituary, he was described as "the most English minister that ever governed England," and Earl Russell praised him on the same occasion as a man who was "English to the backbone."[29] In the 1840s and 1850s, Palmerston dominated "balance of power" diplomacy, always understood according to British interest, and manipulated it in a masterly fashion, which can only be compared to Bismarck's virtuoso leadership of the European alliance system in the 1870s and 1880s. Palmerston perceived the struggle for mastery by any of the European continental powers as a threat to British security, whether the culprit was Russia at the end of the 1820s after the war with the Ottoman Empire, France at the beginning of the 1840s during the Egyptian crisis, or again Russia during the renewed tension over the Eastern Question in 1853. The maintenance of the integrity of the Ottoman Empire, extending over three continents, just like the preservation of Belgian neutrality, was axiomatic to his policy.

In 1833 Palmerston became the first British minister to think through the problems connected with the Eastern Question. Previously he had concentrated on western Europe. To be sure, as early as 1828 Aberdeen had described the maintenance of Ottoman rule in Europe as essential to the balance of power.[30] But no material support followed, so Russia could impose a peace on the Porte at Adrianople which gave her control over the mouths of the Danube, the right of intervention in the semiautonomous principalities of Moldavia and Wallachia, and

increased rights of protection over the Christian subjects of the Sultan. Immediately after the treaty of Unkiar-Skelessi, in which Russia guaranteed Ottoman integrity and thus established herself as the Porte's protector, Palmerston made a speech in the House of Commons in which he laid down a political axiom which remained in force for decades and was even followed to its logical conclusion in war: "The integrity and independence of the Ottoman Empire are necessary to the maintenance of the tranquillity, the liberty and the balance of power in the rest of Europe."[31] As an application of this principle, Russia's unilateral guarantee was replaced in 1839 to 1840 by a collective four-power guarantee (from 1841 France was also included), and as part of the same settlement the closure of the Straits to warships in time of peace was stipulated; later, in 1853 to 1854, the same principle dictated the outbreak of war. Palmerston embodied Britain's suspicion of Russia which had grown since the 1830s, when Russia began to emerge as an imperial rival in Asia, with the contraction of the empty spaces between the two giant empires.

Yet another element is intrinsic to Palmerston's policy, an aspect that points up a less obvious cause of the Crimean War: his belief in the uniquely beneficial effects for politics and society of the British constitution. "He was a steadfast and devoted partisan of constitutional liberty in every part of the Continent," according to the *Times*'s memorial in 1865.[32] This English sense of superiority, nourished by tradition, in the face of a reactionary and autocratic government, such as Nicholas's, was decisive in kindling popular enthusiasm for a war which was interpreted as a crusade against the tyranny of tsarist Russia and its threat to Europe. But it also explains why a statesman like Buol failed when he aimed, as has recently been demonstrated, at a closer alliance between the Hapsburg monarchy and Britain going beyond the limited cooperation of the Crimean War.[33] Even in 1852 to 1853, that is directly before the eastern crisis deteriorated through the Menshikov Mission, Austria was the continental state most hated in Britain, because of her persecution of revolutionary refugees such as Kossuth through demands for repatriation or sequestration. Soon afterwards the Tsar would be stigmatized as evil incarnate. In Britain at that time the names Austria, Russia, and Rome were synonymous with tyranny. To be sure, Austria's image as the jailor of minority groups changed with the outbreak of war and with the rapprochement between Austria and the western powers, but later the pendulum seemed to swing back again: Austria's so-called seesaw policy was held responsible for the transfer of fighting from the Balkans to the Crimea and for the subsequent dragging out of the war; Austria was blamed for staging the premature peace conference in the spring of 1855 and especially for her concordat with Rome in August 1855, directly before Sevastopol.

At the same time, 1855, King Ferdinand II of Naples, "Re Bomba," was also criticized, partly because his regime was regarded as a refuge for reaction and repression, but above all because he demonstrated his neutrality by forbidding British agents to purchase horses, draft animals, and provisions in his kingdom. In September 1855, the British government, following Palmerstonian methods, intended to send a couple of gunboats to cruise off Naples and present allied demands as an ultimatum.[34] And the Greek government was obliged to change its policy, which unquestionably was not strictly neutral, after British and French troops occupied Piraeus.[35]

The main lines of British foreign policy are essential background for understanding Britain's position after Sevastopol and during the peace negotiations. Palmerston's policy of the mailed fist was not approved by all Cabinet members in all situations, especially when it came to decisive questions of war and peace: this possibility for institutionalized dissent was one of the strengths of the British parliamentary monarchy.

The static war aim of maintaining Ottoman integrity implies a dynamic one—Britain's desire to restrict and diminish Russia's power so that there could be no recurrence in the foreseeable future of the policy which had led to war in 1853, that is, presentation of demands as an ultimatum and the seizure of material guarantees from the Ottoman Empire. This goal can be appropriately compared to the notion of "containment" stemming from the political vocabulary of the twentieth century, for the image of damming up implied corresponds entirely to Palmerston's ideas. Directly after the fall of Sevastopol, in a memorandum of September 1855, which up to now has been published only in fragmentary form, Palmerston revealed his conception of the true war aim: "to curb the aggressive ambition of Russia. We went to war not so much to keep the Sultan and his Mussulmans in Turkey as to keep the Russians out of Turkey." Russia's territory must be reduced or at least "hemmed in" by "a long line of circumvallation."[36] "Circumvallation" is an expression from siege engineering. Palmerston's use of it reflects the military experience of that day; it is therefore entirely analogous to the metaphor expressed in the later phrase "containment policy" (or equally *cordon sanitaire*). It is no accident that this modern image carries more meaning for us than that of the line of circumvallation, although the actual sense, in spite of the difference in the words, is identical. This concept demonstrates the continuity between tsarist and Bolshevik foreign policy and the resemblance in the response of western Europe. Today we have long since forgotten that for decades in the first half of the nineteenth century, Russia was viewed as a menace. This oversight is at least partly due to the fact that Russia after the Crimean War was regarded by western Europe as a more or less negligible quantity.

As one means of damming up the Russian drive for expansion, the

sea powers and Austria, soon after the war broke out, decided that it
was essential to revive the collective guarantee of 1841 and to revise the
Straits Convention signed jointly with Russia "in the interest of the
European balance." The peace talks which went on almost uninterruptedly during the war, including the Vienna Conference in the
spring of 1855, foundered on the interpretation of this originally
deliberately vague third point of the "four point program" of 8 August
1854.[37] Russia did not accept the Anglo-French interpretation: neutralization or rather demilitarization of the Black Sea. The western
powers, on their side, rejected Austria's interpretation: a "counter-
weight" or system of balancing Russian and Ottoman-western naval
forces, as well as the project of placing mutual limits on naval potential
in the Black Sea. Yet in the official war aims program this third point
was the crucial demand for Britain as well as France.

In British administrative circles, the notion of a line of circumvallation assumed another form even more appropriate to the image. The
most extreme version was doubtless the demand for "dismemberment"
of the Russian empire along ethnic lines,[38] a goal that surfaced again in
Britain's Russian policy during the intervention in 1918 to 1921. The
discussion in the British Cabinet—we need more evidence here—
seems to have arisen incidentally and probably was not serious. But the
hints that come to hand are significant, for they demonstrate the sense
of menace from the Russian rival which had taken deep root in Britain.
At any rate, it was Palmerston who advocated dissolution. In a
memorandum of 19 March 1854, circulated among Cabinet members,
he sketched out a plan for partitioning Russia which entailed nothing
less than "redrawing . . . the European map."[39] Finland should be restored to Sweden, the Baltic provinces should fall to Prussia, Poland
would be transformed into a "substantive kingdom," Austria would
renounce her north Italian possessions in return for the Danubian
principalities, possibly with Bessarabia thrown in, and the Crimea and
Georgia would be returned to the Porte. Lansdowne and Russell considered this grandiose plan a daydream.[40] Aberdeen, thoroughly upset, predicted that its realization would require a thirty years' war.[41]
Although Palmerston himself regarded it as a "dream," he never gave it
up. In discussions with the French foreign minister, Drouyn de l'Huys,
in autumn 1854, he heartily agreed with the latter that as the war went
on, "small results" would no longer suffice to repay the enormous
common effort and "great territorial changes" would be necessary.[42]
"What of course these remarks pointed out to," as Palmerston summarized the upshot of the conversations, "were Georgia and Circassia,
the mouths of the Danube, Poland and Finland, matters . . . which I
told him were mine personally."

Palmerston anticipated victory at Sevastopol not as the end of the war, but as the first step towards implementing his ideas. He followed the storming of the fortress with anxiety, since he foresaw "a danger of peace" once it fell.[43] Austria would draw Britain into negotiations for an "insufficient peace" before the allies had achieved a result decisive enough to justify Britain in proposing such conditions "as will effectually curb the ambition of Russia for the future." After the naval base had been captured, he let it be known in the Cabinet that "Russia was not yet 'half beaten enough.' "[44] In reaction to the first Austrian peace proposals, he demanded that the war go on for at least another year; not before October 1856 could the Crimea, Georgia, and Circassia be detached from Russia, and Poland's independence be assured.[45] Clarendon was fundamentally in accord with his prime minister's train of thought. Continuing the war was essential: in 1856 a major front must be opened in the Baltic; the war would then assume a European character: "Et alors comme alors. Out of that might spring fresh territorial arrangements."[46]

In preparation for opening a campaign in the Baltic, the British took the necessary military steps during the autumn and also secured their diplomatic position. On 21 November, Britain and France concluded a treaty of alliance with Sweden (November Treaty);[47] the secret articles attached to it arranged for Sweden's entry into the war on the western side.[48]

From these ideas and plans we can draw certain conclusions which have previously been neglected or overlooked. It is clear that the character of the "Crimean" War would have changed in 1856, for the Black Sea and the Crimea would have become a secondary front and the original war aim, the integrity of the Ottoman Empire, would have receded. The conflict with Russia, previously conducted as a cabinet war, would have been transformed into a "war of nationalities" with a scope and consequences hard to calculate—a vision which even at the time began to take shape in the minds of contemporaries.[49] Besides continuing traditional warfare, that is, the military intervention already planned, the western powers might have resorted to kindling a new kind of war by revolutionizing the ethnically distinct portions of the Russian empire from Finland to Poland, Bessarabia, and the Black Sea territories as far as the Caucasus. Russia on her side would have turned the same weapon against the multinational Ottoman and Austrian empires, which were perhaps even more vulnerable: this had been demonstrated with respect to the Ottomans by the Greek legion in Murav'ev's camp and would later be proved in Austria's case.[50]

Yet the role played by such revolutionary programs in the Crimean War has remained unnoticed and therefore uninvestigated, and so there are important questions which still cannot be answered. However, we can already distinguish the shape of plans for insurrection,

along the lines made familiar in the Austro-Prussian War of 1866 and the First World War.[51] In Sweden, a Finnish legion was organized for use in Finland; in the Crimea, an Anglo-Polish and an Anglo-Turkish legion stood in reserve. The latter would be attached to the British expeditionary corps destined for Asia Minor and would be detailed to raise the Caucasus. We are more accurately informed about the plans for the Anglo-Polish legion, because the papers of its inspirer and intellectual leader, Prince Adam Czartoryski, who was living in exile in Paris, have been published in part.[52]

In September 1855 the Prince wrote a memorandum destined for Napoleon, in which he drew on his familiarity with Russian conditions gained as Alexander I's adviser and right-hand man at the Vienna Congress, to advise the Emperor about how to revolutionize the Russian peoples, an approach previously overlooked by the allies.[53] Russia was surrounded by foreign ethnic groups like a girdle "which can victoriously choke her." In these "girdle territories," "masses of auxiliary troops" stood ready; they only needed to be organized and armed. Using them would relieve the allies' anxiety about dividing their own military forces and would substitute for Austrian military aid, thus far vainly awaited; or it might even persuade Austria to participate.

In the following pages, Czartoryski assessed the value of each "nationality" as a military reserve. In the north, it is true, he only discussed Poland, that is, he omitted the Baltic lands and Finland. In the front rank, the Moldavo-Wallachians could be mobilized against Russia. They would have no difficulty in putting twenty-five thousand men in the field with the reserves necessary. All they would demand would be prospects for satisfaction of their "just national claims," an outcome which the Sultan would certainly not oppose. In the south, in the mountains of Abkhazia, the territories of the Don and Kuban Cossacks, the provinces of the Ukraine, indeed even in White Russia, a resounding impression could be made if allied squadrons appeared on the Sea of Azov and destroyed the fortifications there. It would reawaken the spirit of freedom in these peoples, which had manifested itself recently in peasant revolts and had been repressed with difficulty by Muscovite troops. In Poland, finally, the western powers would find the best reservoir of troops. Cadres should be formed immediately from the numerous Polish exiles, prisoners, and deserters. From the outset, each detachment should include cavalry squadrons, infantry battalions, and artillery batteries so that each captive could immediately be integrated into his branch of service. Each ally should provide for a cadre of fifty thousand men. Depots for weapons and equipment would be established in due course in Moldavia or at the Danube mouth; for the Polish provinces, the best location would be Odessa, which was yet to be placed under siege.

The Prince justified his plan again in concluding: "in appealing to the national groups on which they can rely, and which they cannot overlook . . . if they mean to win, the allies will have at their disposal significant forces which will recruit themselves, and only need to be armed." In this memorandum and in numerous further petitions he addressed to Napoleon and Palmerston, Czartoryski asked as reward the restoration of Congress Poland in accordance with the stipulations of 1815.

All these plans came to nothing because peace was concluded abruptly. Yet the fact that they exist, that Palmerston leaned towards a "war of nationalities" and that Napoleon sympathized with the Polish cause, points which have yet to be examined in depth, all suggest certain conclusions about how the war would have been transformed.

From Palmerston's program of war aims jumps out the desire for a "redrawing of the European map," a corollary up to now almost completely disregarded. During these years, this demand was advanced much more emphatically by Palmerston than by Napoleon. Many details which will be discussed later corroborate this impression. Palmerston had studied the European map more intensively, even in a literal sense, and had chewed it over more thoroughly than Napoleon; Napoleon considered all such plans more farsightedly and more cautiously, because he let himself be deflected by the difficulties. In evaluating Napoleon's program, it must of course be remembered that only scanty sources exist as testimony, in contrast to the rich documentation for Palmerston. Napoleon's confidential utterances have been transmitted chiefly at second hand, while Palmerston's thinking is fixed in pages written in his own hand in a fullness not yet fully exploited by scholars. This derives at least partly from the differences in government in Britain and France in those years. The motto "redrawing of the map," which historians conveniently and correctly use to describe the underlying tendencies of Second Empire foreign policy, can be compared with the slogan of "fresh territorial arrangements" which characterized British European policy during the Crimean War, or more precisely Palmerston's plans.

It must appear as a historical irony that Napoleon III preserved Europe from the consequences of a major revolution, such as would have occurred if the war had been continued according to Palmerston's ideas.

The scope and consequences of a war that never happened certainly cannot be ascertained. And Palmerston should not now be baptized the great revolutionary leader of the Crimean War and described as a black sheep in contrast to the white lamb, Napoleon. But this much is sure: Palmerston could not have guaranteed that his far-reaching war aims would have been realized in October 1856 and not later, just as he had not been able to insure in the fall of 1854 that Sevastopol would fall in a couple of weeks, as British military and political experts expected, rather than demanding 349 days of unspeakable sacrifice. Furthermore, it is certain that with implementation of the British war aims outlined above, the Crimean War could no longer have remained localized in the Crimea, but would have become a world war in the full sense of the term and would have buried the Concert of Europe then and there, not sixty years later. The course of European history would have changed dramatically. Aberdeen and other influential British personalities, like Gladstone, who had refused in the spring of 1855 to remain in Palmerston's cabinet, perceived correctly that Britain under Palmerston was being led onto shaky ground. If Palmerston had attained his goal of reducing the power of the tsarist empire to its level before Peter the Great, the European balance would of course have been completely unhinged. Russia presumably would not have been left to fight alone. There were signs enough in the winter of 1855/56 that Britain as well as France would have declared war on the King of Prussia because of his supposedly weak and wavering attitude.[54] This declaration of war would have set in motion the entire machinery of alliance commitments between the German powers. Russo-American relations, which had improved notably, might have become closer and might even have led to a military alliance.[55]

These reflections open a new perspective on Austrian policy during the war. In this chapter it can only be hinted at:[56] Austria, by persistently refusing to participate in the war against Russia, served her own interest, by sparing herself material sacrifice and preserving her shaky imperial structure from possible collapse; and she also defended European interests, by forcing Britain, through Napoleon, to break off hostilities. The Austrian leaders, particularly Count Buol, clung to their position of armed neutrality in a hard-nosed and unyielding fashion because they were profoundly convinced that in so doing they could prevent a world war.[57] Austrian policy in the Crimean War, sharply criticized by contemporaries and generally misunderstood by historians, could hardly be more fundamentally misrepresented than by the assertion, drawn from a widely used historical reference, that Austria, by concluding the alliance of 2 December 1854, caused the war to continue.[58] In his political salon in Vienna, Metternich flung up his hands at the massive stupidity that had led the sea powers, the Ottoman Empire, and Russia into war, and directed the attention of his disciple, Buol, to the confusion and unpredictability of Europe's political situation; the corollary for Austria must be a policy of the free hand. Buol hoped that the December Treaty would put an end to precisely this instability, for he thought he was pledging the sea powers to peace while keeping Austria out of war. France and Britain were determined, however, to continue fighting, with *or without* Austria, at least until the capture of the Crimea; they went into the Vienna Peace Conference with warlike intentions.

NAPOLEON'S WAR AIMS

How did Napoleon react to the fall of Sevastopol and to the new British war aims proposals? What did his own program look like?

In many respects, Napoleon's policy seemed contradictory to contemporaries as well as to historians. It was an indefinable mixture of fixed ideas and indecision, of cool calculation and fantasy. It does not help to label it "sphinxlike," as was generally done in the nineteenth century, because this ambiguous phrase begs the question. As has been said, we have very few sources directly from Napoleon which might divulge the secret of his fashion of governing; yet it is possible to reconstruct his "program" (really more of a vision than a plan of action) by examining his programmatic writing, starting with the *Napoleonic Ideas,* the numerous and typical anonymous pamphlets and brochures, the official speeches, and the conversations with politicians and diplomats, often strikingly candid.

Napoleon's basic goal was to revise the European system of 1815, which in his interpretation had been designed in the interest of the princes in the name of legitimacy, at the expense of the desires of the peoples. This fundamental aim was well known. What bewildered contemporaries was that he could be flexible in executing it. The secret of his policy was that Napoleon knew how to accommodate his plans to changing circumstance and to luck, that in spite of his restlessness, he knew how to leave himself time and how to help things along; he never forced the situation like Palmerston. But in any case, there is an insoluble contradiction inherent in his very form of government, in Bonapartism itself, aptly described by a contemporary as the child born of popular sovereignty and absolutism.[59] Bonapartism inevitably wore a different mask in domestic policy than in foreign policy. Napoleon had risen through revolution, but he had repressed it in blood. He considered it his mission to restore that system in the interior which he planned to overthrow in Europe. This duality was summarized by another observer, Baron Hübner, the Austrian ambassador in Paris, who helped make Louis Napoleon acceptable to the Vienna court: "In his own home Louis Napoleon is necessarily a conservative, in other peoples' homes he is a revolutionary."[60]

In the eastern crisis of 1853, Napoleon III saw a favorable opportunity to get some leverage on the 1815 system. His policy in the war and especially his attitude after Sevastopol can only be understood in the context of his master plan. The eastern crisis and the fate of the Ottoman Empire interested him only to the extent that he could exploit them. His explanation to the Senate on 2 March 1854 was intended solely for effect abroad: "We are going into this war with England to defend the Sultan's cause, and at the same time to protect the rights of Christians. We are going into it to defend freedom of the seas and our legitimate influence in the Mediterranean."[61] It artfully linked the idea of a crusade and a sturdy opportunism with traditional French interest in the Mediterranean, threatened by Russia, all without letting his private hopes be known abroad. The position adopted, since it seemed to spring from the Holy Places question, could be justified to a public conscious of history, whether French interest was traced back to the successful policy of alliance with the Sultan, from Francis I to Napoleon I, or whether it was related along religious lines to Saint Louis or even Charlemagne.

The first important gains appeared swiftly: escape from humiliating isolation in Europe through cooperation with liberal Britain, then destruction of the conservative "alliance of the northern courts," which protected the system of 1815, through the alliance with Austria on 2 December 1854. These were preliminary steps to beginning to realize the major goal, by the detour of the Eastern Question. It was odd, however, that the Eastern Question and the attempted solution did not belong to the Vienna system but, in Treitschke's phrase, "to the many other unresolved questions of the congress."[62] To Napoleon, Ottoman territory in Europe, precisely because it was not included in the system of 1815, could provide a laboratory for the principle of nationalities, where the danger of repercussions would be minimal compared with central Europe between the Po, the Rhine, and the Vistula. The fact that this would soon conflict with the principle of Ottoman integrity, the ostensible basis for French participation in the war, did not weigh heavily on Napoleon as long as he could be sure that his British ally would approve his plans for the Balkans. This was in fact what happened, for he found in Palmerston a fellow believer and developed a lively exchange with him through personal contacts during the war.

Napoleon considered the Eastern Question "a situation which lent itself to territorial compensations": he said as much to Duke Ernest of Saxe-Coburg-Gotha, Prince Albert's brother, in March 1854.[63] He could only be encouraged by the precedent of Greek independence, sanctioned by Nicholas I, although he was one of the most zealous champions of Holy Alliance principles. The Danubian principalities, Moldavia and Wallachia, seemed to him during the Crimean War and thereafter to be the best possible test case for popular sovereignty. According to Napoleon's notions, the Rumanians' attempts to win independence and unity could be rewarded with less danger than would arise anywhere else in Europe: Austria's interests would be served if the united principalities were assigned to an archduke. Ottoman integrity would not be compromised if the archduke accepted the sovereignty of the Porte. Russia's interests did not count because she was the enemy. The price would be paid by Austria in Italy. "If it depended on me," Napoleon confided to the duke, "I would be glad to grant Austria the Danubian Principalities; and if I were Emperor of Austria, I would not be enthusiastic about retaining Lombardy, since it . . . will always cause trouble, always demand sacrifices, until sooner or later there will be a general Italian uprising."[64]

This exchange plan served several functions, not least that of broaching the Italian question, and it occupied Napoleon from the time war began until the peace conference met and even thereafter. Its realization would not have endangered the European state system, that is, the "European balance of power." Consequently Napoleon was sure the British would approve, although they were sensitive about the balance. Palmerston once admitted to the Sardinian envoy in London, d'Azeglio, in relation to a similar question, which the latter had posed "in the way of discussion," that Austrian displacement towards the east would not endanger the European balance.[65]

From this discussion with Duke Ernest in March 1854, we can glimpse other well-known features of Napoleon's plans, in addition to these notions about southeastern Europe and Italy, that is, his schemes for Poland and Germany. Napoleon alluded to the idea of restoring Poland within the boundaries of 1815 without its Prussian and Austrian provinces. He was convinced that Prussia must be built up in Germany, and considered the German Confederation just as defective as the organization of the Apennine peninsula. He also indicated frankly to the duke the price he would ask for France: "On my word, as for France, it is a matter of indifference to me whether they give compensation on the Rhine or in Italy."[66]

These were Napoleon's war aims. The Ottoman Empire, the real object of the war, was of secondary importance to him. The Crimean War provided the first major occasion "to adjust the map of Europe," and opportunity must be seized.[67] It is not necessary to explore other side issues which occupied Napoleon, like the handling of the Iberian peninsula or the idea of a Scandinavian empire, nor to follow the stages of developing, modifying, redoing, and redeveloping the *one* idea during the changing circumstances of the war and the alliance. It pops up throughout the war up to the fall of Sevastopol. For instance, in the spring of 1855 Napoleon launched a pamphlet put together by Granier de Cassagnac in which his true "war aims" were outlined in scarcely veiled form.[68] According to this, Poland should go to Prussia, and the Crimea and the Caucasus should be given to the Ottoman Empire, while Moldavia, Wallachia, and Bessarabia, that is, all the ethnically Rumanian territories, would be assigned to Austria, in return for the cession of Lombardy to Piedmont.

NAPOLEON'S CONGRESS PLAN

Napoleon believed that his life's work consisted in implementing his "doctrine" concerning the unworkability of the European system created forty years before at Vienna. He did not allow himself to be held back by any of his advisers; if they did not agree with him, he dropped them[69] or else worked around them.[70] The foreign policy of the Second Empire in the 1850s was typified by Napoleon's personal, that is to say, authoritarian approach to government. In realizing his ideas, the Crimean War was useful but not necessary, just as a dozen years later Bismarck regarded the Austro-Prussian War as avoidable in thinking about German unification.

All his life, Napoleon cherished the idea of actualizing his "great design" partly or entirely through a general European congress rather than through military means.[70a] Events between 1852 and 1854, that is, from the time the eastern crisis flared up until war broke out, have been investigated intensively by historians in search of the causes of the war, but no comprehensive examination has been made as yet concerning Napoleon's congress plans and their relationship to the procedures of the Concert of Europe, as it functioned in the mid-nineteenth century. In the conversation already mentioned with Duke Ernest directly before war began, Napoleon talked about the subject in general terms: "after the war with Russia had been won, a European peace congress would be absolutely necessary, to solve the questions left unanswered by the Congress of Vienna and to give the peoples a lasting peace."[71] After the Rubicon was crossed, that is, after Russian troops had gone over the Pruth and occupied the left bank of the Danube and after the allied squadrons had sailed through the Dardanelles and the Bosporus, the congress idea, as far as we know now, receded into the background, although the fighting, like the Thirty Years' War, was punctuated with peace talks, mediation, and conferences.

Soon after Sevastopol fell, Napoleon's congress idea surfaced again, as we learn from Duke Ernest, who chanced to stay in Paris in September 1855. The duke had two extensive conversations with the Emperor on 24 and 25 September.[72] Napoleon believed the position of the western powers to be very favorable; he seemed inclined towards peace but did not underestimate the advantages of war. For a peace concluded at that stage would leave behind in both Britain and France a certain aftertaste of "regret"; it would seem like a truce. Napoleon obviously was thinking of a peace focused on the ostensible object of the war, the Eastern Question. This was further indicated as he developed his train of thought: real satisfaction for all European states could only be attained if the peace settlement included a solution of those questions "that had been settled injudiciously by the Vienna Congress, or had arisen since." As examples Napoleon named Poland and Italy. He asked the duke to support the idea of a "big peace congress" and begged him to urge it on the King of Prussia. He further clarified his thinking by saying that it ought to be a congress of princes, "at which all the greater and lesser sovereigns would have to appear in person."

It must have been thanks to Duke Ernest's intervention that Frederick William IV did actually in January 1856 suggest to Napoleon a congress of princes which might meet in Aachen.[73] The author of this idea was not therefore the Prussian king, as previously supposed,[74] but Napoleon himself. The Coburg prince may also have transmitted the congress idea to his uncle, King Leopold of Belgium. The latter mentioned it to the Prussian minister president with the example of the "European conferences" that had indeed provided relative stability for his own country.[75] However, Manteuffel returned the ball; he did regard a European conference as urgent after the shocks of the revolution of 1848, "perhaps the only means which could possibly work against the rising fever in the sick body [of Europe]"; yet he considered it inappropriate to initiate it from the Prussian side. Queen Victoria, who was probably contacted at the same time about the idea, rejected it categorically.[76] Like Duke Ernest himself, she may have judged prospects for the success of such an illustrious gathering as slight, on procedural grounds alone. It could have attained results only if the questions to be handled had been worked out at lower levels to the stage of a treaty or if they were taken in hand by a small group of great powers which would deliberate in private as was done at Vienna in 1815 or Versailles in 1919 so that decisions were then simply accepted by acclamation by the rest. If even one of the powers were absent or excluded, the outcome would be fruitless or at least flawed, as was the Frankfurt Congress of Princes of 1863 within the German Confederation when Prussia was absent or later the Versailles peace in world politics because the United States adopted isolation and Soviet Russia did not participate.

Napoleon further publicized his pet idea in 1855 through a pamphlet, a device he often used. In December 1855 an anonymous brochure appeared in at least four editions entitled *Necessity of a Congress to Pacify Europe*;[77] it advanced Napoleon's congress idea in direct connection with forthcoming peace overtures to Russia. Even at the time diplomats thought they recognized Napoleon's hand in the pamphlet.[78] In fact it later came out that Napoleon had had the text ghostwritten by Charles Duveyrier and had then revised it personally.[79]

In view of the military situation, which had entered a new phase with the capture of Sevastopol, Napoleon, according to the pamphlet, believed that a new congress of sovereigns offered the best means of making and keeping peace. Since the goal had not been achieved by traditional methods of settlement such as mediation or diplomatic conferences, the only solution that suggested itself now was a congress. And it would be the only way to end the war "worthy the magnitude of the struggle."

In calling for such a congress Napoleon conceived himself as the spokesman for European "public opinion." He was convinced that in contemporary civilized Europe, military results would be ephemeral; victory could only come through "public opinion." This notion, essential to his idea of government, had echoed through his public as well as his private utterances in preceding weeks and would recur frequently. In September he explained to Duke Ernest, "in our day it is impossible to wage a great war and to conclude a major political settlement contrary to the interests of the peoples. Their voice will always break through and veto everything against their interests."[80] And in his short speech ending the Paris World's Fair on 15 November, an occasion when Europe was listening attentively, he appealed solemnly to public opinion: Europe would have to judge who was right and who was wrong.[81] In his pamphlet Napoleon described this speech as a public call for a congress. The response, he wrote, confirmed that "Europe is ready for this great spectacle." Napoleon referred here to the visits of important politicians to Paris in preceding weeks and the pressure from a number of neutral governments on the Russian regime for peace.

Yet these were isolated reactions, he went on, and could not be taken as the common voice of Europe. At this point, the circle closed: for this common voice to be heard and to impress, it must "speak out solemnly in a gathering of all the rulers, where ideas can be merged in a universal thought, where the will of all will find a common expression." To put it another way: Europe is personified in the congress.

To disturbing questions about the procedure for calling a congress and about its mandate, Napoleon had concise but not altogether reassuring answers. Speaking with Duke Ernest in September, he had given him to understand that of the two neutral great powers he would prefer Prussia taking the initiative in calling the congress. Austria he rejected as a matter of course, since her relations with France were unsatisfactory: contrary to Napoleon's announced expectation, Austria had persisted in her policy of the free hand, that is, nonparticipation in the war, and Emperor Francis Joseph's congratulations on the victory at Sevastopol had come painfully late. "It is entirely clear, that it is better to cling to a woman who hates us, than to one who has already betrayed us once, like Austria," he remarked to Duke Ernest in explaining his wish for a Prussian initiative.[82] Now, in December 1855, Napoleon adapted to progress in the peace soundings opened in the meantime: he recommended that the "idea of a congress" come from Russia herself. The latter should accept Austria's peace proposals as the base and then suggest entering into discussions "not in simple conferences, but in a gathering of all sovereigns after exchange of solemn and sincere explanations about the origin, character, and results of the conflict."

This demand for a declaration of principles by the belligerents needed closer examination. Napoleon provides it in the pamphlet, when he explains his own conduct. Looking back on history, he tries to convey to contemporary Russia that she will not suffer decline in renouncing her aggressive policy in the Orient and cooperating in the regeneration of the Ottoman Empire. Her legitimate influence will be safeguarded, and once an exhausting eastern policy has been given up, she will be able to import the "wondrous civilization" of the West for her own benefit. Thus seventy years before, Britain's loss of her North American colonies led to limitless development in commerce and navigation. Post-Napoleonic France surpassed the influence exercised under Louis XIV and Napoleon I. Russia must now mend her ways.

After such a declaration Russia would again be accorded an appropriate role in a congress. And now Napoleon abruptly let the cat out of the bag: this congress should solve not only the Eastern Question, "but all the questions which have arisen since the Congress of Vienna." The congress then should not be merely a glamorous mass meeting; it should put through a massive program. How far-reaching can be glimpsed from the "European questions" advanced outside the Paris Peace Congress.[83]

This fifteen-page pamphlet served to announce Napoleon's proposals for ending the war. To him, the necessity of calling a congress followed logically from the incapacity of the five great powers to reach consensus. His conciliatory treatment of Russia is striking. This psychological device, which he employed later in the war with Austria, was not only intended to influence Russia towards peace, but also to dangle the hope of "a new and precious alliance." In contrast to this, the assurances that the Anglo-French alliance was "eternal" ring like a mere duty statement.

This anonymous pamphlet from the second year of the Crimean War exposed Napoleon's basic diplomatic program. It must be taken into account in judging the results of the Paris peace of 1856. Napoleon did not let himself be discouraged by the relative indifference accorded these appeals or by later setbacks: he introduced the idea of a congress on other occasions. And the effort to reinforce official diplomatic initiatives by the anonymous pamphlet remained typical of his foreign policy.[84]

The destruction of the European system created in 1815 through a congress ending the Crimean War—that was Napoleon's aim in war and peace. When compared with Palmerston's, it certainly appears no less ambitious, but it could be realized with less use of force. In any case, Napoleon's unreserved longing for peace, as expressed in the congress idea, was not motivated directly by Sevastopol, as will be demonstrated next.

NAPOLEON CHOOSES PEACE

The Emperor's first reaction to the conquest of Sevastopol, unlike that of his peace-hungry foreign minister, who wished to end the war immediately,[85] was determination to exploit the victory to continue the war.[86] The allied troops ought to expel the Russians from their strongholds outside Sevastopol before winter set in, from their provisions depot, Simferopol, and insofar as possible from the whole peninsula. But at least Sevastopol must be held. From there the entire Russian Black Sea coast could be threatened and decisive blows could be delivered to strategic points in Asia or in Bessarabia. Possessing the Crimea or even just Sevastopol would provide an "important bargaining counter," a "means of negotiation" with Russia. Napoleon gave the Vienna court to understand that he did not wish to resume peace negotiations.[87]

However, the stubborn commanders in the Crimea, Marshal Pélissier and General Simpson, did not let themselves be hurried by instructions from Paris and London, so in the ensuing weeks there were no noteworthy military operations. Meanwhile, Napoleon had shifted the Anglo-French discussion over continuing the war to a new level. He held that the time had come to end the war's specifically "oriental" character and "Europeanize" it. The creation of a Baltic front must be seen as an important step in this direction; however, it would primarily serve British interests since its goal was destruction of the Russian Baltic fleet. But a more comprehensive French war aim could be joined to this or even given priority: the continental war to revolutionize Europe's nationalities. "If France is to continue the war at great sacrifice," Prince Albert summarized Napoleon's latest views as presented to the British government, "she needs goals which are more national, more French: Poland, Italy, the left bank of the Rhine etc."[88]

To be sure, "the left bank of the Rhine" cannot be regarded as part of the revolutionary program, but must be considered a war aim in its own right. Historians have previously disregarded or neglected this goal in connection with the Crimean War, probably because direct evidence cannot yet be adduced or because it did not assume any further practical significance during this short period of the autumn of 1855. But it is just as important to include options that were not implemented when making historical judgments, as it is to be concerned with human purposes that were achieved. It is plausible that Napoleon had designs on the Rhine frontier at this time even if direct evidence should be lacking, in view of the traditional French Rhine policy from Louis XIV to Guizot and Napoleon's own better-known Rhine plans of the 1860s.[89] Yet even the many secondhand testimonials, often the only sources for judging Napoleon, show us Napoleon's propositions here rather clearly, although naturally the details still require examination.

Prince Albert, who was generally well informed, alluded in a letter to his mentor Stockmar to a comment from high-ranking French officers "that Germany will soon meet its usual fate of becoming the theatre of war."[90] In December 1855, Napoleon told the British ambassador, Cowley, that the French army ought to teach Prussia a lesson.[91] One might conjecture that the French troops withdrawn from the Crimea after Sevastopol on Napoleon's orders in spite of British remonstrances (the sources mention one hundred thousand men) were held ready for a continental war. In a speech to the Imperial Guard on 31 December 1855, Napoleon hinted to his officers that they should be prepared: a great French army would be needed again.[92]

In Britain, too, around the turn of the year substantial threats were made against Prussia. On 1 January 1856 there appeared in the *Morning Post,* Palmerston's organ, an article supposedly inspired by Persigny, in which Prussia was challenged to participate in the war against Russia. In that case, according to a reliable source for British attitudes,[93] Napoleon would be allowed to serve his interests by annexing parts of Prussia, Belgium, or any other part of the continent. The anti-Prussian chorus became so vocal that people would have greeted a second Jena with joy.

At that time, a rumor launched in the Belgian capital was going the rounds in Berlin to the effect that Napoleon wanted to make peace with Russia immediately for the price of the Rhine provinces.[94] Supposedly, such a proposition had been made through the mission of the Saxon diplomat Seebach discussed later. Manteuffel and the Vienna regime as well used this report as an opportunity to ascertain the British government's position. Clarendon's answer, that such scheming on Napoleon's part would be "not at all improbable," was not calculated to allay anxiety in Berlin.[95]

In fact this approach by Napoleon may be considered uniquely a device to bring pressure to bear. One cannot understand the range and implications of Napoleon's diplomatic program if one denies the ambivalence of such methods; and one must presume that Napoleon would have made good the threat if his bluff were called and if realization served French interests. Only thus can one appreciate Napoleon's Rhenish plans, as they emerge in this phase of the Crimean War.[96]

Another of Napoleon's actions right after Sevastopol should be judged by the same yardstick: his official demand to the British to include restoration of Poland in the program, previously concerned only with the Eastern Question, as a new war aim for 1856. This initiative too has been wrongly dismissed as only or primarily a means to an end.[97] Despite this surface aspect, there was a genuine purpose at the core.

On 15 September, only a few days after Sevastopol fell, Walewski sent portentous instructions to the French ambassador in London: "The moment has come to prepare ourselves to make the restoration of the Kingdom of Poland according to the stipulations of the Congress of Vienna an essential aim of the peace negotiations, as soon as possible, and at the same time a fundamental base of the peace."[98]

It is not accurate to assume, based on the British response, which consciously or unconsciously involved a misunderstanding, that Napoleon made realization of this aim an absolute condition. Sources recently published by Di Nolfo prove that Napoleon considered himself misconstrued when the British government took his demand as a *conditio sine qua non*. He accordingly explained to the British Cabinet that he did not want anything new, no change in the European map, only reinstatement of a neglected European law.[99] This interpretation does not show the kernel of his demand, for in his program Poland served primarily as the opening wedge for a general remodelling.

The British answer was no, more on practical grounds than from conviction. The Cabinet considered the moment inopportune for a mutual pledge. Apart from the misunderstanding mentioned above, they suffered under the misconception that Napoleon wanted to restore the *independence* of Poland,[100] that is, Poland in the boundaries of 1772. And Clarendon believed that Russia would only agree to such a condition after two or three more campaigns.[101] Palmerston declared that it would suffice to agree upon this demand during the peace conference and to push it there.[102] But far more important than these considerations was the low priority that the Polish question held among British war aims. For the British, after control of the Black Sea, supremacy in the Baltic ranked as the next most important war aim aside from the diversion in the Caucasus. The British Cabinet's refusal demonstrates the now clear divergence in the interests of the two allies.

The British government's reply, officially communicated on 22 September,[103] influenced Napoleon's decision between war and peace: the demand for the restoration of Poland lost one of its functions but now served as a weapon to push Britain towards peace. This judgment made by previous scholars is, in itself, accurate, but, as has been said, one should also remember that Napoleon's Polish demand was not just a trial balloon, sent up to test British attitudes; it must also up to a certain point be taken literally.

Besides the categorical British answer on the Polish question, there were other factors which joined in the weeks after Sevastopol to set Napoleon on a peaceful course. The diplomatic options already well known to scholars read: either continue the war with Britain's aid *and* the help of the revolution—that is, first satisfy British war aims, then shake Europe to its foundations and perhaps remodel it—or negotiate peace through a congress imposed by Prussian or Austrian mediation. This would end the sacrifices for the moment on a modest basis, but would in no way necessitate repudiation of the long-term goal, which could be pursued later through an alliance with Russia and the union of the Danubian principalities.

Choosing the first alternative would have forced Napoleon to assent to British priorities and that implied that the nationalist revolutions would have to be postponed; or, if both allies followed their war aims simultaneously, a serious lack of coordination in the joint military operation might ensue. The second alternative was strongly suggested by motives of domestic policy.

The sources for French internal conditions during the Crimean War are as yet so little explored that we can only sketch a tentative picture of the connections between domestic policy and warmaking. We must be satisfied with hints and with isolated and inconclusive details. We must remember Napoleon's personal conviction that war was contrary to human nature and was particularly anachronistic at the contemporary cultural level. This attitude of Napoleon's became evident during the battles of Magenta and Solferino. It must also be reckoned with in the Crimean War, although it did not become as obvious as in 1859 because in 1855 Napoleon did not personally visit the front as intended. But we can cite Napoleon's remark, relayed by the Prussian major general, von Willisen, one of Frederick William's numerous special emissaries, that "he detested the barbarity inseparable from war."[104]

French public opinion weighed heavily on Napoleon as well, and after Sevastopol the public spoke unanimously for peace. No one has yet analyzed in detail the relevant reports from the prefects and pro-cureurs généraux,[105] but sources available from various quarters permit the conclusion that in the autumn of 1855 the French people called just as decidedly for peace as the British public two years before had demanded war. In Britain even in February 1856 Palmerston asserted that the people were for war from the highest aristocrat down to the last miner in Cornwall;[106] but scholars have been unable up to now to check this crucial assurance of the British prime minister. In France competent witnesses confirm the Duke of Cambridge's observation after an extensive stay in France in January 1856: "the feeling [for peace] extends itself to all classes. The Emperor cannot altogether go against a feeling which so loudly expresses itself on all occasions."[107] French military honor was satisfied, French soldiers had died for Sevastopol, but "die for Kronstadt?" Even the Crimean front seemed very far away for Frenchmen thinking primarily in continental terms. To make sacrifices for the Gulf of Finland—that was hardly comprehensible; it would have been different with military objectives on France's eastern boundary, or at least within "central Europe."

Napoleon's intimates, about whom we know more than about farmers in Provence, were unanimous for peace. For instance, directly after Sevastopol Walewski wrote in this sense to the Emperor vacationing in the summer palace of Saint Cloud; he tried to focus Napoleon's attention on the commanding moral position he had assumed before France and Europe after the storming of the Malakov: "Who can deny that France comes out of all this enhanced and Russia diminished? France *alone* has grown in this struggle. Today she holds first place in Europe."[108]

Historians have suspected that the minister's enthusiasm for peace was closely connected with his stock market speculations. In our opinion, every historian who has suggested such a link is obligated to show proof. It is completely inadequate to appeal to Persigny, Walewski's personal enemy, or to Clarendon, who after the congress called his colleague the worst individual with whom he had ever been obliged to work (probably because of his partiality for the Russians).[109] A dictator like Napoleon, deriving his power from the national will, could not afford to work against such a consensus. It was his minister's duty to confront him with this unanimity.

Napoleon's decision to end the war was affected by two other important considerations: the financial disarray and popular unrest. Here too before we can deliver an assured judgment it will be necessary to investigate the circumstances in greater depth; once again we must be satisfied with suggestions.

Napoleon did not gloss over the country's serious financial situation. On 3 March 1856, he publicly expressed concern to the Senate.[110] During the 1850s France experienced unexpectedly vigorous growth. Through pioneer railroad construction, the rapid progress of industrialization had become visible throughout the country. In 1853 the founding of the Crédit Mobilier revolutionized capital formation through an entirely new way of producing money and credit, mobilization of securities. In the sequel, there were signs of unsound speculation leading to a scarcity of money, accentuated when three war loans were floated.

Napoleon was impressed by this unfavorable turn. In autumn 1855, the Crédit Mobilier asked government approval for emission of a loan of over 72 million francs. The Emperor wanted at first to say no; he finally agreed to allow the raising of half the sum in view of the dangerous consequences of refusal for the Crédit.[111] In October 1855, the gold reserves of the Bank of France sank to 280 million francs; two months before they had amounted to 400 million. Part of the reserve had flowed off to the East, to the troops in the Crimea and to Constantinople, where the old Turkish piaster was being driven out by the French five franc piece.[112]

The scarcity of gold affected the man on the street through a rise in the cost of living. Inflation was intensified by a subaverage grain harvest, following upon two years' middling harvest. The grain harvest, amounting to 8.2 billion kilograms, had to make up a shortfall of 7 million, which, to be sure, was made up for by imports from abroad, but at the price of further financial strain. The annual consumption of grain reached at least 10 billion kilograms. Moreover, in expectation of higher prices, farmers tried to hold back part of the supply.[113]

The natural consequences of inflation were discontent in the country and open disaffection in the cities. In Angers and other places riots occurred, which indeed could be controlled by the police but which were exploited by countless secret societies. Already the prefects were urging a military buildup in the provinces to forestall any problems during the winter, when inflation would increase. By transferring security forces from Boulogne, the garrison at Lille was strengthened by two thousand and the one at Paris by ten thousand (to forty thousand).[114]

Domestic insecurity had not yet become ominous, but it was disquieting. Napoleon had to consider antidotes. The best remedy would be peace. The stale Marxist thesis, that Napoleon let himself be drawn into the Crimean War in order to escape domestic difficulties, can thus be stood on its head: Napoleon had a strong motive after Sevastopol for ending the war because of growing discontent in the country.

In 1857, when talking to General Totleben, the defender of Sevastopol, Napoleon admitted that after Sevastopol another decisive military victory was hardly to be expected and so he had seen no purpose in continuing the war.[115] And one year later he wrote his minister, Walewski: "The war in the East could have touched off the awaited revolution, and it was in just this hope, that I went into it. Major territorial changes could have followed. . . ."[116] Although these confessions point to the strategic and diplomatic situation as Napoleon perceived it, we must not understate the role played in his decision by the domestic considerations outlined above. The final impetus was provided by the British response to Napoleon's question about a new war aim: Poland, the symbol of Napoleon's effort to cure "France's congenital fateful illness," the treaties of 1815.

How did it happen that Britain, prepared for war under a bellicose prime minister, accepted the decision to end the war? The answer: Palmerston was not Britain. This statement must be examined more closely.

BRITAIN DECIDES TO END THE WAR

Both before and after Sevastopol, Palmerston directed his efforts towards continuing the war with energy. His remark in August 1855 was characteristic of his attitude: he feared peace more than war.[117] His first reaction to the French proposal concerning Poland was to agree emphatically:[118] what Napoleon said about Poland was absolutely justified. The allies would have a perfect right to include in the peace terms the demand that Poland be restored according to the stipulations of the 1815 congress. He wrote that if there were anything new to discuss, it would be best to continue the war. "We shall find all our steadiness and skill required to avoid being drawn into a peace which would disappoint the just expectations of the country, and leave unaccomplished the real objects of the war."[119]

Palmerston was backed by the military experts. The War Office, even more than the generals, was eager to wipe out the memory of the catastrophic maladministration in the organizational area and at the front. There was almost unanimous support from public opinion. Even such a firm partisan of peace as Gladstone was obliged to admit this resignedly: "The Government are certainly giving effect to the public opinion of the day."[120] *The Times*, indisputably a shaper of opinion, described the fall of Sevastopol as "a preliminary operation."[121]

Our knowledge of decisionmaking in the British Cabinet relative to the Polish question is fragmentary. The pretext for refusal was the inopportune timing of an official commitment. The real motive, however, was the fear that the short-term goal of controlling the Baltic would recede behind the long-term goal of restoring Poland.

In the following weeks the factor that carried the most weight in forcing British consent to negotiations was Napoleon's decided inclination to peace, which became clear after 22 September and quickly climaxed in the peace project of 14 November 1855 worked out by Buol and Bourqueney. Now the alternatives were to conclude peace or to continue the war alone.

The second choice, examined carefully, had to appear unrealistic. Using the device of a letter from sovereign to sovereign, Napoleon sketched allied strength for the benefit of the British Cabinet.[122] Plain statistics provided an impressive argument: "Your Majesty has in the Orient, I believe, 50,000 men and 10,000 horses. On my side, I have 200,000 men and 34,000 horses. Your Majesty has an immense fleet on the Black Sea, as on the Baltic; I have one which is imposing though less sizeable. Well, in spite of this formidable war machine, it is obvious to everyone that despite hurting Russia a great deal, we are not able to *overwhelm* her with our forces alone."

All the statistical juggling of, for example, Palmerston or Prince Albert did not erase the fact that, if French ground forces were to be withdrawn, the British expeditionary corps, a hodgepodge of British and Sardinian troops plus foreign legionaries numbering some eighty thousand men, according to Albert's calculation,[123] would not be able to accomplish anything against the Russian continent and a two-million-man army. Certainly such statistics taken in themselves are fallacious, and there are other factors to consider, such as control of communications, technical equipment, advantages and disadvantages of the vast space, economic warfare, the possibility of recruiting allies and so on. But except for Palmerston, and perhaps Clarendon and the War Office, no one in the British government judged the anticipated sacrifices acceptable in relation to war aims going beyond the Franco-Austrian peace project.

We do not know whether Palmerston solicited opinions from the War Office concerning military prospects if war were continued without the French. In any event, he informed the French emperor officially that Britain would not consent to a bad peace and would prefer to continue the war alone with the Ottoman Empire.[124] He attempted also to persuade his colleagues in the Cabinet, but he met with unanimous opposition.[125] A conversation he had with the Sardinian king makes it clear that his diagnosis was no impulsive reaction to the Austrian peace proposal. Victor Emmanuel reported Palmerston's comments to the French emperor in detail, and Napoleon, already irritated by the first letter, became so angry that he threatened to make it a matter of state.[126] Palmerston had explained that Napoleon was in the hands of a "parcel of adventurers" and was going to conclude a disgraceful peace dictated by the schemes of this band. He could just withdraw his army from the Crimea; England "did not care a fig for the French" and if Sardinia only stood fast, would continue the war alone to an "honoura-ble" conclusion.

At this point, when the British government was coming to a decision between war and peace, an inestimable advantage of the British constitution as compared with continental European systems proved its worth: the interplay of forces provided by a system of checks and balances at the highest governmental level. The Cabinet, the principal decisionmaking body, was collegially organized and its power was restricted by the influence of the Crown, and by its responsibility to Parliament and the administrative departments. The prime minister was only a *primus inter pares*. His power cannot be compared with that of an autocrat like Alexander II or a dictator like Napoleon III. If Palmerston had had the power of a Russian tsar, he undoubtedly would have opted for war. Nonetheless, in autumn 1855 the British Cabinet decided for peace in agreement with the Crown and the parliamentary opposition and against the advice of the prime minister, the war department, and the temper of public opinion.

The peace proposals set forth in the Buol-Bourqueney memorandum of 14 November arrived in London on 18 November. They consisted of the Four Points, now clarified in contrast to the earlier, purposely vague formulation, and sharpened. Contrary to the dominant but erroneous opinion, which evidently goes back to Temperley, they were supplemented by a fifth point important for Britain.[127] Clarendon's first reaction, communicated to Palmerston by letter that very evening, was to regard the peace proposals as suspect, since they emanated from Austria.[128] However, he did not underrate the extent to which they fulfilled British war aims and found British interests eminently provided for, above all in the third point, which demanded neutralization of the Black Sea. He alluded to Napoleon's inflexibility and recognized that the alliance with France would be endangered by refusal. Under these circumstances, he pleaded for acceptance, although he admitted he would have been happier if the proposals had never been made.

Queen Victoria admonished them not to brush aside the peace initiative; she adduced the same substantial reason, the fact that France threatened desertion.[129] She was convinced that it would be "the height of impolicy" to reject the proposals.

Both Clarendon and Victoria immediately brought up a noteworthy psychological calculation likely to shake Palmerston's firm stand: the conditions were so harsh one could hardly imagine Russia accepting them. It was to be expected that this peace project would fail like all the previous ones and would not interrupt Britain's pursuit of her war aims; this analysis must have made it easier to concur in French and Austrian wishes. The motive recurs in the following weeks[130] and can even be discerned during the peace negotiations next spring.[131] Clarendon actually believed that he could improve British prospects in conducting the war through Austria's new position. The demand made in the first point for the cession of half Bessarabia would dig an unbridgeable gulf between Vienna and Petersburg; Austria would accordingly have to act more closely with the western powers and would have to be "less neutral."[132] Austria's attitude indicated to him that she currently feared Russia less strongly, since she must guess that Russia was practically exhausted. This less cautious handling of Russia demonstrated that Austria had won a feeling of independence relative to the rest of Germany, another sign that Russian prestige in Germany had fallen sharply. From this line of thought Clarendon concluded that after the expected Russian refusal of the peace proposals, Germany would excommunicate Russia and it would then be possible to continue and end the war on a "really solid foundation."

This conclusion was very questionable, since it rested on too many interdependent variables. But its point of departure, the expectation of Russian intransigeance, apparently was widely accepted in the British Cabinet[133] and, ironically, contributed to the decision for peace.

Like the Queen and the foreign secretary, the Prince Consort favored acceptance of the Austro-French peace proposals.[134] Even today scholars do not fully agree how much influence the Crown, especially Prince Albert, exerted on cabinet decisions in the nineteenth century. Historians have given up the earlier interpretation, advanced by Bagehot, that "royalty [was] not essential," for the effective functioning of cabinet government.[135] Especially since the publication of Queen Victoria's correspondence, the pendulum has swung part way back towards the other side. As for Prince Albert, it has been suggested that if he had lived longer, he would have "Prussianized" the British constitution. It has also been said that the Prince exercised more political power than any British sovereign since Charles II. The evidence available today, which is especially rich for the Crimean War, confirms this more recent interpretation.[136] In this particular question, the Prince's evaluation coincided with that of the Cabinet majority.

It is not necessary to analyze the opinions of individual Cabinet members based on the sources we have. It is enough to inquire into the grounds for the decision, in so far as they have not been considered above.

As to Palmerston's comprehensive war aims program, Cabinet members pointed out that Britain's goal in the war had been presented to European public opinion as restoration of the European balance; could this explanation still be credible if Britain rejected the peace project? For example, Gladstone writing to the Duke of Argyll, then postmaster general, doubted Britain's right "to rectify the distribution of political power by bloodshed which carry it far beyond just bounds."[137] Argyll agreed with this point of view and alluded to the arbitrariness of the concept of "just" and "unjust bounds." He sympathized as little as Gladstone with Palmerston's radical interpretation of the "balance of power" as meaning that Russia should be reduced to a great power in name only. The time might come when people would reproach Britain with the same overweening ambition which had been the excuse for war with Russia.

As the Cabinet evaluated the situation, there emerged a diplomatic consideration which also influenced Napoleon in a related but opposite way: they feared that if the war continued on French terms, France would achieve military and political preponderance which would upset the balance of power and reduce Britain to the status of a junior partner in the alliance.

Finally they discussed the repercussions of the war on the Ottoman Empire. The exhaustion of the Ottomans' already insufficient resources could only be hastened by lengthening the war. Their position as protégés would become more explicit. The concern for the Sultan's independence and honor would become farcical, and his position would ultimately be untenable. In other words, the war could lead to a second Unkiar-Skelessi, this time with the West. As already mentioned, this was precisely the outcome Ottoman statesmen had feared.[138]

Second only to these anxieties, the Cabinet worried about detrimental effects on Britain's internal affairs. Scholars have convincingly demonstrated—see Lamer's recent work on German views for an example—that on the continent Britain's nineteenth-century constitution was misunderstood by everyone, from conservatives to liberals. Inflexible habits of thought, an overemphasis on doctrine, and reference to European constitutional monarchies as the standard explain this faulty grasp. An example is Lothar Bucher's treatise appearing in 1855, during the Crimean War, *The Truth about Parliamentary Government*. In France, Auguste Comte had already contributed to the misapprehension of British parliamentary institutions.[139] The British form of government was just the opposite of a system based on abstract principles like Nicholas I's autocracy, neoabsolutism in Austria, the constitutional monarchy of the Prussian reaction, or Napoleon's Caesarism; it was a conglomeration of rules and institutions derived from tradition, or, as Gladstone said, a fortuitous "heap of absurdities."[140]

Like political theorists, practicing politicians on the continent rated the British form of government very low. In Frankfurt, Bismarck deplored the lost "ancestral wisdom" of the Englanders in a tone at once ironic and contemptuous.[141] His impression of Britain during the Crimean War does not resemble at all his later view, which has been praised by historians as very realistic. In Vienna, Metternich regarded the critical condition of British political and military leadership at the beginning of 1855 as symptomatic of social revolution. He wrote Buol in perplexity, "Old England no longer exists and a new England has not yet been made."[142]

The notable thing about the British constitutional situation in 1855 is not so much the way it was perceived on the continent as the way it was perceived in Britain itself. The Crimean War unloosed a lively debate over the constitution of the country. Some blamed the parliamentary system of government for the disastrous conduct of the war in the winter of 1854/55 and called for a dictator; they woke a resounding echo in public opinion. They considered the appeal to Palmerston not so radical as they wished; but it was still salvation in the hour of need. When Prince Albert said on 9 June 1855: "Our constitutional government is on trial,"[143] he used a phrase which was not demagogic but did express the anxiety of the moderate majority. The attacks had begun with criticism of the army leadership; then deeper causes were sought in the failure of the civilian administration reaching to the highest level. Confidence in the existing system had never been so deeply shaken. The impact of the crisis was as serious as the Prussian constitutional conflict of 1862 or the Dreyfus Affair in France.[144]

Continuing the war would have intensified the problem. Placing Palmerston, the idol of bellicose public opinion, at the head of the government had brought a certain calm. However, it could hardly be more than buying time. In autumn 1855, in spite of the changes, average to below average leaders continued to head the army. Another setback in the field, for example before Kronstadt, could loose the storm again. Shortly after the fall of Kars, ominous calls for a committee of inquiry were heard. In the Cabinet itself, contrary to the general impression, Palmerston enjoyed less confidence than Aberdeen at any time prior to his fall. One might say that the fall of Sevastopol prevented a second greater catastrophe in Britain. About details we can only speculate.

Such considerations demonstrably influenced the Cabinet's decision on 20 November to accept the Franco-Austrian peace project.[145] In the decisive Cabinet meeting, certain conditions were set on implementation of the project;[146] this naturally made it easier for each participant to agree. Special stipulations were appended to the third and fifth points: neutralization of the Black Sea was not to be the subject of a separate convention between Russia and the Ottoman Empire but should be part of the general treaty; also the Sea of Azov must be subject to the rule of neutrality. The broad fifth point was to be understood as covering a pledge by Russia not to rebuild the fortress of Bomarsund on the Aland Islands, which had been destroyed by the British navy, and the right of the allies to discuss the fate of the provinces on the east coast of the Black Sea. Palmerston was outvoted by an overwhelming majority. So he capitulated: "He was far too able and too wise a man not to see that he could not fight against both our

French ally and the prevalent feeling of his own Cabinet," in the words of his colleague, Argyll.[147]

The fundamental decision had been taken. Even if the British prime minister tried to cheat, the success of the peace effort now hinged on Russia's reaction. Before discussing this, it is necessary to go into the origins of the peace initiative.

Austria's Peace Initiative

Background

In a letter of 18 November 1855 to Palmerston, Foreign Secretary Clarendon tried to understand Austria's motives as an aid in reaching his own decision.[148] From Austria's viewpoint, seizing the peace initiative must seem safer now than before, despite the sacrifice demanded of Russia. The fact that Austria now felt able to act independently of the German Confederation proved that she must consider Russia seriously weakened. In the spring, Russia's military prestige in Germany and in the Austrian army had apparently been great enough that Austria would have faced isolation in Germany had she proceeded actively against Russia. At the time when every soldier of the French and British army was needed in the Crimea, Austria presumably had feared, reasonably, that she would have to bear the brunt of a European war and that the slightest reverse would put Vienna at the mercy of the Russian army. All this was different now, since military affairs had taken a new turn. The German courts evidently realized that their idol was broken and that Russian troops were being transferred from the German border to the south. It would be natural for Austria to wish for peace and to offer extensive concessions to the western powers to get it. For she distrusted the liberal tendencies in Germany which would be encouraged if the war were prolonged; she suspected that Louis Napoleon would not continue the war in the Crimea, but might look elsewhere for compensation for his sacrifices. So Austria threatened to break relations with Russia in case she rejected the peace conditions; that is, she would declare a "war without battles." It might seem absurd and typically Austrian, but one must remember that Austria had said from the beginning that she would not go to war without effective military support from the allies.

There is much truth in these reflections, but not the whole truth. To understand the Austrian position in 1855 to 1856, we must examine Clarendon's remarks more closely. No part of nineteenth-century Austrian history has been so profoundly misconstrued until very recently as the Crimean War. Understanding the Austrian position, and specifically understanding Count Buol's policy, has been hindered by traditional misconceptions. The first steps towards reevaluating Austrian policy and revising Buol's image have been made;[149] but it is clear that they have had very little impact, since it could be said even very recently that Buol led the Viennese war party,[150] and that he wanted to use the Crimean War "to finish the work of Prince Eugene and to extend Austria's rule over the neighboring Balkan provinces, to achieve and exploit the downfall of the Ottoman Empire in Europe."[151] On the last point we might simply change Buol's name with the diplomatically insignificant Count Coronini, who commanded the Austrian occupation troops in the Danubian principalities and whose Eugenian dreams[152] Buol worked to combat. The first misconception, however, has profound roots.

It may reflect the limits of Prussian historiography that Buol, as the more or less unsuccessful mediator in the Crimean War, was compared unfavorably with trigger-happy activists like Bismarck. A Social Darwinist attitude and a historiography dedicated to Bismarck worship would naturally see nothing else in the Austrian administration's unreserved desire for peace except effeminacy and neurosis. In gross oversimplification, the collapse of Buol's policy in 1859 is then linked all-too-directly to Austria's isolation as result of the war. Buol has also suffered at the hands of pro-Austrian grossdeutsch historiography, since his policy, with its lack of sensitivity towards Prussia and the small German states, inevitably presages 1866.

Even contemporary judgments of Buol and his policy in Germany were overwhelmingly negative. Heinrich Leo described Austria's seeming inability to choose between the belligerents as "political bill-jobbing."[153] Bismarck called Buol a cipher.[154] In December 1855 Pfordten compared him to a locomotive "that does not know where it's going and whenever it's set in motion, just puffs and whistles."[155]

It was largely from such sources that the Austrian historian Heinrich Friedjung constructed his interpretation of Austrian policy, appearing in 1907. Naturally he arrived at a negative view of the foreign minister, which was adopted unquestioningly by subsequent scholars. From the daily records of the Vienna Haus-, Hof-, und Staatsarchiv, it is possible to prove that Friedjung did not look at a single one of Buol's instructions.[156] Friedjung and his followers also used contemporary publications which were biased because they relied almost exclusively on Austrian and German authorities, who as a rule judged Buol unfavorably. In fact, Buol cannot be identified with any of the factions at the corrupt Vienna court; he was isolated there, opposed by military leaders and by his own colleagues, except for Bach. In contrast, foreign diplomats and politicans evaluated his political competence in overwhelmingly favorable terms.[157] At the Paris Congress he developed a good working relationship with Clarendon,[158] and even Cavour believed that Austria and Sardinia would agree, if it depended solely on Buol.[159]

Buol's outlook had been molded by Metternich: this was especially true in the Crimean War, even when he seemed to go against his mentor's advice, as in the December Treaty. He appealed to Schwarzenberg's German and Russian policy only when he wished to demonstrate Austrian consistency to counter the reproach of betraying the Holy Alliance or deserting Russia.

It is precisely this reproach, made even at the time, which historians have adopted without examination. However, the corollary is a view of the Holy Alliance that does not really apply to those years, the era of Nicholas I. The Holy Alliance or, in the plainer and more appropriate phrase used by contemporary diplomats, the alliance of the three northern courts, has not yet been investigated in depth,[160] but its basic structure and functions are clear: in its political capacity it protected the European balance of power; in the social sphere it defended regimes guided by tradition and legitimacy against the forces of the revolution. Nicholas's support for the Greek war of independence shows that these principles could be overwhelmed by strong national interest. In fact, from that time on, the Holy Alliance also enabled the Tsar to dominate his own allies. The relationship between them, particularly after 1848, followed the model of two wards dependent on their guardian, a pattern which Austria in turn sought to impose on Prussia. The phrase allegedly coming from Schwarzenberg about Austria's "ingratitude" to Russia must be understood in this context; under whatever circumstances it was uttered, it aptly expresses his efforts to escape from Russian tutelage.

Both before and during the Crimean War, Buol pursued this policy of gradual withdrawal from reliance on Russia.[161] Buol and his likeminded colleague Hübner considered the most important result of the war for Austria to be "liberation from Russian dominance."[162] Up to now historians have failed to see Buol's "destruction" of the Holy Alliance from this vantage point. What remained to be destroyed in 1854 was hardly a Holy Alliance; rather it was a case of ending a de facto unholy alliance de jure.[163] In the Greek war of independence as well as in the Crimean War, Nicholas distorted the basic idea of the alliance founded by his brother. In 1853 he wanted to make Francis Joseph his accomplice in rousing the Balkan Christians against Ottoman rule.[164] Francis Joseph and his foreign minister rejected this demand by appealing to the principles of the Holy Alliance. This sprang naturally from Austria's instinct for self-preservation.

Outright alienation from Russia certainly did contrast with Metternich's ideas; during his term of office, he had been able to keep a high degree of independence within the alliance of the three eastern powers. However after 1848 to 1849, relations between the European powers changed fundamentally. The Tsar now vaunted himself as the despot of eastern and central Europe. Partly as payment for the suppression of the Hungarian Revolution, he demanded at the outset of the Crimean War that Austria do what he wanted. But Austria rejected the demand and refused to participate in the partition of the Ottoman territories in southeastern Europe.

Buol was able to retain Metternich's axiom that preservation of the Balkan status quo was necessary for the Hapsburg empire's survival. This interpretation conflicts with the view of previous scholars. Even the most recent major revisionist attempt asserts more strongly than ever that Buol endeavored to continue Schwarzenberg's active policy in southeastern Europe.[165] However, the documents on which this study is based permit, more plausibly, the contrary interpretation, as has recently been demonstrated in relation to the Danubian principalities[166] and as will be shown below.[167]

The obstacle to evaluating Count Buol's policy is the fact that there are very few sources that indubitably demonstrate creative thinking on his part. In the numerous instructions to ambassadors abroad one seldom finds reflections about motives and goals. Where they do exist, it is hard to decide whether they express inner conviction or merely the attitudes of the Emperor. Buol was an unconditionally loyal servant; he was not a statesman who, when faced with fundamental political divergences, fought for his opinions, like Bismarck against William I or Palmerston against Queen Victoria. Besides, the old controversy about whether the young emperor or his minister directed foreign policy in the Crimean War cannot yet be resolved conclusively for the entire period; the two latest works based on archival research reach opposite conclusions.[168]

In our opinion, Buol's eastern policy in the Crimean War agreed fundamentally with Metternich's axioms and advice. The conditions of the multinational empire's survival dictated two principles: the territorial status quo in the Balkans must not be attacked by foreign influence nor must it be altered even with Austria's cooperation. At the beginning of the eastern crisis, on 9 February 1853, Metternich wrote to Buol: "fruits nourishing to our empire do not grow in any field in the Orient. . . . There is only one course we must cling to and that is *the political* which means in fact *the maintenance of treaties* and the *prevention of a European war, from Oriental causes!*"[169] When war broke out, in spite of Austrian efforts to prevent it, the primary task was *"the quickest possible restoration of the peace."*[170] The best method would be through diplomatic conferences, preferably in Vienna, with a carefully conceived agenda.[171] Austria must not become actively involved in the conflict under any circumstances. This did not imply strict neutrality but "waiting with a free hand."

Since Metternich considered the consequences of the struggle to be totally incalculable, he warned against leaning toward either of the belligerents. The idea of unpredictability and the consequent need for Austria to keep freedom of action recur again and again in his advice to Buol. "Austria can only find the one [attitude] practical for herself when she secures freedom of action. In today's unhallowed war—a war whose origin rests on errors and whose end cannot be foreseen—the geography of our empire should suffice to determine our position in the quicksand. The state *in the middle* must not be towed off either to the east or to the west. . . . We are called to the task *of restoring peace* . . . but we must never let ourselves be used as the shock troops of east against west or west against east."[172]

These opinions, or rather stereotyped formulas, recur again and again in Buol's correspondence with his ambassadors, opinions which they were to use with foreign governments. In the phrase appearing in a letter to Hübner: "in having escaped from one form of dependence we have no desire to embark upon another,"[173] we can see both Buol's satisfaction at the escape from Russian tutelage which Schwarzenberg had initiated and he had continued as well as Metternich's warning against exchanging the present waiting game for dependence on the western powers. When the failure of the last Vienna conference, in 1855, was followed by pressure from the West to enter the war, Buol wrote again to Hübner: "it would be better yet to return to dependence on Russia. The idea that the interests of the continent ought to be discussed and decided upon in London is out of date."[174]

This statement provides a key to interpreting the December Treaty of the preceding year between Austria and the sea powers and brings us closer to understanding this step than Buol's alleged and certainly overworked phrase, "diplomatic revolution." Metternich decided that in concluding this treaty, Austria had abandoned the course he had advised, and so he castigated Buol.[175] Appealing to the hopes aroused by the treaty in Britain and France, some scholars have erroneously wished to read into it Austrian readiness for war with Russia. On the contrary Buol intended a purely moral tilt towards the West, designed to save her from the isolation which threatened on all sides—Russia, Germany, the West. A further aspect was the fact that Austria might now be able to exert some influence on allied war aims, which were assuming an extravagance potentially dangerous for Austria since Austro-Russian relations might be further embittered.[176]

This interpretation of the treaty is confirmed by the fact that Buol was able in the very same month to carry out his intention of bringing the belligerents to the conference table. In any event the sea powers concurred in secretly expecting that negotiations would fail and war could continue. The mistake that can, perhaps, be cast up to Buol is that he did not state *unambiguously* in advance to the allies that Austria, in the event the conference failed, would not *automatically* enter the war. Anyhow Austrian entry into the war could not be construed from the text of the treaty. If the western powers cherished that hope, that was their error. On 16 April 1855 Buol wrote his ambassador in London: "Austria is a great power who can make war for her own interests or for those of Europe, but she cannot expose herself to the reproach of doing it unnecessarily or for the convenience of an ally."[177]

As we know, the western powers interpreted the December Treaty differently than Buol. This is demonstrated by Clarendon's secret letter to Palmerston, mentioned earlier.[178] In an analogous situation in autumn 1855, when the Franco-Austrian memorandum pledged the sea powers and Austria "to consult" about measures to be taken in case Russia rejected the peace project, Buol emphasized that Russia's refusal and the subsequent rupture of diplomatic relations would not in themselves entail Austrian entry into the war. Thus he underscored to Bourqueney, the French ambassador in Vienna—in order to avoid any ambiguity "and in order to avoid the misunderstandings which arose from the treaty of 2 December"—that the means of pressure to be used against Russia (breaking relations and discussions with the western powers) *did not* include a *commitment* to fight.[179] Austrian participation would completely change the character of the war and would bring incalculable consequences; this could only occur after all other expedients had been exhausted.

Again this notion of incalculability, the "incalculable risks," traces back to Metternich's advice;[180] it recurs in Austrian documents throughout the war like a refrain. Just as frequently one meets the consensus against entering the war. For instance, in November 1855 Buol reminded the French ambassador of the basic principle "which we have constantly advanced, that Austria cannot take such a weighty decision except for reasons which would directly involve *her own interests,* or which would be imposed on us by *the general interests of Europe.*"[181]

What did this facade of generalities mean in practice? Count Buol, like Metternich his teacher, was a representative of the traditional European community, and thinking in European terms seemed to both of them an obvious procedure.[182] He is poles away from Bismarck, who commented: "I always hear the word 'Europe' on the lips of those politicians, who want something from other powers, which they don't dare ask in their own name."[183] A European approach followed almost inescapably from these presuppositions: Austria, as the most historic and most prestigious, though no longer materially the strongest of the great powers, saw herself as the political as well as cultural link between

East and West thanks to her geographical position.[184] Based on the Danube basin with German and Italian states as buttresses, she tried to hold the balance politically between the fringe powers, Britain and Russia, whose mutual opposition surfaced at the end of the eighteenth century and dominated the nineteenth. Culturally, she regarded herself as the channel for the spiritual and material overflow from the West to the East.[185]

In domestic policy, this European vision expressed itself in the desire to repress the forces of revolution, which since the French Revolution had threatened to overwhelm the traditional social order of the Hapsburg empire, particularly through liberalism and nationalism. Buol and his monarch were profoundly persuaded of the importance of this mission. This is obvious from their statements about the difficulties of the Austrian position at the Paris Congress. When on 11 February 1856, the council of ministers discussed possible internal arrangements for the Danubian principalities,[186] which would be set in place by the congress, the Emperor instructed his foreign minister to block every attempt "to introduce democratic or modern liberal institutions into the principalities or to make them a haven for political refugees and agitators." With respect to Serbia, it must be declared in the negotiations that "the basis of princely power . . . comes from the Sultan and that the use of any sort of popular choice must be excluded."[187]

This fear of revolution is the neglected motive behind Austria's political position during the Crimean War. In contrast, a Yugoslav scholar has recently termed this fear of revolution a "myth."[188] He agrees that there were certain conditions for revolution among the Balkan Christians at the time of the Crimean War: hunger, and a striving toward social justice and national independence; but insurrections thus motivated would not have touched off a European revolution. This suggestion does not disprove the plausibility of the Austrian government's anxiety, since it focused on a small area—Bosnia, Herzegovina, and especially Montenegro—and was concerned in a cultural sense with the peasants and mountain clans of the western Balkans. More important would be an examination of revolutionary symptoms in the "nation states" of the Hapsburg empire, such as Hungary. Only when scholars have provided this can we reach a definitive judgment as to whether the Austrian government's fear of revolution was justified or not. But in any event, the Hapsburgs worried primarily about revolution in their own empire, not revolution in Europe.

Indeed one can speak of a "revolutionary nightmare" haunting Buol and Francis Joseph during the Crimean War.[189] It was only too well founded domestically and diplomatically: at the beginning of the eastern crisis, only four years separated Austria from the most difficult domestic passage of the empire's existence. The consequences of the revolution had affected every citizen and lasted into the war years. The state of siege in Vienna and Prague was lifted only on 1 September 1853, in Galicia, in Hungary, in the Banat, and in Lombardy-Venetia on 1 May 1854, while in Transylvania it continued until 15 December 1854. Nineteenth-century Austria was not a unitary state like France; it was an imperial structure, a multinational empire on the Ottoman or the Russian model. Like them, its unity had been in constant danger since the French Revolution because of the explosive force of nationalism. Dahlmann at Frankfurt in 1848[190] had called for the dissolution of the clumsy imperial body; Mazzini had made it his life's work; Pogodin, Russia's most important journalist, never tired of asserting during the war that the shortest road to Constantinople lay through Vienna.[191] The view that nationalism in the Hapsburg empire could never have been satisfied short of its collapse is deterministic and hence unhistorical.[192] The tsarist empire was overthrown, but the Russian multinational state still exists. Certainly as compared with the Hapsburg empire, it possessed the advantage of a broader territorial expanse and a frontier position which protected it better from outside influence, and conditions in the tsarist empire may have made its minorities more susceptible to Russification in comparison with the obstacles to Germanization (or Magyarization) in Austria; but the contagion of nationalism was basically just as dangerous to Russia's cohesion as to Austria's. This is demonstrated by the Polish revolutions of the nineteenth century, the decades needed to subjugate the mountain tribes of the Caucasus, and the compulsion to secede in the civil war after 1918. Nobody in the nineteenth century, except one or two Turcophiles, believed in the survival of the Ottoman Empire, the greatest empire since the *imperium Romanum,* for Turkey was not only menaced like Austria and Russia by the explosive force of nationalism, but was further threatened by the confrontation of two world religions and the unavoidable symbiosis with a foreign—western—civilization.

Several considerations made it impossible for the Austrian rulers, assuming they were not suicidal, to opt for participation in the war on one side or the other; these factors included overawareness of the structural laws of an imperial system in the nineteenth century, recent experiences during the revolutions of 1848 to 1849, and Napoleon's radical plans for Europe, which were common knowledge in Vienna along with those of the Tsar for the Balkans. If Austria had cooperated with Nicholas's partition plans for the Balkans, she would have become an accomplice in the dissolution of the Ottoman Empire and would have conjured up, with the radicalization of the Balkan peoples, the danger of a revolutionary flare-up in the Slavic portion of her own empire; and meanwhile it would have provoked Napoleon into revolutionizing the Hapsburg empire in Italy, and perhaps in Hungary and Galicia as well. But if Austria had collaborated in the war on the western side, she would have borne the brunt of the fighting, her finances, already in disarray, would have been ruined, and the first defeat, likely to be quick in view of Russian military superiority, would have been the signal for revolution. For the Austrian administration there was only one real alternative, the only choice whose results were at all calculable, that is the position of expectancy, "waiting with a free hand." Every demand for assistance in the war, from Petersburg, Paris, London, or wherever else, originated either in blunt egoism or in a misunderstanding of the elements of survival for the Hapsburg empire. Historians' condemnations of Austrian policy in the Crimean War are therefore simplistic, that is to say, unhistorical.

Some remarkable firsthand testimony illustrates the fear of revolution. In the summer of 1853, even before hostilities broke out, when there was still hope for a peaceful solution, Buol wrote to Hübner and Colloredo: "if we were to throw ourselves completely into the arms of France and England, that would definitely mean war. . . . in putting ourselves at Russia's disposal and sharing all the consequences of her more than rash policy, we should face not merely war, but the general disruption of Europe—maybe even the triumph of the revolution."[193] The Leiningen Mission to Constantinople some time before had supplied the precedent for the more famous Menshikov Mission; it explicitly pursued the goal of stopping an Ottoman war of conquest in Montenegro, which, so people feared in Vienna, might give the signal for revolution to the "subversive party" of the Kossuths and Mazzinis.[194] Napoleon's warning to Hübner at the end of 1853: "I will raise Italy"[195] parallels Nicholas's simultaneous threat: "I will march in the name of our holy faith to deliver Christianity from the Moslem yoke; and I appeal to everyone who is Christian."[196] In Frankfurt the Prussian delegate to the Bundestag, who was not exactly well disposed towards Austria in general or Count Buol in particular, had to admit after months of observing developments in the East, that Buol's foreign policy was wise. He believed that France's motive in seeking Austrian military assistance was not so much to control Russia as to damage Austria.[197] "As soon as Austria goes to war against Russia, she is 'under the thumb' of France and must accept whatever is imposed on her with regard to her position in Italy, in the Orient, or in Poland by the Allies, who are sitting on the long end of the lever." The same dangers would arise if Austria opted for Russia. The procedures of the Holy Alliance in previous years had sufficiently proved Austria's second-rank, subordinate position when paired with Russia.

Austria's diplomatic sphere of action was severely restricted as much by Petersburg's warning that Austria is "the Achilles whose heel is everywhere"[198] as by Napoleon's threat, in the witty formula of an Italian contemporary, that he had "in hand the torch for burning and the pump for extinguishing."[199] Austria's orientation was rigidly prescribed: the path of peace, of neutrality in the eastern war. This was the policy that offered the Hapsburg empire the greatest chance for endurance. Buol thought and acted very realistically in accordance with the rules for survival of a multinational empire. *Realpolitik* in the nineteenth century did not just mean seizing the initiative in a favorable moment like Cavour or Bismarck;[200] it also meant keeping quiet during general pandemonium or initiating a disciplined retreat.[201]

Tribute is due Austria for her role in the Crimean War, a recognition denied her by contemporaries as well as historians: she kept the war away from the Balkan powder keg by occupying the Danubian principalities in 1854 and localizing hostilities in the Crimea. She earned additional merit by limiting the time of the war and seizing the initiative for peace in autumn 1855. In so doing, she saved Europe from a world war.

It is appropriate now to examine the Austrian peace initiative, with emphasis on certain little-known details.

Implementation

In sorting out the multitude of peace initiatives in the autumn of 1855, it is essential to establish the chronological sequence. Previous accounts suffer by disregarding this fundamental rule; as a result they posit a false causal connection or they ascribe too much weight to one attempt by omitting others. An example is Friedjung's interpretation, dominant for decades, to the effect that Buol seized the initiative because he feared a direct understanding between Petersburg and Paris through the Seebach-Nesselrode and Morny-Gorchakov connection;[202] this hypothesis does not pass the test of chronology. Likewise, given the ambiguity of the expression and its context,[203] it is inadmissable without more evidence to construe a demand addressed to Austria to seize the peace initiative from the remarks passed between Walewski and Hübner on 13 September, when the French foreign minister said: "When it becomes a question of making peace, it will be the moment for Austria to play an important role by resolutely supporting the sea powers."[204] As late as the beginning of October, Buol declared to another diplomat that the time had not yet come "to step between two enemies with a compromise, when one side shows no sign of weariness, and the other has been encouraged by successes."[205] Nonetheless, some weeks later Bourqueney ascribed to Count Buol "the honor of first formulating" the peace proposals which he brought to Paris at the beginning of October.[206]

Until all the documents have been analyzed, the last word about the peace initiative cannot be spoken. It would be sounder to omit as far as possible any previous discussions of this subject in historical studies, since they are too abbreviated and are misleading in emphasis. In fact, it may never be possible to decide exactly where the initiative origi-nated. Rather, one must recognize numerous more or less independent soundings during the weeks after Sevastopol.

The same may be said of the unofficial efforts in Paris and Petersburg to enter into direct conversation. The question about initia-tive can be answered unequivocally here: each side believed that the other would take it. France could not step forward officially because of her alliance commitments; Russia considered it dishonorable to sue for peace given the existing military situation. So on both sides there was no more than the readiness to listen to the other side. On 12 September Gorchakov circulated a quip in Vienna that describes the subsequent bilateral soundings: "We will be mute, but not deaf."[207] He added in German: "We must above all guard our new emperor against humilia-tion." Likewise Nesselrode let it be known in Petersburg: "We are waiting . . . for someone to offer us reasonable conditions—we will accept."[208] However, a glance at the military situation made it clear that Russia was in no hurry to come forward with peace proposals. In Petersburg people cherished the hope that Napoleon, having won an important victory, would now make up his quarrel with Russia.[209]

In Paris the foreign minister told the Austrian envoy that he did not expect Austria to initiate peace negotiations at the present time.[210] These were the days when Napoleon was urging London to enlarge allied war aims through inclusion of the Polish question; he envisioned occupation of the entire Crimea as the next step. French hopes with regard to Poland fell through in September because Britain said no, much to Walewski's relief, since he did not share his master's ambitions. Only then did the minister speak to Hübner about the advantages of a quick peace: "It [peace] would resolve the Eastern Question, without opening the Russian Question."[211] To open the "Russian question" meant taking Palmerston's program seriously; it meant perhaps that after the invasion of the Crimea, the bulk of Anglo-French troops would be transferred to Bessarabia to continue fighting there, or as Hübner put it: "The major front will be in Poland and the minor one in the Crimea." Walewski completed Hübner's thought: "It will be neces-sary to try to make peace before larger questions arise."[212]

For Buol all this raised the spectre of a war which could no longer be localized, but would become European. He had to act. The details of his decision are not known. Buol wished first to inform himself exactly concerning allied war aims; then, following a hint from Bourqueney, he entertained the idea of breaking diplomatic relations with Russia as Austria's best means of pressure on Petersburg.[213] His own proposals about war aims he summarized as follows: of the Four Points, the first two should be stiffened, so that the Danubian principalities would form a more effective bulwark against Russia. Fortifications could be constructed in these provinces; Russia should be removed entirely from the left bank of the Danube through the cession of a strip of territory and should be excluded from participation in arrangements about Danube shipping. The third point must be understood as meaning neutralization of the Black Sea. The fourth point should be negotiated in Constantinople without Russia.[214]

At the beginning of October, Bourqueney brought these proposals to Paris. It was four weeks before he could return to Vienna with counterproposals. In the meantime, Napoleon must have stopped hoping that the military situation in the Crimea would improve for the sea powers. The only French revisions concerned the first two points: Moldavia and Wallachia should be united under a foreign prince recognizing suzerainty of the Porte; Russia must return Bessarabia, ceded in 1829 to Russia, to the united principalities.[215]

This idea of a rectification of frontiers between Russia and the Ottoman Empire was not entirely new. It had been broached at the Vienna Conference in the spring by the plenipotentiaries of Britain and France, but no concrete formula had emerged. The stimulus to discussion was now provided by Buol and picked up by France. Since the peace treaty of Adrianople had stipulated only the cession of the Danube mouths to Russia, not any part of Bessarabia, Buol evidently pressed for revision in subsequent conversations with Bourqueney. In Bourqueney's memorandum of 7 November, a line between Lippesani[216] and Kilia was proposed as a new boundary; Buol changed this in his own hand to the line pushed farther forward from Chotin to Lake Sasyk.[217] The cession was justified in the document as an "exchange for the fortresses and territories captured by the allied army."

Therefore the extension of territorial cessions from Russia indubitably goes back to Austrian influence. This demand, it seems to us, was Austria's greatest mistake during the Crimean War.

The neutralization of the Black Sea has generally been regarded as the heaviest sacrifice imposed on Russia. The semiofficial Russian narrative of the war supports this interpretation. But the course of the peace negotiations shows that the cession of territory in Bessarabia posed the real question of honor for Russia. Russia had long accustomed herself to the prospect of dismantling her power on the Black Sea. Neutralization could not change the conditions that actually prevailed in 1855 to 1856, since there were no Russian ships left. On the other hand, no territory had been ceded since Peter the Great. It would be the first territorial cession by Russia to the Ottoman Empire, the hereditary enemy.

In nineteenth-century European history down to the peace of Versailles, cessions of territory imposed by the enemy have been more wounding to national pride than any other admission of defeat. After the Second World War, with the weakening of national feeling, there has been a change of consciousness in such questions. In the Crimean War, the demand for territory must have been an even greater blow to Russia, since it was no secret that the requirement originated with the Austrians, who had not fired a shot. Moreover the territory to be ceded included the fortress of Ismail, captured by Suvorov under Catharine the Great in a brilliant example of Russian prowess.

Buol certainly did not underestimate the severity of the sacrifice asked of Russia; however, he apparently thought it less serious than the neutralization of the Black Sea. "To submit to these conditions," he reported on 9 November to the Emperor, "will fall very hard on Russia. . . . The renunciation of her preponderance in the Black Sea and the plans associated with it is the hardest sacrifice for Russia. However, the sea powers will never give up this demand. If Russia makes up her mind to this sacrifice, then it seems to me that we can attain the territorial cession, which promises such incalculable advantages."[218]

According to preceding utterances, Buol evidently counted among the "incalculable advantages" the fact that Russia would now withdraw from the Danube. "The Danube would become a German river all the way to the delta." It was the main artery for Hapsburg commerce, and as long as Russia had her hand on it, it was choked at the mouth. For while Russia had had possession, she had allowed the Danube estuary to become virtually impassable to favor the rising port of Odessa.[219] If it had been a question of "*freedom* of shipping on the Danube," Austria would have had to be satisfied with demanding a narrow strip of territory on the left bank or just the left bank itself (the Kilia arm), following the Ottoman-Russian boundary before 1829. But the present demand rested on a major self-deception. It would inevitably destroy the trust between the two powers, which had indeed been severely strained by previous experiences, but had by no means disappeared.

To what extent Buol himself was responsible for this territorial demand is not yet clear. His choice of the phrase, "incalculable advantages," in no way implies that Buol agreed with the extent of the territorial cession. Some sources hint that Buol found himself in the same situation as Bismarck in 1871 with regard to Metz.[220] At the beginning of January 1856, the Prussian government learned that top

Austrian generals had rejected the river boundary.[221] A memorandum from Quartermaster General Hess dated 22 January 1856 disclosed that the delimitation in the north around Chotin was based on military considerations, since this key fortress could be tied into the Austrian fortification system in Galicia and Bukovina.[222] It was the military also who demanded that Austria be granted two important rights: the right to navigate the Danube to its mouth with warships in time of peace and the right to station Austrian garrisons at certain strong points. Since the Emperor adopted this wish, Buol expressed only feeble objections;[223] but his attitude towards Russia in January and in the subsequent peace negotiations suggests that he tried to moderate the harshness of Austrian demands. That he did not from the outset reduce them to the minimum (left bank of the Danube) is another proof of his unconditional loyalty to the Emperor.

However that may be, the French government approved the demand for "boundary rectification." In Bourqueney's memorandum of 7 November, the passage concerning unification of the Danubian principalities was omitted on Buol's insistence. But Buol did agree to add a fifth point: "The belligerent powers reserve the right vested in them to bring forward in the European interest special conditions in addition to the Four Points."

This dangerously ambiguous point encapsulates French strategy vis-à-vis their British allies. It was supposed to cover the proposed British war aims without recognizing them individually. To specify them would have required a great deal of time, since everything would be negotiated between three cabinets. Discussions might have extended to the British Parliament and that could have entailed further undesirable delays. Secrecy and speed during the winter break, when no decisive military action could take place thanks to the contemporary state of military technology, were essential to success in making peace.

Austria, wishing to transmit the peace conditions, had no interest in adopting Britain's new demands, which grew directly out of the military situation. Therefore a vague formulation was chosen for Point Five, so that new conditions would be clearly the requirements of the belligerents, not of Austria. Buol did expressly ascertain through Bourqueney that such demands would not present an "insurmountable obstacle to the restoration of peace."[224] France and Britain would have to agree between themselves as to the content.

Buol and Bourqueney initialled the Five Points in Vienna on 14 November 1855 as "Projet de préliminaires de paix." At the same time a "memorandum" was drawn up which sketched the origin of the peace initiative and the allies' future procedure towards Russia.[225] Austria would present the peace program to the Russian government for unconditional acceptance within a set time; if Russia refused, Austria would break diplomatic relations and would consult with her allies over further measures.

This "draft preliminary peace treaty" fulfilled all the legal requirements of an ultimatum although it was not officially so designated. Reprisals were couched in the form of breaking diplomatic relations, rather than declaring war, out of deference to Austria's treaty ties with Prussia (April Treaty 1854) and the German Confederation (accession to the April Treaty, July 1854): if Austria declared war on Russia, that would open a war "foreign to the Confederation" according to the legal provisions laid down in Article 46 of the Vienna Final Act, but in reverse, Russia could not attack Austria at any point without calling the German Confederation, including Prussia, into action on the basis of the various alliance pledges.

With the ultimatum, Austria stepped out of her previous position as mediator between East and West, adopted in the spring of 1855. She had committed herself to a peace demarche backed by the threat of decidedly hostile, though not necessarily military, action. But it is not this step which precludes considering Buol as an "honest broker"; it is the fact that Austria hoped to be paid for intervention at a price that did not follow directly from the course of the war. Like Buol up to the autumn of 1855, Bismarck could not prevent a new phase of alienation from Russia as the consequence of his mediation in the Russo-Turkish War in 1878. But Buol transformed the unavoidable chill in Austro-Russian relations into an unnecessary freeze through his demand for territorial cessions in Bessarabia, a demand which, it was generally recognized, originated in Austrian selfishness. He assumed a heavy responsibility in deciding on the ultimatum; because he added the demand for territory, his entire role was compromised.

Paris officially communicated the peace project initialled on 14 November to the British government according to the procedures agreed upon by Buol and Bourqueney. The British Cabinet, after lively internal discussions, felt obliged to subscribe to it. Some revisions were suggested especially concerning the third and fifth points;[226] they were accepted in Vienna in essentials except for the demand that the special conditions be spelled out. On 16 December, Count Valentin Esterházy, the Austrian ambassador at the tsarist court, brought the ultimatum to Petersburg. He was provided with secret instructions which carefully prescribed his conduct.[227] If, eight days after delivery of the ultimatum, he had not received an unconditional answer, he was to inform the imperial chancellor that in case of refusal he would leave Petersburg in two weeks' time with the embassy personnel. With regard to the fifth point, the instructions empowered him to explain in confidence that the special conditions would not involve either territorial cessions or a war indemnity and also would not present any "serious obstacle to the conclusion of peace."

Lack of explicit testimony makes it difficult to determine whether the Austrian administration had prepared for the eventuality of Russia's nonacceptance. The question is all the more important because Buol and Francis Joseph do not seem to have been sanguine concerning the prospects of their demarche. After the memorandum had been initialled, Bourqueney announced in Paris that the Emperor was convinced Russia would not accept, while Buol considered the chances about even.[228] The Bavarian representative in Vienna went away from a talk with Buol in mid-December with the "troubling conviction, that Count Buol himself does not believe in the success of the peace attempt now underway."[229] Buol wrote to Duke Ernest on the day the ultimatum was sent: "Whether Russian pride will permit its acceptance is outside my calculations."[230]

To the minister, making any diagnosis seemed difficult, since it could not rest on any solid information. Existing techniques of reporting and spying did not permit a reliable picture of Russian opinions. Francis Joseph did not have a military plenipotentiary personally attached to the Tsar, who could have reported from the Tsar's immediate circle (parallel to the Prussian plenipotentiary, Count Münster, although it is true the latter spent most of his time in Berlin at the end of 1855). The Austrian ambassador at Petersburg had been on leave since September 1855, and when he returned at the end of December, he was treated like a pariah for weeks. Buol was therefore reduced to conjecture. "We know only this much," he said to the Bavarian representative, "the military superiority which Emperor Nicholas bragged of, and thanks to which every Russian arrogantly thought to be the judge in European matters, has not stood up, and since the war began, the Russian cabinet has always been three months behind events with its concessions, and has let slip the right moment for accepting the conditions proposed to it. I am afraid . . . that the same thing will happen this time too."

In spite of this uncertainty, it is obvious that no military preparations were initiated in Austria. Austrian military participation was out of the question. Besides the reasons mentioned above, the empire's financial plight, in case of war, would have led to public bankruptcy. The budgetary deficit, chronic since the 1830s, had been one of Metternich's greatest anxieties. In his advice to Buol during the Crimean War, references to this sore point are not lacking: "Among the worst problems of the day is the domestic situation and particularly our financial position." This reason too suggested that the only possible option for Austria was "standing . . . her own ground and acting within her sphere of moral freedom, as a rational choice."[231]

In the years of peace after 1849, the army ate up almost half the revenue. Mobilization doubled the military budget for 1855.[232] The finance minister, Baumgartner, explained in January that "such a military expenditure [must] unavoidably bring the state to collapse."[233] The new finance minister, Bruck, believed that a return to sane fiscal practices would be possible only if the state kept within the allocation of 110 million [florin] for the military, that is to say, the normal peacetime allotment. Bruck's program was recognized by the ministerial conference as inescapable. Reducing the size of the army, already imperative because of the poor health situation in the third army (Hungary) and the fourth army (Galicia),[234] would be the most important way of doing this. Further measures which the industrious finance minister originated or continued included sale of state properties (railroads, domain lands) and founding of a new bank in the form of a credit institute.

In fact this last measure, initiated in autumn 1855 on the French model (Crédit Mobilier) in the hope of mobilizing private credit, worked like an electric shock. At the beginning of December 1855 the subscription opened for shares in the new credit bank of commerce and industry. In contrast to the feeble response to the emission of the national loan in 1854, all the propertied classes participated in the new exchange of securities. The rush on the credit bank was so great in December that every evening thousands of people queued in the street to gain entry next morning; police and soldiers were called out and maintained law and order only with difficulty.[235]

For Bruck's comprehensive program of financial stability to succeed, the most important prerequisite was a quick peace. Buol evidently believed that promising diplomatic activity could follow a Russian refusal, and the Russian administration might modify its decision. The neutral states of Europe would have to be asked to put pressure on the Russian government through demarches in Petersburg. Then Russia's growing moral "isolation" in Europe would take effect.[236] It was a daring scheme, dictated by the rigid constraints on Austrian foreign policy.

On the day the Austrian ultimatum was sent, Francis Joseph wrote King Frederick William of Prussia and King Max of Bavaria a letter in his own hand in which he asked that they support the demarche.[237] Since the two German cabinets had not participated in drafting the Austrian peace proposals, they considered themselves to have been presented with a fait accompli. Accordingly, their support in Petersburg, especially Bavaria's, was lukewarm. They hardly influenced decisionmaking in Petersburg; in no way did they give the deciding nudge, as Frederick William proclaimed later and as historians have sometimes asserted.[238]

Before examining the historic decision taken by the Russian Crown

Council on 15 January 1856 and the motives which determined it, the other peace initiatives of the autumn of 1855, simultaneous with the Austrian peace efforts, must be examined.

NEUTRAL POWERS ATTEMPT TO MEDIATE AND FRANCE TAKES SOUNDINGS

In autumn 1855, the Prussian government tried on several occasions to tie up the threads of the peace conversations cut since spring. On 12 September, King Frederick William spoke with his minister, Manteuffel, about directing an inquiry to Vienna concerning a joint offer of good offices in Paris and London to restore peace.[239] Vienna considered such a demarche premature.[240] Meanwhile in Berlin Lord Loftus and Baron Malaret, the chargés d'affaires of the two sea powers, were informed of the King's idea in confidence. However, their governments rejected it. Walewski asked Count Hatzfeldt, the Prussian envoy in Paris, the key question, whether Prussia would be willing, in case the Russians refused the peace terms, to support these conditions with force.[241]

After Napoleon had decided on peace, the French government in early October sounded out Berlin to see whether some conciliatory statements had been received from Petersburg; the line was that it was a shame nobody wanted to take the first step towards peace.[242] These hints were transmitted to Petersburg, but stirred no echo. Nesselrode confessed himself puzzled as to how they might clarify matters from the Russian side.[243]

In the autumn of 1855, Berlin became the center for reports and rumors from West and East. Frederick William had learned from Paris that the French emperor made it his first priority to implement the third point by neutralizing the Black Sea. At the end of November he had sent Petersburg a despatch which he had drafted himself, in which he exhorted his nephew the tsar to take the first step and call for peace with explicit conditions concerning the Black Sea: the "Pontus Euxinus" would become "mare clausum (neutrum)" for everyone, a direct agreement would be made between Russia and the Porte concerning this, and the arrangement would be guaranteed by the powers.[244]

It is characteristic of Prussia's diplomatic style that the King wanted contacts through his intimates in addition to direct intervention between sovereigns and efforts through usual diplomatic channels. Many times he asked his adjutant general, General Leopold von Gerlach, to write the military plenipotentiary at Petersburg in the sense of peace.[245]

In the next months, the Prussian king was all the more eager for peace, because he had concluded, on the basis of reports reaching him, that during 1856 the war would change not only its location but its character. It was no secret that if the peace efforts were fruitless the allies planned to conduct the spring campaign in the Baltic. Once an allied expeditionary force landed on the coast of Courland and Livonia, the war would come close to the Prussian frontier. It would then become very difficult to preserve Prussian neutrality. In his speech on 15 November at the close of the Paris World Fair, Napoleon menaced Europe's neutral states: in the middle of a total war, "indifference [would be] a bad risk and silence an error."[246] At the end of November the alliance between Sweden, previously neutral, and the sea powers was concluded.[247] After 16 December the King realized that Austria was ready to take a genuinely hostile step by threatening to break relations with Russia. He was also afraid, like the Austrians, that Napoleon would use the revolutionizing of ethnic groups as a new weapon.[248] For Prussia this meant endangering its eastern flank and its own Polish provinces. What is more, at the beginning of January a rumor reached him through diplomatic channels about Napoleon's designs for war on the Rhine.[249]

These reports and their ramifications suggest that in 1856 Prussia would probably be forced to choose one of the belligerent camps. The first real sign that Frederick William was beginning to accept this conclusion is his despatch to the Tsar at the end of November already mentioned. That this became a conviction, probably jelling during December, is proved by his second personal letter, directed to Alexander II on 6 January 1856, following the Austrian ultimatum.[250] Apparently bitter about Austria's preemption of the peace operation, which he had not helped to prepare, he spoke in the first letter, of 30 December, about "propositions unknown to me" and merely alluded to the responsibility weighing on him and on Alexander ("I tremble . . . when contemplating the responsibility which rests on the two of us").[251] Now he was so impressed by the slender prospects for the near future that his letter was almost an appeal to the Tsar to accept peace to ward off the danger threatening *Prussia*. The three allies would regard Prussia as the "Christmas turkey. . . . I firmly believe that it has been decided. . . . France wants the Rhine, Austria Silesia[252] and England the ruin of our industry." He mentioned the arguments affecting Russia only secondarily: the dim prospects for the next campaign, the danger to Kronstadt and Petersburg, and "the projected rising in Poland."

Like Prussia, the other German states faced a serious danger of war in 1856. Bavaria and Saxony especially took energetic steps to banish it. The two courts believed that they were entitled to mediate not just because of the respect they enjoyed in German politics; their claim resulted from the simple fact that during the war the Bavarian representative in Petersburg, Count Bray, had taken care of French interests in Russia and the Saxon representative in Paris, Baron Seebach, had taken care of Russian interests in France.

In the summer and autumn of 1855, Paris was the fulcrum of European diplomacy because the world fair was organized there. Both the Saxon minister, von Beust, and the Bavarian minister, von der Pfordten, travelled to the French capital at the end of October 1855. That they met there "purely by chance" and that Pfordten professed to be "painfully surprised," an assertion which historians have accepted,[253] is a deliberate lie. Beust had planned to visit Paris for a long time. When Pfordten learned this in October from Dresden,[254] he hastened to ask the King for permission to make a visit himself,[255] so that Beust would not "anticipate" him. The trip could be presented as "improvised," since he first attended the railroad opening in the Palatinate on 23 October and then made a "side trip" to Paris. The industrial fair would give an adequate pretext.

The two German ministers had a double motive for their journey: first, after the western powers' victory in the Crimea, to erase any reproach for pro-Russian inclinations and to cover themselves in Paris—a natural concern given Napoleon's plans for 1856; and second, to test the political terrain and transmit to Petersburg the views prevailing in Paris. In so doing, they might play a role in European diplomacy—in the words of King Maximilian, "speak up in the councils of the great powers."[256] Thus in a memorandum to King Max, Pfordten extolled as potential benefits "consolidation of a good relationship with France, defense of the Greek question and perhaps some small cooperation in the restoration of peace."

In subsequent weeks a caricature was circulated in Munich which captures the impression the German ministers' trip made on the public.[257] Louis Napoleon was depicted with Pfordten and Beust in front of him like twin children, and underneath it the comment: "Let the little ones come to me for theirs is the German empire."

In Paris, in addition to talking with Walewski, with Bourqueney, who was still there, and with Prince Jerome, Pfordten had two long conversations with the Emperor. He summarized them in a document intended for the Russian chancellor, which he handed Count Bray, who was returning to Petersburg.[258] France would be ready to embark on peace negotiations immediately but she could not take the first step; she would await one from Petersburg. She would not demand either that Russia cede territory or that she be humiliated in any other way. As the basis for peace she still accepted the Four Points, but they should be spelled out. To meet the third point, France preferred neutralization of the Black Sea, so that neither Russia, nor the Ottoman Empire, nor any other naval power could maintain a war fleet there. If peace were not concluded by the following spring, the western powers would "continue the war with all energy, seek to extend its sphere, work especially for Austria's participation, at first through ordinary diplomatic channels, but ultimately perhaps through appeal to the nationalities in Italy, Hungary, and most of all Poland."

Pfordten presented the fruit of his observations as "an accurate summary of the Emperor Napoleon's views." In France, he wrote, people were not bitter against Russia. After the victory at Sevastopol, the inclination to peace was "decidedly stronger" there than in Britain; however, people believed that Britain would have to follow France's lead. Despite this, the desire for peace was not so intense "as to preclude continuing the war"; Napoleon would be able to count on the nation's support next spring.

Talking to Bismarck on 14 December, Pfordten expressed the same views as to Nesselrode.[259] He cited a remark of Napoleon's which aptly describes the nature of the war as it had actually unfolded in 1854 and 1855, and contrasts the character it might assume in the following year: if the war continued into the next year, it would no longer be based on "European law, but [on] the egoism of individual states."

This expression veiled a menace to the German states and their policy of neutrality which Pfordten hardly needed to communicate to Petersburg. In the reports concerning the conversations between Napoleon and Beust, this emerges even more plainly.[260] Napoleon reproached the Saxon minister for the position adopted by the German Confederation which had scarcely been pro-French. If the confederation persisted in this attitude, the war would take on larger proportions. Beust was not intimidated and seems to have energetically defended German neutrality to Napoleon, just like Pfordten.

The two German ministers' reports concerning their Paris journey reached Petersburg at the end of November[261] and once again, like the previous Prussian communications, underlined Napoleon's inclination towards peace. But the Russian government's reaction was unequivocally negative. The imperial chancellor and also the Tsar explained to the Prussian representative, Baron Werther, on 28 November, that at the present moment they could not offer "a peace proposal springing from Russia."[262] In a letter sent to Beust some two days earlier, Nesselrode had refused to meet the demand for neutralization of the Black Sea.[263] According to the Russian interpretation, already expressed during the Vienna Conference in spring 1855, accepting this demand would be dishonorable, since it would imply restriction of Russian sovereignty. Like Emperor Napoleon, Russia could not go beyond a certain point in concession.

The Russian refusal reflected the Tsar's personal decision. He had just returned in the second half of November from an extensive inspection of southern Russia. Nesselrode had taken earlier Prussian peace probes ad referendum with the explanation that he must await the Tsar's return. The Russian imperial chancellor, like the Austrian foreign minister, was his master's faithful servant and sincerely believed foreign policy (like the army) to be the archetype of imperial power. It was a matter of course to him that the Tsar in solitary plenitude of power must answer the decisive question: war or peace? He could only advise. He could not mention his own moderate opinions now, since Alexander's eagerness for war was undaunted.

The evacuation of the fortress of Sevastopol, anticipated for weeks, had neither shaken the Tsar nor awakened any inclination towards peace. His attitude was reinforced by the bellicosity of his intimates, primarily military advisers. After the fortress fell, he sent a message to Prince M. D. Gorchakov, the commander at Sevastopol, couched in comforting allusions: "Let not your courage fail, but think of the year 1812 and trust in God. Sevastopol is not Moscow, and the Crimea is not Russia. Two years after Moscow burned, our victorious army entered Paris. We are still the same Russians and God is with us."[264] During the tour, reports reached him about the bad harvest and lower-class discontent in France. He believed that this was the first sign of serious unrest. Indeed, his misunderstanding of France's domestic situation went even further: "Previous revolutions have almost always begun this way, therefore perhaps it will not be much longer before there is a general collapse. This is the likeliest end of the present war, for a genuine desire for peace, on conditions appropriate to Russia's honor, I expect neither from Napoleon nor from Britain, and so long as I live, I will accept nothing less." So he wrote Gorchakov on 28 October from Nikolaev.[265]

Alexander and his companions brought back a favorable impression from the tour. Everywhere, the young tsar was greeted enthusiastically by the people and the soldiers. He found the troops at Nikolaev and in the Crimea in good shape. The important fortress of Nikolaev, which could easily have been set on fire from the ocean side two months before, had been made impregnable according to experts by fortifications and a barrage of ships. Evacuation of the Crimea, which many Russians had predicted in September, was now unthinkable. According to Nesselrode, the army was equipped with enough munitions and provisions for months, and construction of a military road to facilitate resupply was making rapid progress.[266]

These were the factors motivating Alexander's decision at the end of November to refuse all mediatory proposals from Berlin, Dresden, and Munich. And there was another reason: Napoleon had made direct overtures.

Napoleon had suggested the first Prussian sounding at the beginning of October, but after the simultaneous Austrian initiative the plan had been dropped. Beust and Pfordten's peace efforts proved to be self-initiated actions through usual diplomatic channels; they were not unwelcome to Napoleon, but were unsought by Petersburg. Just when Napoleon secretly began to weave direct threads between Paris and Petersburg is not now discoverable; it may never be possible to determine, given the nature of such contacts. Evidently, the decision was reached sometime in October and led to two parallel intrigues about which Alexander was informed on his tour of inspection. He was more sanguine about them than about the intervention of the Prussian government or other lesser courts. Apparently, according to Alexander's letter written on 24 October in Nikolaev the Tsar had just then learned of Napoleon's direct feelers: "We have information that Napoleon is inclined to open negotiations directly with us, but I do not entirely trust the situation. If something comes of it, then naturally I would prefer direct negotiations with him to interference from any other side.[267] The exchange of views anticipated here between the Tuileries and Petersburg was already in progress when the various German courts' mediation attempt, and then concrete proposals, came through at the end of November. Alexander therefore ordered that this overture be refused.

In spite of the state of war, the threads between the French and Russian ruling elites had never been completely snapped. There had always been a significant Russian colony in Paris; its leading personalities had left Paris when war broke out, but they had soon returned to the capital. For example Princess Lieven, the "Sibyl of Europe," who had sponsored an important political salon in Paris since 1839, emigrated to Brussels but after only a few months returned with Napoleon's express permission. She kept connections open between Paris and Petersburg during the war. In Paris she stayed in especially close touch with the Duke of Morny, the "second man" in the Second Empire, president of the Corps Législatif since 1854.[268] Besides the Russian colony in Paris, there were also contacts through the diplomatic missions to neutral governments, above all in the Belgian capital, Berlin, Vienna, and the other German posts like Munich, Stuttgart, Hanover, and the German Diet in Frankfurt.

After the capture of Sevastopol, or more accurately, after his decision for peace at the end of September or early October, Napoleon opened two of these channels in order to study the views of the Russian government and let his own seep through. For some time they played an important role in his maneuvering for peace, along with conversations with numerous sovereigns, princes, and ministers of Europe, public speeches and anonymous pamphlets, soundings through neutral governments, and the approach through Vienna. One channel ran between Morny and the Russian ambassador in Vienna, A. M. Gorchakov; the other was the bridge between Baron Seebach, with Walewski as the contact, and Nesselrode.

These connections complemented each other, since they implied different degrees of confidentiality. Because of his unofficial position, Morny could go further in his remarks and could be more concrete than the foreign minister. However, he could be more easily disavowed. Morny, who was an outspoken Russophile, had regretted the war simply because of his position in the business and financial world. As demonstrated by his recently published correspondence with Princess Lieven, he hoped for an early end to hostilities. When he learned of the fall of Sevastopol, he wrote the Princess: "Since we have nothing to gain materially and we have won all the honors of the campaign, . . . we can only lose by continuing."[269] In this spirit, he sought to advance the peacemaking.

It was perhaps this letter which initiated confidential probings through Gorchakov or it may have been the subsequent, apparently no longer extant, correspondence with the Princess, which she could have transmitted in summary to Vienna or Petersburg. However, it may just as well have started with Gorchakov, as has previously been more or less accepted.[270] The partially published correspondence between Morny and Gorchakov, which begins in the second half of November, does not clarify this.[271] Two Viennese bankers, Eskeles and Sina, acted as intermediaries. Both were members of the board of directors of the company which had purchased a part of the Austrian state railroads with the help of the Crédit Mobilier. In autumn 1855, Eskeles was in Paris on several occasions and could unobtrusively transmit correspondence, which otherwise was forwarded with business mailings.

Morny's chief goal, it appears in his letters to Gorchakov, was to convince the Russian government that it was necessary to accept the new draft of the crucial third point.[272] Britain would not make peace unless the Black Sea was neutralized. Morny asserted that the new phrasing was more advantageous than the old formula of limitation. It was vaguer; it did indeed conceal a restriction, but precisely because of its less explicit form it would be less dishonorable. As a further argument he appealed to history. The traditional signs of defeat were indemnity payments and territorial cessions. A demand for a limitation of power such as the present instance was scarcely critical if one considered how long it could be enforced. Try to cite a case in which such treaty provisions had been strictly observed. Morny may have been thinking of the drastic reduction of the Prussian army laid down in the peace of Tilsit and its evasion in practice. In any event, he ascribed no long duration to such stipulations: after just a couple of years, they would be untenable. "Often indeed, it is the nation which has imposed the limiting condition which is the first to demand its violation." Finally Morny, using yet another, not very relevant historical comparison, alluded to the change of ruler in Russia in the spring of 1855 and its implication for peace: if the tsar were named Francis I, he would not accept the conditions; if he were Charles V, then he would do it all the faster.

In his answer, Gorchakov really did not seem to put much stock in Morny's arguments, yet he made no secret of his "Napoleonic sympathies" and using the example of the good relations between Napoleon I and Alexander I,[273] climaxing at Erfurt, he indicated that a rapprochement between the two powers could be fruitful.

According to Morny's proposals, this first, written exchange of ideas should be followed by a personal meeting in a German city, perhaps Dresden; but the Morny-Gorchakov link was snapped at the beginning of December on instructions from Petersburg.[274] The reason for this was that Nesselrode now wished to let the connection through Seebach directly to Walewski operate undisturbed. The Russian chancellor may have spotted his successor in Gorchakov and he did not seem inclined to give this political rival a free hand in peacemaking.

Although up to now little has been known about the relations between Nesselrode and Gorchakov, it is certain that the contrasting political outlooks of the two statesmen had already surfaced. Even in the Crimean War, Nesselrode sponsored the principles of the Holy Alliance, his guide in conducting Russian foreign policy for three decades. One of its controlling ideas was the need to isolate France from the alliance system, since she seemed to be a breeding ground for revolutionary movements. Gorchakov, on the contrary, had acquired in Vienna a profound hatred for everything Austrian—he called Buol and the other ministers "infamous scoundrels"[275]—he often admitted in 1855 in his correspondence with Petersburg his preference for a tie with France, Russia's "natural" ally, and he seemed to find support for the idea. It was now revived in his correspondence with Morny and emerged more clearly than ever before.

The Morny-Gorchakov contact was cut at the moment it began to take on more explicit form, and consequently it remained just an episode. In earlier Russian historiography, it has been given greater significance than it deserves. This overestimate can be traced to the semiofficial narrative of Russian wartime diplomacy which Gorchakov himself inspired.

The peace feeler from Paris through Seebach is more important: first, it went through only one absolutely necessary intermediary, and second, Napoleon kept it available throughout the entire Austrian peace initiative, though with differing purposes. However, it is the most mysterious of all the attempts to prepare for peace at the end of the Crimean War. None of the letters exchanged between Seebach and Nesselrode have yet been published. We cannot assume that it will ever be possible to reconstruct the Seebach mission completely. Its crucial phase, the trip to Petersburg at the end of 1855/beginning of January 1856, just when the Austrian ultimatum was being delivered, presumably originated with an oral message from Napoleon transmitted by Seebach, also by word of mouth. Unless Seebach wrote private notes which might some day come to light, the veil of secrecy will never be lifted.

So there are important questions which cannot be resolved with the evidence at hand. What were Napoleon's expectations concerning this peace feeler? Did he have any accurate notions about what was involved if Russia and France ended the war directly? What role would fall to Britain? Or was the only function to lay the groundwork, as Buol apparently supposed: to support the Austrian peace initiative through conversations in Petersburg which should remove all doubt that France was serious in identifying with Buol's peace project? Or were they designed to put pressure on Austria through the threat of a direct Franco-Russian understanding and so force the Austrian initiative? Through whom, at what point, and with what motive were Francis Joseph and Buol informed of the contact? Such questions cannot be answered conclusively on the basis of official documents.

The initiative seems this time to have originated with Nesselrode.[276] Seebach was his son-in-law and had already served after Nicholas's death the preceding March as Napoleon's messenger to express sympathy to the new tsar. Perhaps the Prussian communications after Sevastopol encouraged Nesselrode at the end of October or some time in November to open this channel for preliminary soundings. Nesselrode found previous reports about Napoleon's inclination towards peace to be confirmed. Walewski asked him to draw up proposals and for his part divulged French ideas about the third point: Russia would either have to agree directly with the Porte about limiting its naval power on the Black Sea or else accept neutralization. Although he preferred the first alternative, he remarked that the second would after all allow Russia to maintain warships in the Sea of Azov, while the Ottoman Empire would be able to do likewise in the Sea of Marmara.[277] Nesselrode's answer was noncommittal. He rejected limitation, since it would humiliate Russia; neutralization was a vague formula needing definition.

Meanwhile, Nesselrode and Alexander had learned from Gorchakov in Vienna that an ultimatum was to be expected from the Austrians. This report worried the Tsar. If it proved right, he wrote on 25

November to his commander-in-chief in the Crimea, Russia's situation in the spring would "look even more difficult."[278]

This was the first sign of alarm from Alexander; the favorable impressions gathered during the inspection tour began to alter. On 24 November,[279] Gorchakov reported a modification of French ideas on the third point:[280] Napoleon had now decided on neutralization, since it coincided more exactly with the Franco-Austrian peace project of 14 November, and he understood by it the nonpresence of warships in the Black Sea "with the exception of the forces which Russia and the Porte will judge necessary for coastal security." The special convention originally envisioned by Walewski for limitation would therefore be transferred to neutralization.[281] The Tsar noted: "This clause completely changes the question as it has been presented to us up to now; I don't see any obstacle to it on my side." Gorchakov considered it important that the number of naval forces be established through a *direct* agreement between the riparian states without any *ostensible* participation of the western powers, since this would not compromise Russia's sovereign rights. The Tsar agreed.

Gorchakov's report continued: the Russian Black Sea fleet no longer exists. To reconstruct it would be a task for the future. It was a question whether Russia's interests demanded that a future fleet attain a strength which Europe would again consider a threat or whether there might not be other, more effective ways of displaying Russia's might: this question must be examined by His Majesty. If Napoleon's ideas on other important details did not hinder discussions, should this one point be the grounds for rejecting such negotiations out of hand? Alexander wrote: "No."

Now the Russian Cabinet stepped out of its reserve. The modified neutralization formula finally offered an exit which at least in appearance would not compromise "the dignity of the Emperor" and "the self-esteem of the Russian people." In the nineteenth century these phrases were not just stereotypes concealing a will to power. Added to this came the rumor of the Austrian ultimatum. It demanded quick action. The following Russian proposal about the third point was accordingly transmitted to Walewski by Seebach:[281a] closure of the Straits; no war fleets in the Black Sea except vessels which might be judged necessary by Russia and the Porte; determination of the number of these vessels by a convention concluded directly between Russia and the Porte without open participation of the other powers.

A comparison of the date of completion of the Austrian peace initiative with the date when this Russian peace proposal emerged demonstrates the error of the previous assertion that the Austrian government was pushed into its peace initiative by the direct Franco-

Russian conversations and by fear of their possible consequences.[282] Rather the reverse is *correct,* that the Russian government was scared into its peace proposal by reports about the Austrian plan,[283] and it is *possible* that the Vienna government, informed about the Russian demarche, recognized that rather than turning back, a hasty advance was demanded.[284]

In Vienna Gorchakov, who was also informed of his government's proposal to Walewski,[285] had indicated[286] that the special convention, at the sea powers' demand, would be annexed to the general peace treaty with the proviso that its stipulations could not be altered without concurrence of all the signatories. Although this again introduced the ostensible participation of the other powers in the solution of this crucial question,[287] Gorchakov was empowered to communicate the Russian proposal to the Austrian Cabinet. Shortly thereafter it was transmitted to other German courts.[288]

On 6 December, Gorchakov communicated the Russian peace proposal orally to Buol, saying that he brought peace; Buol, however, simply noted the information and sent it on to Paris and London with the hope that the three cabinets might agree as soon as possible on their own project.[289] In Paris, Seebach apparently had not received an answer to the Russian proposal. Meanwhile Napoleon learned the British Cabinet's decision—on 26 November he was also informed by the Queen: Britain would not agree to a special convention between the Ottoman Empire and Russia concerning the Black Sea.[290] This demand was part of the British counterproposals to the 18 November communication of the Franco-Austrian memorandum. Napoleon therefore did not wish to react to the Russian initiative before the imminent final drafting of the Austrian ultimatum.

On 16 December, the day the Austrian ultimatum was sent, Walewski informed Seebach that the Russian proposals did not go far enough.[291] According to treaty commitments for an interallied agreement, he would transmit the demarche to Vienna and London. For the rest, comprehensive peace proposals worked out jointly by the three allies were on the way to Petersburg.[292]

This did not mean that the Seebach mission was terminated; it entered a new phase, the most mysterious, concerning which only secondhand sources are now available. Previously the chief aim had been to get the peace talks going between Paris and Petersburg. The goal was either to reach a direct Russo-French understanding or to force the London Cabinet by calculated indiscretions to make peace through fear of a Russo-French rapprochement and to manipulate the Vienna Cabinet. Now its function, directly shaped by Napoleon, was to explain the Austrian ultimatum to the Russians, to hold out the hope, never put in writing, of conciliatory treatment at the peace congress, and to induce her to accept the ultimatum unconditionally through a mixture of flattery and menace—a good example of Napoleon's diplomatic style.

Both Vienna and London detected these aspects in Seebach's Petersburg journey. Buol believed that Seebach was to inform Russia about the British special conditions which *he* had not wanted to include in the ultimatum.[293] Clarendon thought Seebach was to tell the Russians that Napoleon was serious about the Austrian ultimatum and stood behind its demands.[294]

The Prussian government interpreted the Seebach mission quite differently. At the beginning of January, Manteuffel had heard a rumor from Brussels[295] that Napoleon had promised Russia to secede from the British alliance in return for the Prussian Rhine provinces and that Russia had agreed. Clarendon, in response to Bernstorff's inquiry, said it was plausible; however, he guessed that such a proposition would have originated with Russia, not Napoleon. He was firmly convinced that Russia would not hesitate a moment to pay this price, if it would bring a separate peace. Manteuffel naturally connected this rumor with Seebach's mission. It found its way into Frederick William's letter to Alexander of 6 January 1856, though, of course, without explicitly mentioning the Seebach mission.[296]

There is further evidence that such a suggestion may have been made to France by Russia at this time. In August 1856 Gorchakov drew up a secret special instruction for Count Kiselev, the Russian ambassador to Paris; it was published in abbreviated form in a neglected source in 1909. We read: If Napoleon wants to go ahead with plans for Italy, Nice, and Savoy, he may do so with confidence. If he wants to tackle Austria, Russia will not oppose. "If he were to think of restoring the old Rhine frontier, he should know that Russia will not abandon Prussia. She will offer her good offices *without going any further.*"[297]

So in the summer of 1856 Russia was actually prepared to allow Napoleon to extend the French boundary to the Rhine. Whether she was ready at the beginning of 1856 cannot be stated for certain. However, one may suppose such feelings in view of the Russian efforts to pry France loose from the western coalition. Russia's continuing effort to make a separate peace with France emerges clearly from the semiofficial Russian account of the Crimean War.[298] The price of the Rhine frontier obviously could not be mentioned in print. The mystery which still cloaks this episode can be dispelled only by the Russian documents, if at all. Hardly any information is likely from French sources, since Napoleon's secret diplomacy has left very few traces in the French archives.

However that may be, Jomini and various diplomatic sources tell us about Seebach's delivery of his message during his journey to

Petersburg. On 19 or 20 December, Napoleon received Seebach in a farewell audience.[299] The Emperor explained his ideas thus: there were two ways to end a major war, one of the two parties could be reduced to exhaustion or else the fight could be broken off when the parties were still equally strong, so both could save their honor.[300] In his opinion, they had reached this point. In the Baltic, the allies had accomplished little; in the Crimea, they had won a victory, but at a very high price. The Russians had put up courageous resistance. Thanks to Prince Gorchakov's strategy, Russia would hold the Crimea through the winter. The allies could have occupied it in September, if they had been stronger.

After this purposely flattering summary, Napoleon turned to the future: next year the war would probably go better for the allies than for Russia. Previous experience suggested that they could not carry the war into the interior; but they could use technical advances in naval warfare to destroy Kronstadt. In the Black Sea, the blockade would be continued, forcing Russia to build up her strength. All this would mean useless bloodshed. He would prefer a permanent tie with the Russians; however, they would have to sacrifice something, since they had no allies. The peace conditions transmitted would be the least the allies could ask. Acceptance was dictated by political necessity.

Napoleon hinted at problems with London. Only with great difficulty had he sidetracked a British demand to extend neutralization to the Sea of Azov and to require destruction of Nikolaev. In London they hoped that the peace conditions would be rejected.[301]

Seebach dropped the remark that he did not see any room for negotiation in the face of such unconditional demands. Napoleon left it with the comment "that he wanted to move closer to us, and that he would prove it in the course of the negotiations."

So runs the semiofficial Russian account, which is probably based on Seebach's report. If it is accurate, although possibly not complete, we must conclude that Napoleon sent a signal for a rapprochement or maybe even an alliance. If Alexander had not done so earlier, perhaps at the end of November, he could now have amplified and suggested a separate peace at the price of the Rhine province. Napoleon's hint to Baron Hübner in the middle of January, "Russia is making advances to me," should be connected with this.[302]

Whether or not Seebach received such a secret instruction from Alexander[303] and brought it back to Paris, he did have an ostensible message, which was no secret in diplomatic circles.[304] Napoleon was informed that Russia would not go beyond her counterproject to the Austrian ultimatum.[305] In this counterproposal, which was also sent to Austria, Russia accepted Points Two, Three, and Four, deleted in Point

One the demand for territorial cession in Bessarabia, and flatly rejected Point Five.

In a letter to Walewski (probably entrusted to Seebach), Nesselrode proposed a conference in Paris to sanction the Russian project as a preliminary peace.[306] He described Napoleon as "the arbiter of the situation." He also alluded to the "natural sympathies of the two nations"—a departure from form in which Nesselrode recognized that his life's work lay in ruins, and sketched the theme of future Russian diplomacy. In this answer, Alexander thus accepted the French invitation to a rapprochement, as Seebach had transmitted it to him and as it had been publicized in the pamphlet *Necessity of a Congress to Pacify Europe.*

Napoleon was inclined to adopt the Russian counterproposal to the Austrian ultimatum even though it meant departing from the procedure concerted with Austria. On 14 January he expressed his views to Queen Victoria in an unduly neglected letter.[307] He outlined frankly for the Queen the unpleasant options which he foresaw. According to the stipulations, Austria ought really to break off diplomatic relations. And Britain and France? They must continue the war! For a "purely Austrian interest" which could in no way consolidate the Ottoman Empire! This surely meant the territorial cession in Bessarabia. That Napoleon linked this question to the decision on war or peace, demonstrates Austria's false position. Napoleon suggested a solution: since Russia was ready to evacuate all of Asia Minor, the allies should limit themselves to demanding for the Porte some fortifications on the Danube, like Ismail and Kilia in place of the cession of territory in Bessarabia. Concerning the fifth point, they should insist that the Aland Islands not be fortified and that the (Crimean) Tartars be amnestied. French public opinion would not accept further risks on account of a few acres of Bessarabian wasteland.

If one supposes that in addition to the Russian counterproposal, Seebach brought back a secret alliance offer, there may be still another motive for Napoleon's letter to Queen Victoria beyond the obvious function of persuading Britain to make peace in accordance with Russian conditions. Napoleon held up the Bessarabian question as the only justification for continuing the war. Russia had met all the other allied war aims (the Four Points). He saw no other obstacle to ending the war. If Britain concurred, peace could be concluded without Austria. If she refused—possible, since the British war aims were definitely not limited to Bessarabia—then Napoleon could show that the Anglo-French alliance had been invalidated, since it forbade pursuit of particular interests—that is, the Austrian interest in Bessarabia and the British private agenda. Justified before public opinion in France and

Europe, he could begin to implement his own grand design with the help of a new Franco-Russian alliance.

In writing this letter, Napoleon must have had such motives unless one supposes that he had not really understood the procedure attached to the Austrian ultimatum. Buol's instructions to Esterházy had envisioned two distinct phases: first, "the phase of persuasion,"[308] when Esterházy might make confidential communications about the first and fifth points, and a second, "that of menace." Only in the second might Esterházy threaten a rupture, to compel "acceptance, pure and simple." This phase had not expired on 14 January, so unconditional acceptance by Russia, that is withdrawal of the Russian counter-proposal, was still possible. That Buol set great store by this procedure was well known both in Paris and London because of information received regularly by telegraph from Vienna. Therefore Napoleon's sketch of the alternatives on 14 January to Queen Victoria was either incorrect or premature.

The Queen and her ministers could simply refer to this chronology and avoid the decision asked. Victoria, who expected and indeed hoped for continuation of the war,[309] answered Napoleon next day in the following terms: "We have reached the 15th; on the 18th diplomatic relations between Austria and Russia should be broken off; I believe that our position relative to Russia will be stronger if we discuss her propositions after the rupture'and after having seen its effects."[310]

The climax of the last act of this drama was played out the following day. On 16 January at one o'clock the announcement of unconditional acceptance of the Austrian ultimatum was wired from Petersburg to Vienna and from there to the other two capitals.[311]

"Russia's submissiveness amazed the world then, and has perplexed historians since that day," wrote the English Crimean War scholar Harold Temperley in 1938.[312] The documents confirm the first proposition many times over; the second, hardly questioned up to now, is no longer valid.

To demonstrate this, we must examine the complex motives which actuated the Russian leaders' decision for peace at this fateful moment. Many details are still lacking, but the main threads explaining the momentous decision can be exposed.

RUSSIA DECIDES ON PEACE

A few days after the Austrian ultimatum was delivered, Tsar Alexander called a "Crown Council." It met at eight o'clock on 1 January 1856 in the Imperial Cabinet at the Winter Palace.[313] Besides the Tsar, those present included Grand Duke Constantine Nikolaevich, head of the navy, State Chancellor Count Nesselrode, the minister for state property, Count Kiselev, the adjutants general, Prince Voroncov and Count Orlov, State Secretary Count Bludov, and the former ambassador to Vienna, Baron Meyendorff. The Tsar read the text of the Austrian ultimatum and asked the council meeting whether Russia's situation dictated acceptance or permitted continued hostilities.

Nesselrode, as the first to speak, mentioned that a new campaign would lead to far less favorable peace conditions;[314] he suggested that they try to evade the critical fifth point. Kiselev alluded to Russian finances and commerce, which would deteriorate as the war went on. All the other advisers except Bludov spoke for acceptance of the ultimatum with the alteration indicated by Nesselrode. Bludov said that accepting the Austrian conditions was incompatible with Russia's honor. The meeting agreed to reply that Russia would accept the conditions except for Point Five and the territorial cession in Point One.

Prince Gorchakov delivered the answer in Vienna on 11 January.[315] Buol insisted on unconditional acceptance and noted that diplomatic relations would be broken off on 18 January in case of refusal. Esterházy was reminded again of the secret instructions enabling him to provide confidential explanations about the dubious points. The fifth point would not commit Russia. It would give the same latitude to all the belligerents; therefore it would be in Russia's interest. This was a reference to the capture of Kars, not yet known when the Austrian ultimatum was drafted; Russia could use this victory to win better peace conditions. Concerning Bessarabia, Buol let it be understood that the final delimitation would be negotiable.[316]

On 15 January, Tsar Alexander called another Crown Council. There are enough sources about this historic meeting[317] to permit a pretty complete summary of the reasons adduced by individual participants[318] for unconditional acceptance. The ministers' comments were exceptionally realistic and responsible.

Count Bludov was the only one whose views were distorted by emotion. His remarks reflect the bias of Petersburg and Moscow intellectuals[319] such as the Slavophiles: like Ivan Aksakov, they judged peace scandalous but war hopeless. They believed however that only continuation of the war to the bitter end could reveal the bankruptcy of the Nicholaian system. This was an extraordinary moral situation, repeated later in other countries (for example the German resistance fighters in the Third Reich): patriotic men and women have been obliged to desire total defeat in order to expose the impossibility of the existing system. Count Bludov's comments in January 1856 cannot be equated exactly with such ideas; however, his despair was summed up in Choiseul's witticism at the end of the Seven Years' War: if we do not know how to make war, we will have to make peace.

It is useless to rank the arguments advanced in the second Crown Council for ending the war and to debate which was more important, diplomacy, as the older accounts assert, or the economy, as the Marxists now say. Either one was weighty enough to make peace the only sensible alternative.

It is typical of Nesselrode and indeed of the way things were done in Russia that the imperial chancellor commented essentially on politics and diplomacy and did not give a comprehensive analysis. Nesselrode's failure to achieve greatness as a statesman stemmed less from his own lack of creativity than from the autocratic governmental structure of tsarist Russia. The power of decision and the final responsibility rested with the Tsar alone. Nesselrode's position as imperial chancellor is not comparable to that later held by the German imperial chancellor, who shared responsibility with the ruler. Departments were more sharply separated in Russia than in other countries. Nesselrode held the same rank as other ministers and was elevated only to the extent that foreign policy under Nicholas was more significant than any other area.

In presenting the diplomatic situation, Nesselrode pointed to some ominous developments: the hostile attitudes recently adopted by Austria and Sweden.

We can see from his letters to the Crimean commander-in-chief that Alexander was profoundly impressed by news of the Austrian ultimatum. Since he had learned that the Austrian army had been reduced, he did not expect Austria to enter the war immediately, but he prepared himself for the worst in 1856 and believed that Russia's situation would be "very critical" and "very difficult."[320]

The treaty between Sweden and the western powers of 21 November 1855 left a hardly less important psychological mark.[321] Since the start of the war, the two western capitals had been aware of King Oscar I's anti-Russian inclinations and Crown Prince Karl's bellicose attitude. Alliance negotiations had started many times but had always foundered on exaggerated Swedish demands (a British subsidy, return of Finland to Sweden, Sweden's entry into the war to be coordinated with Austria's). In November 1855 the negotiations finally led to a treaty: the western powers guaranteed Swedish-Norwegian integrity and an offensive alliance was planned. King Oscar intended an early entry into the war. The treaty was officially communicated to the Russian government on 17 December by the Swedish representative, Major General Nordin.[322] Nesselrode was surprised; he fumbled: "What! There's a treaty?" He suspected a further secret agreement arranging Sweden's entry into the war. Article 2 especially seemed to encourage this apprehension. But the main point of the Stockholm Treaty for Nesselrode was that Sweden was the first of the phalanx of neutral states to choose sides.

In his remarks to the Crown Council, Nesselrode concluded that the western coalition would soon add the Scandinavian states (possibly with Denmark) and Austria with the entire German Confederation. Perhaps Austria would not formally adhere to the military coalition during 1856; but apparently the allied military council in Paris had decided to occupy the entire Crimea and to press forward with French troops over the Danube towards Bessarabia.[323] This would bring the war to the Austrian borders and would facilitate Austrian entanglement. Prussia too would not be able to withstand the pressure. Little by little all Europe would unite against Russia, and sooner or later she would have to accept peace conditions; only later, they would be harsher in proportion to enemy successes. Even now Britain had grave doubts about the Five Points. If Russia accepted them now, she would be able to exploit the disunity within the enemy coalition which would increase once peace was concluded. Napoleon had already made overtures to Russia. Refusing the peace conditions would throw him back into Britain's arms, perhaps forever, whereas acceptance would make it possible for Russia and France "to start down a road, that would further the interests of both."

So Nesselrode did not want to lose the opportunity to throw the devil, that is the British, out of the Russian house with Beelzebub's help. In conclusion, Nesselrode again spoke for peace, adducing secret Austrian assurances. The final boundary in Bessarabia would be negotiable. Nothing had been said about Kars and Nikolaev. These questions were still open. Here Nesselrode gambled on Napoleon's support.

Speaking next, Prince Voroncov argued emphatically for peace. The veteran governor of the Caucasus could credibly suggest the grim prospect that if the war continued, Russia might lose the Crimea, the Caucasus, Finland, and Poland. Count Kiselev, one of the next to speak, developed this idea. From Meyendorff's summary of the Crown Council it appears that the participants thought that these border provinces might betray the Russian empire not because of military defeats but because of their peculiar political status and ethnic composition. As Kiselev said, Russia had conquered these provinces only half a century before; in that short span of time it had not been possible to forge an organic union. Foreign emissaries were already at work in Volhynia and Podolia; Finland was a "doubtful possession" in spite of testimony showing the inhabitants' good will; Poland would rise as soon as the allies mounted military operations in the area.[324]

These comments are striking proof that the Russian administration reckoned with the prospect of border revolutions in 1856. They feared that these provinces would secede just as they did briefly after 1917. Russia would have had to renounce half or three-quarters of a century's worth of conquests and would have been reduced to her territorial status before the time of Catherine the Great or, if Palmerston's threats about the Baltic provinces materialized, before Peter the Great. Kiselev's comparison stands out in high relief: in relation to such losses, the present conditions were "minimal."

Baron Meyendorff advanced a range of ominous historical comparisons. If the war continued, then the financial sacrifice would parallel Austria's situation after the Congress of Vienna, when Austria had been so exhausted by the long revolutionary wars that she had been obliged to stay absolutely quiet. In 1847 Metternich wanted to send thirty thousand soldiers to Switzerland to suppress the revolution, but had to give it up because bankruptcy threatened. The revolution won in Switzerland, and shortly after in Paris and Vienna. Meyendorff hinted here at the spectre of revolution in Russia. The further reference to Charles XII again exemplified how the financial drain of protracted warfare could diminish a great power. At the beginning of the last century Sweden had been a significant power; after Charles XII's wars it sank to the level of a third-rate state and had never risen again. The conclusions were obvious to Meyendorff: a war ended now would not injure development of Russian power or prejudice Russia's future. Peace now would be a truce only; after it expired, Russia could attain what seemed impossible now. However, were peace postponed, Russia would be so depleted that she would not recover for fifty years.

Unfortunately Meyendorff in his brief sketch did not provide any conclusive statistics about Russia's financial situation, about war costs, their relation to the total budget and their inflationary effects. He merely cited Finance Minister von Brock's opinion that if the war continued, Russia would inevitably go bankrupt; the war had cost 300 million silver rubles so far and created an enormous deficit.

There is no economic or financial history of Russia dealing with the Crimean War period. If the war had continued and if the economic and financial implications had emerged more clearly, scholars would probably have investigated these important aspects already. Even though this relatively short war did not spell economic and fiscal ruin for Russia, such problems should be analyzed in depth, so that their influence on the war can be established and the prognoses of Brock, Meyendorff, and others evaluated.

The Russian national debt, not disproportionately high before the war, was officially estimated at 400 million rubles in 1852;[325] it shot up during the war. The military expenses, even in peace the largest budget item, preempted four-fifths of the revenue, contrasted with about one-half in Austria. In 1851 to 1853 they averaged about 220 million rubles per annum;[326] in both war years 1854 and 1855 they increased by about 500 million, that is to say they tripled. According to the finance minister's calculations, the overrun in the third war year would be at least as much.[327] But government revenues had remained about constant. For 1855 they showed a slight decrease (206 in comparison to 220 million). The consequence was a deficit of 307 million in 1856, eleven times as high as the average for 1851 to 1853. The only way to satisfy the greater need for money was by issuing bank notes and floating loans, mostly abroad in Berlin and Amsterdam. Money in circulation doubled between 1853 and 1856 to 600 million. The rate of inflation in 1856 stood at 30 percent for exports and 13 percent for imports.

Beginning in the autumn of 1855, prices rose considerably. Inflation remained significant in 1856. Prices varied in different parts of the country: they were steepest in the southern provinces, that is, the war area, and in the western military districts. Agricultural products were more strongly affected than manufactures; in 1856, for example, rye meal was up 270 percent, while the average increase on sixty finished wares at the Nižnij-Novgorod fair was only 15 percent.

Naturally the export trade was most seriously affected. The total volume of exports declined by half between 1853 and 1854 and at least four-fifths between 1853 and 1855.[328] Britain, the best trading partner, was eliminated to a large extent because of the blockade. Prussia, and to a lesser degree Austria, took its place, but the details have not yet been investigated.

The war had a very different impact on individual branches of the economy. According to the Soviet economic historian Strumilin, the Crimean War initially dealt a "heavy blow" to the Russian economy and especially its industry. But in 1855 and 1856 there was actually an upswing, especially in the northern provinces, resulting partly from military orders.[329] Agriculture suffered most, since it lost hundreds of thousands of workers and just as many draft animals.

As for the different social classes, few were mortally affected.[330] The exceptions were those coast dwellers who suffered from the destruction and plundering practiced by the British navy and the Ottoman soldateska, and those farmers who paid the *obrok* (ground rent), since they were obliged to buy high-priced corn for subsistence but could not sell their own labor or their craft products dearer than before. The economic impact of the war on the average farmer must have been considerably less than that of a bad harvest. In the autumn of 1855 there was a rather good harvest.

From a financial point of view the great loser was the Russian state. *It* paid the bill through a drastic increase in the national debt. The

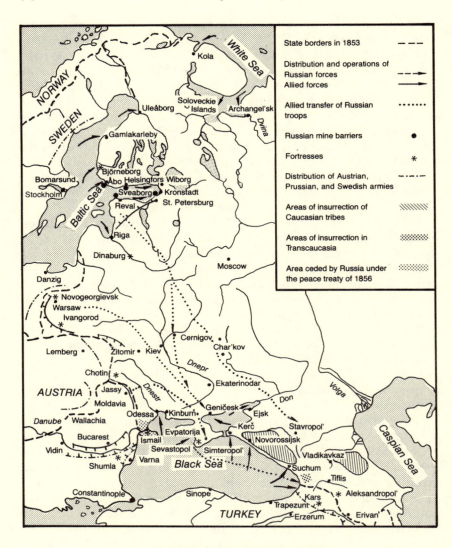

4. European Russia 1853–1856

balance between revenues and expenditures, already disturbed before the war, was fundamentally deranged. The finance minister's prognosis, quoted by Meyendorff in the Crown Council, was fully justified: if the war continued, the state would go bankrupt.

The Crimean War ended just in time for the Russian economy and indeed, with the exception of Britain, for the European economy. There seems to have been no long-term damage to the Russian economy. In the first two years of peace the export trade rose to a value far exceeding the prewar level, even if we adjust for inflation. The worldwide economic crisis of 1857 affected Russia only the following year, and very slightly by comparison with other countries.

The state's grim financial prospects, conjured up on 15 January 1856 by several speakers in the Crown Council, did influence the decision between war and peace. Although we possess no direct testimony, the report of the war minister, Prince Dolgorukov, must have been even more crushing. Recently there came to light a long-neglected report drawn up around the turn of the year 1855/56 concerning Russia's war economy. It was written by Major General D. A. Miljutin of the General Staff, the great army reformer of the 1860s and 1870s. Towards the end of the war, Miljutin was attached to the war minister for special service. The memorandum, entitled "The Dangers of Continuing the War in the Year 1856,"[331] marshalled impressive statistics. From the conclusions which Miljutin himself drew more or less explicitly, certain fundamental considerations emerge concerning the social structure of the Russian army. And Miljutin's statistics can be expanded by details learned later.

The basic theme running through Miljutin's brief is the conviction that Russia was incapable of successfully conducting a long war based on its serf economy against two fully industrialized powers. As proof Miljutin adduces the following arguments:

1. The number of troops, extraordinarily increased since the beginning of the war, had remained constant despite heavy battle losses and much illness. (Miljutin placed troop strength at 1.8 million men. In addition there were about 400,000 militia.) But the mass of recruits enrolled at the beginning of the war (some 400,000 men) were raw. Officers were lacking to train them. Miljutin's conclusion is that "the human reserves for reinforcing the troops are exhausted; in continuing the war our troops cannot increase in numbers but must unavoidably decline."

The number of troops, over 2 million men, constituted a little more than 3 percent of the population. In 1854 and 1855, from 1,000 males of military age, 55 were taken into service, 10 to 12 more than in peacetime. In other words, at least 800,000 men had been withdrawn from the labor force. Such a sudden and extensive diminution of the work force was very nearly a catastrophe for the Russian serf economy with its low productivity. The peasants were liable not only

for military service but for many other duties. The peasants in
military districts were especially severely affected by the quartering
of troops, the delivery of agricultural products, and forced transport. Further recruiting would have destroyed Russian agriculture,
the backbone of the economy.

Miljutin's evidence implies the high toll of lives. Today the human
losses can be calculated more accurately through documents from
the inspection division of the War Ministry.[332] In the thirty months of
war 256,295 men died. From this figure the "normal" mortality rate
should be deducted (35 per 1000 each year, twice as high as in the
western armies[333]). Genuine war losses accordingly numbered about
150,000 men. The mass of disabled cannot be ascertained from
official figures but can be approximated through accurate reports
from the Sevastopol garrison during the 349-day siege. The losses
among the 130,000 men consist of 15,000 killed in action or dead of
wounds, over 4,000 missing, over 70,000 wounded and 40,000 sick
(of whom over 8,000 eventually died). The ratio of dead to wounded
is about 1:4. Extended to all fronts this gives a figure of about 120,000
to 130,000 injured. In addition 50,000 invalids were discharged from
military hospitals at the end of 1856. Together with the losses among
the civilian population this gives at least 300,000 men. Using strict
methods, therefore, the total loss comes to half a million workers.

According to analogous calculations the losses in horses and draft
animals should run about one-third or one-half a million—an
equally heavy blow for Russian agriculture.

2.   In his memorandum Miljutin also considers stocks of weapons
and munitions.[334] Here Russia's inferiority to the industrial West was
striking. The army's equipment determined its defensive strength.
The war hit the army when rearmament had just begun. The battles
at the Alma and at Inkerman inflicted unusually heavy losses on the
infantry because it still carried obsolete flintlocks, basically unchanged since the seventeenth century, while the enemy troops already had the modern Minié guns with rifled barrels, providing a
longer range and greater accuracy. At the end of 1855 the stocks of
weapons and munitions were almost exhausted. At the beginning of
the war 1 million guns had been stockpiled; now only 90,000 were
left. Of the 1,656 field guns, only 253 were available. The backward,
indeed primitive, weapons industry could not begin to furnish the
army's needs. Modernization and expansion could not be accomplished overnight. Purchasing weapons abroad in Belgium and the
United States did not alleviate the situation, as the British blockade
tightened.

3.   Stocks of powder and shot were in even worse shape. To be sure, in 1855 powder production increased four to five fold over peacetime (from 60,000 to 80,000 up to 300,000 pud); but the increase did not mean much in terms of the needs at Sevastopol alone (250,000 pud). It has been calculated that when the Russians fired one round of artillery, the allies fired eight to ten. The lack of raw materials was catastrophic. There just was not enough saltpetre and sulphur.[335] Stocks of lead would have covered exactly half the requirements for 1856.

4.   Miljutin considered the condition of the commissariat problematic for the coming year. Provisions would soon run out in the war districts. Transport from the interior would be expensive and slow.

In fact, the Crimean army could not meet its need for grain locally. Grain had to be brought hundreds of kilometers. Since transport had to be overland, and a horse would eat more corn than he could haul, resupply was in effect impossible.[336] Most of the wagon loads from southern Russia to the Crimea did not reach their destination. In 1854 ten thousand wagon loads supposedly went out from the three southern provinces, but no one knows what happened to them. In the second half of 1855 forty thousand wagon loads were to go out from the same area, but their arrival was equally uncertain.[337]

5.   Finally he took up transportation, the most fundamental problem. Miljutin alluded to the fact that inadequate communications made it impossible to provide either provisions or troops in the quantities and at the speed necessary. Therefore the Russian army could not profit by having the inner lines. It was a grotesque situation: allied troops from France and England could be sent by sea to the Crimea in three weeks, whereas Russian troops from around Moscow needed three months to march to the front.[338]

In the prewar years the government's neglect of railroad construction had been criminal.[339] Strategic railroads running in a star formation from the center to the periphery had been projected, but during the war only the Moscow-Petersburg and part of the Moscow-Warsaw lines were ready. The trunk line to Feodosija in the Crimea and the important branch lines to Riga and to Kremenčug on the Dnieper had been approved in 1851, but work had never started. An observer in Petersburg wrote at the end of 1854: "No oversight is now more obviously punishing than the failure to build railroads, since in Russia more than in any other European country the 'fight against space' is a government responsibility. . . . Only with steam power could troops and materials be brought quickly to threatened points in adequate quantities; now the all too numerous army is scattered in the vast space. There is almost no place where it can be concentrated against enemy attack at the right moment."[340]

We do not know what immediate impression Miljutin's memorandum made on the participants in the Crown Council, but we can guess. Perhaps the memorandum had already circulated, for all the speakers from Nesselrode to Meyendorff mentioned the financial and commercial situation and all agreed that prospects for a new campaign in 1856 were unfavorable. The statistics presented left no doubt. Russia had neither the troops nor the equipment necessary to continue the war successfully. Never before had Russia's great power status seemed so vulnerable as at the beginning of 1856, when Austria's demarche forced the Russian administration to a pitilessly realistic analysis.

Alexander, who had inherited a situation he did not create, drew from this disinterested critique the only conclusion possible if he wanted to maintain his regime: he must accept the Austrian ultimatum.

Miljutin had not addressed the sociological side of the question. But doubtless his colleagues were more or less aware of it. Soviet scholarship has demonstrated that peasant revolts were twice as common at the end of 1854 as the average a year earlier.[341] Especially when the militia was called in, revolts sometimes snowballed to involve whole provinces, and in some cases could only be suppressed by troops in battalion and regiment strength, supported by cavalry and artillery. The vision of a peasant war must have presented itself clearly to the Crown Council.

Alexander believed that the army should be the symbol and guarantor of Russian greatness; already in the summer of 1855 he had asked the adjutant general, Count Rüdiger, to suggest reforms.[342] Rüdiger's memoranda, submitted in June, were superficial; they laid the blame on individual abuses. Once again it was Miljutin, as a member of the "special commission for the improvement of the army" since February 1856, who in a March 1856 memorandum discussed the essential structural problem; he criticized the lack of territorial organization and the practice of maintaining enormous peacetime strength without effective reserves, in contrast to other continental states. To obviate this, Miljutin proposed reducing the length of service to two or three years and garrisoning most of the army in the interior. But there were three problems: Russia's huge size, its multinational character, and serfdom. Only the last could be changed. "Serfdom," wrote Miljutin, "makes it impossible for us to reduce the time of service and to raise the number of trainees beyond a certain limit." In other words, to create a conscript army, serfdom must be abolished.

The regular soldier during the Crimean War was differentiated from the militia by the fact that he was not a serf. A feudal bond between territorial lord and peasant could not be reconciled with the procedures of a modern army. A rural economy based on serfdom—peasants comprised almost 80 percent of the population—could only release a limited number of laborers to the army. The army should not consist of short-term conscripts, since as serfs they might be a dangerous element after demobilization; they must be professional soldiers enrolled for up to twenty-five years. To avoid economic and social disaster, the proportion of the army to the total population could not exceed 2 to 3 percent. For mid-nineteenth century Russia with a population of about 60 million[343] this dictated an army no larger than 1.5 to 2 million men. In fact, this was the actual strength of the army during the Crimean War.

Before the war, about 80,000 recruits were drafted annually. They received one year of training in the reserves before entering the regular army. An effective reserve could not be developed under this system. To enlarge the army after war broke out and to compensate for losses several hundred thousand men were needed every year; because of the reasons mentioned, only a limited number could be serfs. The government tried to escape by calling up the militia. During military service the militiaman was differentiated from the regular soldier only by his uniform; but upon demobilization his status was very different, since he remained a serf. In 1812, this expedient was employed with some success, but the nature and brevity of the war precluded social problems. In 1854 the maneuver could not be repeated with impunity. The peasants joined the militia gladly, but expected to be freed. They demonstrated in support of this demand, and there was a real danger that the protests might eventually escalate into a real peasant war. The militia was no longer useful.

The government's situation was grim: a regular army of 1.5 or 2 million men was not adequate for a larger war. Of this army no less than half a million men were required to maintain order, that is to curb peasant unrest. A further 250,000 men had to be stationed in the Caucasus (against Shamil) and in Turkestan. From the rest 250,000 soldiers were not available for service in the field—they were used for communications, in the medical service, for training recruits, etc. Only about 700,000, or about 1 million with the militia, were left for frontline duty. Russia's economic structure made it impossible to better these figures. So there were two alternatives: either abolish serfdom and reconstruct the army on a new basis or give up an expansionist foreign policy, which was equivalent to renouncing great power status and sinking to the level of the Ottoman Empire.

So not only social but also diplomatic and military insights and needs argued for abolition of serfdom. All clear-sighted Russian leaders grasped this as a result of the Crimean War. Miljutin was one of the first to point out the lesson. Alexander plucked up the moral courage to reach the only wise decision: to end the war at once.

The way lay open for peace negotiations.

NOTES

Full citations appear in the bibliography.

I. The Road to Peace

1. Graham to Clarendon, 1 March 1854 (J. B. Conacher, *The Aberdeen Coalition 1852–1855*, p. 256).
2. Cf. I. V. Bestužev, "Krymskaja vojna i revoljucionnaja situacija," pp. 190–91.
3. Memorandum by Nesselrode, 15 January 1856 (S. S. Tatiščev, *Imperator Aleksandr II*, 1: 171).
4. Theodore Martin, *The Life of His Royal Highness the Prince Consort*, 3: 379.
5. Bestužev, "Krymskaja vojna," p. 192.
6. The Bavarian minister in Petersburg, Count Bray, wrote on 28 December 1855 to King Max II: "When the capture of Kars was announced, Count Nesselrode cried: 'At last, we have something *to return.*' Hence he considered that town as a bargaining counter" (BGSA, MA I 598).
7. Queen Victoria to Clarendon, 12 December 1855 (Martin, 3: 379n.).
8. The Turkish defenders were under British leadership.
9. Cf. François Charles-Roux, *Alexandre II, Gortchakoff et Napoléon III*, p. 33.
10. Winfried Baumgart, "Das Kaspi-Unternehmen."
11. Such concerns seem to have been generally expressed in diplomatic circles. On 25 January 1856 the minister of Baden, von Meysenbug, wrote from Berlin to his foreign minister, Rüdt: "To end this situation [the fluid Russo-Turkish boundary in the Caucasus], to set a precise limit, guaranteed by a European treaty, to the progress of Russian rule, and if possible to bar access for ever to the sources of the Euphrates and the route to Asia Minor and to Bagdad—is an exceptionally great interest for Britain, since she feels insecure in her Asian empire." (GLA, Abt. 48, No. 2653.)
12. Granville to Stratford de Redcliffe (about the Cabinet meeting of 19 December 1855), London, 19 December 1855 (Edmond Fitzmaurice, *The Life of Granville George Leveson Gower*, 1: 132); Granville to Stratford de Redcliffe (about the Cabinet meeting of 3 January 1856), 3 January 1856 (*ibid.*, p. 137); Granville to Stratford de Redcliffe (about the Cabinet meeting of 5 January 1856), London, 5 January 1856 (*ibid.*, p. 138). See also George Douglas Eighth Duke of Argyll, *Autobiography and Memoirs*, 1: 602 (about the Cabinet meeting of 13 December 1855).
13. Breakdown of these figures in Martin, 3: 417 (Prince Albert to King Leopold, Windsor, 24 December 1855). See also Germain Bapst, *Le Maréchal Canrobert*, 3: 79; further Emil Daniels, *Geschichte der Kriegskunst*, p. 175.

14. Granville to Stratford de Redcliffe, London, 5 January 1856 (Fitzmaurice, 1: 138).

15. As examples of contradictory accounts, cf. Alexandre de Jomini, *Étude diplomatique sur la guerre de Crimée (1852 à 1856)*, 2: 392, and Bapst, 3: 78–79. Brison D. Gooch, *The New Bonapartist Generals in the Crimean War* (pp. 256–59), used no archival sources for his presentation. See Winfried Baumgart, "Ein Kriegsrat Napoleons III."

16. Queen Victoria to Clarendon, Windsor, 15 January 1856 (Victoria, *The Letters of Queen Victoria*, 3: 163). See also Queen Victoria to Clarendon, Windsor, [middle of] January 1856 (Martin, 3: 425).

17. On 31 January 1856. Cf. *Hansard Parliamentary Debates*, 3rd series, 140: 47; further Herbert Maxwell, *The Life and Letters of George William Frederick Fourth Earl of Clarendon*, 2: 116.

18. Prince Albert to Stockmar, Windsor, 19 November 1855 (Martin, 3: 389). See also Winfried Baumgart, "Der Krimkrieg in der angelsächsischen und russischen militärgeschichtlichen Literatur der sechziger Jahre," p. 188.

19. Cowley to Clarendon (about conversation with Napoleon), December 1855 (Henry Richard Charles Wellesley, *The Paris Embassy during the Second Empire*, p. 86).

20. Hübner to Buol (about conversation with Napoleon), Paris, 17 December 1855 (*Akten zur Geschichte des Krimkriegs*, ed. Winfried Baumgart, I, 3: 176–77. Hereinafter cited as AGKK). See also E. von Manteuffel to King Frederick William IV, Vienna, [beginning of] January 1856 (Leopold von Gerlach, *Denkwürdigkeiten aus dem Leben Leopold von Gerlachs*, 2: 379).

21. Cowley to Clarendon (about conversation with Napoleon), Paris, 10 December 1855 (*Le Relazioni diplomatiche fra la Gran Bretagna e il regno di Sardegna*, series III: 1848–1860, ed. Federico Curato, 98: 189. Hereinafter cited as Fonti).

22. Bapst, 3: 79.

23. *Ibid.*, p. 81.

24. Cf. Edgar Hösch, "Neuere Literatur (1940–1960) über den Krimkrieg," p. 429.

25. Bestužev, "Krymskaja vojna," p. 192.

26. Cf. Winfried Baumgart, "Probleme der Krimkriegsforschung," pp. 249–52.

27. Koller to Buol (about conversation with Fuad Pasha), Buyukdere, 20 September 1855 (AGKK I, 3: 57).

28. Donald Southgate, '*The Most English Minister* . . . ,' p. xxiii.

29. Cited *ibid.*, p. 566.

30. Cf. Conacher, p. 139.

31. Southgate, p. 65.

32. *Ibid.*, p. xxiii.

33. Waltraut Heindl, *Graf Buol-Schauenstein in St. Petersburg und London (1848–1852)*, p. 105, pp. 123–28.

34. [Charles Cavendish Fulke] Greville, *The Greville Memoirs 1814–1860*, 7: 158 (diary entry of 17 September 1855). See also Palmerston's letter to his brother, London, 25 August 1855 (Evelyn Ashley, *The Life of Henry John Temple, Viscount Palmerston: 1846–1865*, 2: 101).

35. Cf. Baumgart, "Probleme," pp. 373–74. The British government also quarrelled with the United States in the autumn of 1855 because of the recruitment of American citizens into the British Foreign Legion, which was to be used against Russia. Palmerston once again reacted by sending a squadron to the West Indies. Cf. documentation in Richard W. Van Alstyne, "Anglo-American Relations, 1853–1857," *passim.*

36. W. E. Mosse, *The Rise and Fall of the Crimean System 1855–71*, p. 1.

37. The minimal program for future negotiations in the form of a note directed by the British and French representatives to Count Buol poses these conditions: abolition of the protectorate previously exercised by Russia over the principalities of Moldavia and Wallachia (also Serbia, nonetheless subordinate) and establishment of a great power guarantee of the privileges granted to these principalities by the sultans; freeing of the navigation of the Danube at its mouths; revision of the Straits Convention of 1841 "in the interest of the European balance of power"; Russia's renunciation of her claim to a protectorate over the Greek Orthodox subjects of Turkey and guarantee of the religious privileges of the different Christian communities granted by the Sultan and confirmed by all the great powers. Text: *Recueil des traités et conventions conclus par la Russie avec les puissances étrangères,* 15: 544. Hereinafter cited as F. de Martens.

38. Cf. Argyll to Clarendon, London, October 1854 (Argyll, 1: 492).

39. John Russell, *The Later Correspondence of Lord John Russell 1840–1878*, 2: 160–61.

40. *Ibid.*, pp. 159–60. See also Conacher, p. 256.

41. Aberdeen to Russell, end March/beginning April 1854 (Frances Balfour, *The Life of George, Fourth Earl of Aberdeen*, 2: 206). See also Southgate, p. 346.

42. Conacher, pp. 441–42.

43. Palmerston to his brother, London, 25 August 1855 (Ashley, 2: 100): "Our danger will then begin—a danger of peace, and not a danger of war."

44. Argyll, 1:589. This is obviously the memorandum also mentioned in n. 36.

45. D'Azeglio to Cibrario (about conversation with Palmerston), London, 3 October 1855 (Ennio Di Nolfo, *Europa e Italia nel 1855–1856*, p. 117, n. 6); Palmerston to Clarendon, 9 October 1855 (Harold Temperley, "Austria, England, and the Ultimatum to Russia 16. Dec. 1855," p. 629 n. 1; see also *ibid.*, p. 630 n.1).

46. Clarendon to Hudson, London, 20 December 1855 (Fonti, 98: 193).

47. F. de Martens, 15: 628–31.

48. King Oscar's secret memorandum, November 1855 (Carl Hallendorf, *Konung Oscar I's politik under Krimkriget*, pp. 89–97; see also *ibid.*, pp. 87–89, King Oscar's diary entry for 17 November 1855). Cf. *ibid.*, pp. 7–15; further Carl Hallendorf, *Oscar I, Napoleon och Nikolaus*, pp. 112–25.

49. Greville's diary entry for 6 December 1855 (Greville, 7: 173): "I suspect Palmerston would wish the war to glide imperceptibly into a war of nationalities, as it is called, but would not like to profess it openly now." The term *war* and its transformation in the nineteenth century would be worth a study.

50. Cf. above p. 5 and below pp. 43–46.

51. Egmont Zechlin, "Friedensbestrebungen und Revolutionierungs-versuche."

52. Ennio Di Nolfo, *Adam J. Czartoryski e il congresso di Parigi.* On Britain's use of foreign legions see the new study by C. C. Bayley, *Mercenaries for the Crimea.*

53. Di Nolfo, *Adam J. Czartoryski,* pp. 137–45.

54. Cf. below p. 26.

55. See on this point the striking remarks of Erwin Hölzle, *Russland und Amerika,* pp. 182–94; further Frank A. Golder, "Russian-American Relations during the Crimean War."

56. More precise treatment below pp. 37–46.

57. Buol to Mensdorff, 2 December 1852 (Heindl, p. 110): "For the time being we cannot believe blindly in a peace policy of the emperor's; though he doesn't go along with ideas of *world wars* at this moment, yet his policy will become an aggressive one; it is just a question of where he will try it." Persigny to Napoleon (about a conversation with Clarendon), London, 16 January 1856 (L. Thouvenel, *Pages de l'histoire du Second Empire,* p. 207): If the war is continued, there will be a *"bouleversement immense* ou . . . une guerre de trente ans."" Hübner's diary entry of 26 January 1856 about a conversation with Empress Eugénie ([Joseph Alexander von] Hübner, Count Hübner, *Neuf ans de souvenirs d'un ambassadeur d'Autriche à Paris sous le Second Empire 1851–1859,* 1: 386): "If they let you have your way, Madame . . . we would have a *world war.*" Italics mine. For further relevant passages cf. AGKK I, 3: 644 (entry "Weltkrieg").

58. *Konferenzen und Verträge, Vertrags-Ploetz,* part II, vol. 3, ed. Helmuth K. G. Rönnefarth, p. 305.

59. L. von Gerlach to Manteuffel, Berlin, 18 February 1856 (Otto Freiherr von Manteuffel, *Preussens auswärtige Politik 1850 bis 1858,* 3: 218).

60. Cited by Franco Valsecchi, "Das Zeitalter Napoleons III. und Bismarcks 1854–1878," p. 61.

61. Cited by Monika Ritter, "Frankreichs Griechenland-Politik während des Krimkrieges," p. 1.

62. Heinrich von Treitschke, *Deutsche Geschichte im Neunzehnten Jahrhundert,* 1: 665.

63. Ernest II, Duke of Saxe-Coburg-Gotha, *Aus meinem Leben und aus meiner Zeit,* 2: 140.

64. *Ibid.,* p. 139.

65. D'Azeglio to Cavour, London, 7 March 1856 ([Camille Benso] Cavour, *Cavour e l'Inghilterra,* 7: 273).

66. Ernest, 2: 141.

67. *Ibid.*

68. Heinrich Euler, *Napoleon III in seiner Zeit,* 2: 951. I thank Mr. Euler for his friendly communication of the manuscript of the second volume of his major biography of Napoleon and for permission to quote from it.

69. Drouyn de l'Huys in the spring of 1855.

70. The most famous example is the conversation at Plombières, which took place without Walewski's knowledge.

70a. For the period up to 1863 see William E. Echard, "Napoleon III and the Concert of Europe."

71. Ernest, 2: 139.

72. *Ibid.*, pp. 281–83. See also Schweizer to Rüdt, Paris, 28 September 1855 (GLA, Abt. 48, No. 2050 f. 582): "The future is therefore war, and as to the eventualities of peace, which must arise sooner or later, they still nourish the secret hope here . . . that a major European settlement, in erasing the terms of the treaties of 1815 and arranging anew the future condition of Europe, will strengthen the foundations of the Imperial throne in France."

73. Manteuffel's note, [end] January 1856 (Manteuffel, 3: 206); King Frederick William's draft telegram, Berlin, 28 January 1856 (*ibid.*, pp. 206–7).

74. Kurt Borries, *Preussen im Krimkrieg (1853–1856)*, pp. 320, 336.

75. King Leopold to Manteuffel, Laeken, 2 February 1856 (Manteuffel, 3: 208–9). For the remarks following see Manteuffel's answering letter, Berlin, 16 February 1856 (*ibid.*, pp. 212–14).

76. Queen Victoria to Palmerston, London, 6 March 1856 (Victoria, 3: 181).

77. The copy to be found in the Vienna archives, used in what follows, is the fourth edition. It has a foreword dated 25 December 1855. On 27 December Hübner sent it to Vienna (HHSA, PA IX 50 f. 430). See also [Charles-Frédéric] de Grovestins, *Le Congrès de Vienne en 1814 et 1815, et le Congrès de Paris en 1856*.

78. Schweizer to Rüdt, Paris, 30 December 1855 (GLA, Abt. 48, No. 2050 f. 835). Schweizer already suspected Duveyrier to be the author.

79. Taxile Delord, *Histoire du Second Empire 1848–1869*, 1: 629.

80. Duke Ernest's note, Paris, 25 September 1855 (Ernest, 2: 282).

81. *Moniteur*, 16 November 1855.

82. Ernest, 2: 282.

83. See below p. 138.

84. Well-known later example: *Le Pape et le Congrès*, Paris, 1859. For a general account see Natalie Isser, *The Second Empire and the Press.*

85. Walewski to Napoleon, Paris, 11 September 1855 ([Alexandre-Florian-Joseph Colonna, Count Walewski], "Les Papiers inédits du Comte Walewski," p. 488).

86. Napoleon to Walewski, St.-Cloud, 14 September 1855 (*ibid.*, pp. 489–90). See further Charles-Roux, p. 34; F. A. Simpson, *Louis Napoleon and the Recovery of France*, p. 333.

87. Hübner to Buol (secret), Paris, 21 September 1855 (AGKK I, 3: 60–61).

88. Prince Albert to Stockmar, Windsor, 29 October 1855 (Martin 3: 385).

89. On this point cf. Hermann Oncken, *Die Rheinpolitik Kaiser Napoleons III. von 1863 bis 1870 und der Ursprung des Krieges von 1870/71*, vol. I; Gerhard Ritter, "Bismarck und die Rhein-Politik Napoleons III"; Herbert Geuss, *Bismarck und Napoleon III.*

90. Prince Albert to Stockmar, Windsor, 24 January 1856 (Martin, 3: 428–29).

91. Cowley to Clarendon, Paris, December 1855 (Wellesley, p. 86).

92. Greville's diary entry of 2 January 1856 (Greville, 7: 186). See also Napoleon III, *Discours, messages, lettres et proclamations de S. M. Napoléon III, Empereur des Français*, 3:124.

93. Greville, 7: 186.

94. Manteuffel to Hatzfeldt, Berlin, 1 January 1856 (Manteuffel, 3: 187). In Germany people considered Napoleon III's designs on the Rhine as a matter of course. Cf. Bismarck to Manteuffel, 19 January 1856, about a conversation with

the Bundestag representative from Electoral Hesse, returned from a trip to Paris ([Prince Otto von] Bismarck, *Die gesammelten Werke,* 2: 95 [No. 108]): "Dörnberg regards the Rhine boundary as an immutable program of Napoleon's." See also Bismarck to Carl Friedrich Ernst von Canitz und Dallwitz, Frankfurt, 29 May 1855 (*Neue Quellen zur Geschichte Preussens im 19. Jahrhundert,* ed. Hans-Joachim Schoeps, p. 465): "Whether they attack us . . . on the Rhine on the grounds of domestic French policy, only time will tell."

95. Bernstorff to Manteuffel, London, 6 January 1856 (Manteuffel, 3: 190–93). See also Greville's diary entry for 9 January 1856 (Greville, 7: 188); further below p. 65.

96. The same argument applies to Napoleon's hitherto only partially verifiable intention, if Prussia entered the war on the Russian side, to lure Austria out of her reserve with Prussian territory (Silesia). Cf. Prince Albert to King Leopold, Windsor, 24 December 1855 (Martin, 3: 418).

97. Euler, 2: 979. See also Di Nolfo, *Czartoryski,* pp. 47–54; Charles-Roux, pp. 39–40; Simpson, pp. 336–38.

98. Di Nolfo, *Czartoryski,* p. 48.

99. Cowley to Clarendon (about conversation with Napoleon), Paris, 24 September 1855 (Di Nolfo, *Czartoryski,* p. 155).

100. Clarendon to Cowley, London, 22 September 1855 (*ibid.,* p. 152).

101. Persigny to Walewski (about conversation with Clarendon), London, 17 September 1855 (*ibid.,* p. 148).

102. Persigny to Walewski (about conversation with Palmerston), London, 18 September 1855 (*ibid.,* p. 150).

103. Cf. n. 100.

104. Von Willisen to King Frederick William, Paris, 3 November 1855 (Manteuffel, 3: 165).

105. Cf. Lynn M. Case, *French Opinion on War and Diplomacy during the Second Empire,* pp. 38–43; Pierre de la Gorce, *Histoire du Second Empire,* 1: 451–53; Simpson, p. 335, n. 2.

106. D'Azeglio to Cavour (about conversation with Palmerston), London, 23 February 1856 (Cavour, 7: 207).

107. Duke of Cambridge to Queen Victoria, Paris, 20 January 1856 (Victoria, 3: 167). Bismarck, who had visited Paris in September 1855, wrote on 15 September 1855 from Frankfurt to L. von Gerlach: "I didn't speak to a single Frenchman who didn't want peace, most of all the military" (Bismarck, XIV, 1: 415).

108. Cf. n. 85.

109. Di Nolfo, *Europa,* p. 236.

110. *Moniteur,* "Supplément extraordinaire," 3 March 1856.

111. Hübner to Buol (secret), Paris, 21 September 1855 (AGKK I, 3: 63–64).

112. Schweizer to Rüdt, Paris, 22 October 1855 (GLA, Abt. 48, No. 2050 f. 653–55).

113. Cf. n. 111 (p. 63); further Schweizer to Rüdt, Paris, 22 September 1855 and 5 October 1855 (GLA, Abt. 48, No. 2050 f. 555 and 594–95).

114. Schweizer to Rüdt, Paris, 5 October 1855 (GLA, Abt. 48, No. 2050 f. 593–94); Pergler von Perglas to King Max (conversation with Count Platen about his trip to Paris), Hanover, 6 October 1855 (BGSA, MA I 597 No. 101).

115. "Razgovor imperatora Napoleona III s gen.-ad. Totlebenom v 1857 g.," ed. N. K. Šilder, p. 719.

116. Napoleon III's note to Walewski, 24 December 1858 (Franco Valsecchi, *L'unificazione italiana e la politica europea dalla guerra di Crimea alla guerra di Lombardia 1854–1859*, p. 338).

117. See n. 43.

118. Palmerston to Clarendon, 16 September 1855 (Di Nolfo, *Europa*, p. 121).

119. Cited by Southgate, p. 384.

120. Gladstone to Argyll, Hawarden, 18 October 1855 (Argyll, 2: 38).

121. Simpson, p. 330, 333.

122. Napoleon to Victoria, Paris, 22 November 1855 (Martin, 3: 525–26).

123. See above p. 6.

124. Palmerston to Persigny, London, 21 November 1855 (Ashley, 2: 103–4). See also on this point Clarendon to Granville, Paris, 12 March 1856 (Maxwell, p. 119).

125. Greville's diary entry of 27 November 1855 (Greville, 7:170): "C[harles] V[illiers] told me that P[almerston] had already thrown out a feeler to the Cabinet to ascertain if they would be willing to carry on the war without France, but this was unanimously declined."

126. Cowley to Clarendon (about conversation with Napoleon), Paris, 10 December 1855 (Fonti, 98: 186–91).

127. Harold Temperley, "The Treaty of Paris of 1856 and its Execution," pp. 391–92; Di Nolfo, *Europa*, p. 130; Southgate, p. 385. The fifth point reads: "Special conditions. The belligerent powers reserve the right which is vested in them to produce special conditions in the interests of Europe in addition to the Four Points" (AGKK I, 3: 107).

128. Di Nolfo, *Europa*, pp. 464–66. For the following remarks see the important account in Schroeder, *Austria, Great Britain*, pp. 321–30.

129. Victoria to Clarendon, Windsor, 19 November 1855 (Victoria, 3: 152).

130. People called the memorandum "a second edition of the Vienna Conferences," that is to say, the conferences that had failed (Greville's diary entry of 27 November 1855, Greville, 7: 169).

131. Cf. Clarendon to Hudson, London, 5 February 1856 (Fonti, 98: 222): "I have no idea as to whether the Russians have accepted the terms honestly or whether they mean to wriggle out of them all in the Conference. The latter is the probable course, and we are not relaxing in our preparations for another campaign." See also Clarendon to Stratford de Redcliffe, 18 January and 8 February 1856 (Stanley Lane-Poole, *The Life of the Right Honourable Stratford Canning Viscount Stratford de Redcliffe*, 2: 434, 435).

132. Clarendon to Hudson, London, 20 December 1855 (Fonti, 98: 192–93).

133. Granville to Canning, London, 20 December 1855 (Fitzmaurice, 1: 133): "Cupid [Palmerston] hopes and believes that the Russians will not accept our ultimatum. That they will refuse, seems to be the general opinion." See also Greville's diary entries of 6 and 11 December 1855 (Greville, 7: 172 and 175).

134. Cf. n. 128.

135. The most recent scholarly view is offered by John P. Mackintosh, *The British Cabinet*, pp. 118–37 (chapter "The Influence of the Crown").

136. Cf. Gavin Burns Henderson, *Crimean War Diplomacy and Other Historical Essays,* pp. 68–97 (chapter "The Influence of the Crown, 1854–1856").

137. Hawarden, 18 October 1855 (Argyll, 2: 37–39). For the following, Argyll to Gladstone, Rosneath, 24 October and 1 November 1855 (*ibid.,* pp. 39–43).

138. See above p. 9.

139. Cf. Olive Anderson, *A Liberal State at War,* p. 90.

140. W. E. Gladstone, *Gleanings of Past Years, 1843–78,* 1: 245.

141. See for example the letters to L. von Gerlach, Frankfurt, 29 October and 8 April 1856 (Bismarck, XIV, 1: 419 and 439–40): "Since the Reform Bill and the decay of parties the clockwork is obviously paralyzed; the forces neutralize each other domestically and Palmerston drives the foreign policy of this mighty nation like an angry old drunkard, who smashes pots and cups, because he has gambled away his money" (*ibid.,* p. 440).

142. [Klemens Wenzel Nepomuk Lothar von] Metternich, *Briefe des Staatskanzlers Fürsten Metternich-Winneburg an den österreichischen Minister des Allerhöchsten Hauses und des Äussern, Grafen Buol-Schauenstein aus den Jahren 1852–1859,* p. 161 (No. 113). See also *ibid.,* p. 160 (No. 112), pp. 162–64 (Nos. 114–116). For Metternich's picture of England, see most recently Eva-Renate Rohl, "Metternich und England."

143. Cited by O. Anderson, *A Liberal State,* p. 91.

144. Its dimensions have been splendidly examined by O. Anderson in her book *A Liberal State at War.*

145. Cf. n. 137.

146. About this Cabinet meeting up to now only very few sources have been available. Cf. Argyll, 1: 596–97.

147. *Ibid.,* p. 597. Paul W. Schroeder (*Austria, Great Britain, and the Crimean War,* pp. 321–30) claims on the basis of his knowledge of the sources to be unable to detect any isolation of Palmerston in the Cabinet. Concerning Britain's concurrence in the Austrian ultimatum he assumes that the British government was convinced of the Russian refusal. When the ultimatum had been sent off, Britain and France did all they could to exclude Austria from the future peace negotiations.

148. Di Nolfo, *Europa,* pp. 464–66.

149. Cf. Baumgart, "Probleme," pp. 243–48.

150. Hans-Joachim Schoeps, *Der Weg ins deutsche Kaiserreich,* p. 251 n. 61.

151. Hugo Hantsch, *Die Geschichte Österreichs,* 2: 353–54.

152. Cf. Coronini to Prokesch, Bucharest, 19 February 1856: "Through noble, well-conducted immigration and colonization of agricultural German elements in the Danube Valley [the prerequisites will be created for the Danubian principalities to fall like a] ripe fruit in the lap of the lordly, mighty *German empire* . . . then the daring dreams of Eugenian and Josephine policy will for the first time become a glittering reality" (*Corespondenţa lui Coronini din Principate,* ed. Ion I. Nistor, No. 757 p. 906; AGKK I, 3: 398).

153. Cited by Schoeps, p. 37.

154. E. L. von Gerlach's diary entry of 13 May 1854 about a conversation with Bismarck (Ernst Ludwig von Gerlach, *Von der Revolution zum Norddeutschen Bund,* 1: 350).

155. Bismarck to Leopold von Gerlach, Frankfurt, 21 December 1855 (Bismarck, XIV, 1: 423).

156. Cf. Heindl, pp. 21–22.

157. Numerous examples *ibid.*, pp. 123–25.

158. Cf. Di Nolfo, *Europa*, p. 231.

159. Cavour to D'Azeglio, Paris, 8 March 1856 (Cavour, 7: 285).

160. An interpretive history for this period is very much needed. For the most recent interpretation see Heinz Gollwitzer, "Ideologische Blockbildung als Bestandteil internationaler Politik im 19. Jahrhundert," pp. 313–14 (n.). We are proceeding on the assumption that the term *Holy Alliance* is also applicable to the period after Alexander I's death and after the Greek war of independence.

161. It has been admirably described by Bernhard Unckel, *Österreich und der Krimkrieg.*

162. Hübner's diary entry of 21 April 1856 (Hübner, 1: 424).

163. Strictly speaking, it has never been abrogated by a new agreement, even de jure.

164. Unckel, pp. 85–93 (especially the passages about the exchange of letters between Francis Joseph and Nicholas I). See also Nesselrode to Meyendorff, Petersburg, 9 June 1854 ([Karl Vasil'evič, Carl Robert von] Nesselrode, *Lettres et papiers du chancelier Comte de Nesselrode 1760–1856*, 11: 66): "The Emperor has not yet renounced the hope of seeing the Christian peoples rise up en masse."

165. Unckel.

166. Paul W. Schroeder, "Austria and the Danubian Principalities, 1853–1856."

167. See below pp. 116–25; further AGKK I, 3: 32–35; Winfried Baumgart, "Die Aktenedition zur Geschichte des Krimkriegs."

168. Unckel, p. 292: "Austrian foreign policy during the Crimean War was the foreign policy of Emperor Francis Joseph." Heindl, p. 115: "In the Crimean War however, it was Buol's policy which prevailed unquestioned." See now my introduction in AGKK I, 3: pp. 28–32.

169. Metternich, p. 64. Italics original. See also Metternich to Buol, 18 November 1853 (*ibid.*, p. 145): "Austria stands in relation to Ottoman affairs in an attitude belonging to her alone. Austria can only desire the maintenance of the Turkish empire in Europe;—not out of love for it, but because she would suffer harm from any other neighbor and would win nothing from territorial enlargement at its expense."

170. Metternich to Buol, 18 November 1853 (*ibid.*, p. 144). Italics original.

171. *Ibid.*, p. 147 (No. 101); further *ibid.*, p. 149 (No. 103), Metternich to Buol, 23 November 1853.

172. *Ibid.*, pp. 158–59, Metternich to Buol, 3 June 1854. Italics original. See also *ibid.*, p. 156 (No. 108), Metternich to Buol, Vienna, 29 March 1854; *ibid.*, p. 159 (No. 111), undated note by Metternich.

173. Lettre particulière (copy), Vienna, 7 March 1854 (HHSA, PA IX 48 f. 112).

174. Vienna, 6 June 1855 (Di Nolfo, *Europa*, p. 460).

175. Kübeck's diary entry of 9 December 1854 (Carl Friedrich Kübeck von Kübau, *Aus dem Nachlass des Freiherrn Carl Friedrich Kübeck von Kübau*, p. 166).

176. Cf. Unckel, pp. 167–68. A very thorough treatment and a somewhat different evaluation of the December Treaty is offered by Schroeder, *Austria, Great Britain*, pp. 83–114. Cf. also Winfried Baumgart, Österreich und Preussen im Krimkrieg."

177. Unckel, p. 214. In a private letter of the same day Buol wrote to Colloredo (HHSA, PA VIII 42 f. 17): "The principal part of the war would fall on us, along with the dangers and the consequences; it is fair therefore that they consult us and listen to our opinion."

178. P. 38 above.

179. Buol to Hübner (lettre particulière), Vienna, 17 November 1855 (AGKK I, 3: 117–19).

180. See also Buol's despatch to Hübner (draft), Vienna, 29 December 1855 (*ibid.*, p. 200): "A calm and impartial review of the totality of the situation does not allow His Majesty to consider his immediate participation in the war, which would open many risks, as the most effective method of speedily restoring to Europe, without shaking her to her foundations, the repose which is so generally felt to be needed." Cf. my introductory remarks in AGKK I, 3: 21.

181. See n. 179. Italics mine.

182. Cf. Heinz Gollwitzer, *Europabild und Europagedanke*, pp. 183–91 (chapter "Metternich und sein Lager," which needs a complementary section on Buol).

183. Bismarck's note, Varzin, 9 November 1876 (*Die Grosse Politik der Europäischen Kabinette 1871–1914*, 2: 88 No. 256). Cf. Theodor Schieder, "Bismarck und Europa," p. 32 on this point.

184. Cf. Metternich to Buol, Vienna, 27 May 1854 (Metternich, p. 157): "Under the pressure of the events of the years 1811 and 1812 and during those of 1853 and 1854, Austria's position on material grounds was *a middle position*, as it will always be in the case of wars between the Occident and the Orient." Italics original.

185. See the pamphlet conceived in this sense which appeared during the Crimean War from the pen of the political scientist Lorenz Stein, *Österreich und der Frieden*, especially pp. 30–46.

186. The protocol is now printed in AGKK I, 3: 369–71.

187. Instructions to Buol, Vienna, 25 February 1856 (*ibid.*, p. 422).

188. Milorad Ekmečić, "Mit o revoluciji i Austrijska politika prema Bosni, Hercegovini i Crnoj Gori u vrijeme Krimskog rata 1853–1856."

189. Cf. Francis Joseph to Frederick William IV, 16 July 1853 (Franz Eckhart, *Die deutsche Frage und der Krimkrieg*, p. 5): "Let us not forget, moreover, that today's Christian world has a worse archenemy than the Turks. This enemy of all divine and human order is the Revolution. As long as it is not entirely conquered, would not fragmentation of the Continental forces through remodelling of the Orient call forth renewed impulses of destruction in the West?" See also Baumgart, "Aktenedition."

190. Rudolf Haym, *Die deutsche Nationalversammlung von den Septemberereignissen bis zur Kaiserwahl*, p. 63.

191. For recent scholarship on Pogodin, see Baumgart, "Probleme," pp. 391–93.

192. Cf. A. J. P. Taylor, *The Hapsburg Monarchy 1809–1918*, p. 7: "The conflict between a super-national dynastic state and the national principle had to be fought to the finish. . . . The national principle, once launched, had to work itself out to its conclusion." A penetrating, carefully weighed and extended presentation of the problem mentioned here is provided by Robert A. Kann, *The Multinational Empire.* See especially his conclusions in vol. II, pp. 286–98. A position in opposition to Taylor is also assumed by Böhm (cf. Wilhelm Böhm, *Konservative Umbaupläne im alten Österreich,* especially pp. 251–52).

193. Lettre particulière (copy), Vienna, 21 June 1853 (HHSA, PA VIII 38 f. 47). Cf. also Unckel, p. 94.

194. Unckel, p. 75.

195. Friedrich Engel-Janosi, *Der Freiherr von Hübner 1811–1892*, p. 114.

196. Nicholas to Francis Joseph, Petersburg, 24 December 1853 (A. M. Zajončkovskij, *Vostočnaja vojna 1853–1856 gg. v svjazi s sovremennoj ej političeskoj obstanovkoj,* 2: 254). See also Unckel, pp. 110–12.

197. Bismarck to Leopold von Gerlach, Frankfurt, 27 April 1855 (Bismarck, XIV, 1: 399). See also the following passage in Bismarck's letter to his longtime friend, Carl Friedrich Ernst von Canitz und Dallwitz of 27 April 1854 (*Neue Quellen,* p. 462): "If Germany is once led to war against Russia, the situation is very tempting for France, she can easily reach an agreement with Russia over our head, or at least through the threat of doing it, force the major burden of the war on us, but demand the eventual advantages of the peace for herself, even at our expense."

198. An epigram of F. I. Tjutčev, cited by Frank Fadner, *Seventy Years of Pan-Slavism in Russia,* p. 289.

199. From the diary of Margherita Provana di Collegno, cited by Di Nolfo, *Europa,* p. 8.

200. Cf. Siegfried A. Kaehler ("Realpolitik zur Zeit des Krimkrieges," pp. 142–48, 164–65), who contrasts the "Realpolitik" of Bismarck and Cavour, in our opinion inadmissibly, to Buol's "Kabinettspolitik."

201. Buol's German policy, which can be treated only marginally here, did not pursue the goal ascribed to it, to secure for Austria the support of the German Confederation and above all Prussia with a view to the (then less dangerous) entry into the war. On the contrary, the policy was designed to bring pressure to bear on the West as well as on the East for peace. On this point, there are only two supporting passages (italics mine). In January 1854 Buol reported to the Emperor (Unckel, p. 121): "If it were possible . . . , to bring the whole of Mitteleuropa, which can dispose of highly imposing military forces, to one and the same *moral* attitude *with the goal of the maintenance of world peace,* then such a result would be very useful materially to support the language which we ought to use in Petersburg and also to counter with energy and dignity every impatient drive of England and France." Towards Beust, Buol defended his policy in the summer of 1855 in the following way (Bismarck, XIV, 1: 424): "we *never thought of wanting to make war,* and even if France had accepted our proposals through Drouyn de l'Huys, we would never have fired a shot; Austria's *'demonstration'* would have taken effect without that, *if only*

Germany had joined it." For a brief discussion of Buol's German policy see AGKK I, 3: 25–28.

202. Heinrich Friedjung, *Der Krimkrieg und die österreichische Politik,* pp. 173–74. Friedjung depended in part on the semiofficial Russian treatment of Jomini (p. 375), who should be used with caution with regard to chronology. As an example of the literature since Friedjung, see Borries, p. 315.

203. As Unckel most recently has done (p. 228; there reference to earlier scholarship).

204. Hübner's account, Paris, 13 September 1855 (AGKK I, 3: 52 No. 3).

205. Wich von der Reuth to King Max, Vienna, 4 October 1855 (BGSA, MA I 597 No. 100). See also despatch (draft) Buol to Koller, Vienna, 1 October 1855 (AGKK I, 3: 73): "For the moment we are hardly in a position to calculate how far the capture of Sevastopol may have advanced the task of peacemaking; for up to now neither the western powers nor Russia have shown themselves disposed to halt on the bloody road of war in order to turn to negotiations. It will therefore be necessary to wait until one or the other of the belligerents considers it suitable to take the initiative with proposals."

206. Lerchenfeld to King Max, Vienna, 22 December 1855 (BGSA, MA I 598 No. 50).

207. Wich von der Reuth to King Max, Vienna, 13 September 1855 (BGSA, MA I 597 No. 73). Gorchakov, it is true, alluded primarily to the Austro-Russian contacts.

208. Hompesch to King Max, Petersburg, 21 September 1855 (BGSA, MA I, 597).

209. Nesselrode to Gorchakov, Petersburg, 21 September 1855 (cited in the report from Schweizer to Rüdt, Paris, 10 October 1855. GLA, Abt. 48, No. 2050 f. 604–605).

210. On 15 and 18 September. Hübner to Buol (secret), Paris, 21 September 1855 (AGKK I, 3: 61, 62).

211. Hübner to Buol, Paris, 2 October 1855 (*ibid.,* pp. 78–80).

212. Temperley's quotes ("Austria," p. 628) from this report are thoroughly misleading. Hübner's words: "Austria was determined to impose peace on Russia by force of arms" are taken out of context and give a false impression. The next words quoted by Temperley do not reflect the domestic circumstances of France, but of Britain, and could not have been meant "for the private edification of Buol." Rather they express the scepticism predominant on the continent at this time about the viability of the British constitutional system. (See above p. 35.)

213. Despatch (draft) Buol to Hübner, Vienna, 1 October 1855 (AGKK I, 3: 72).

214. Temperley, "Austria," p. 629, quoting from a letter from Cowley to Clarendon of 13 October 1855. The proposals here ascribed to Buol are to be weighed especially carefully, since they rest not on a direct, but on an indirect communication transmitted through many stages (Buol to Bourqueney, Bourqueney to Cowley, Cowley to Clarendon).

215. Cowley to Clarendon, 30 October 1855 (*Conversations with Napoleon III,* ed. Sir Victor Wellesley and Robert Sencourt, p. 97).

216. Obviously a reference to the locality called Lipkany on the upper Pruth.

217. AGKK I, 3: 106.

218. *Ibid.*, p. 103.

219. See p. 126 below.

220. On this, most recently Eberhard Kolb, "Kriegführung und Politik 1870/1871" (especially pp. 107–8).

221. Diary entry of Leopold von Gerlach of 7 January based on a letter from E. von Manteuffel from Vienna (L. von Gerlach, 2: 379).

222. *Corespondenţa lui Coronini*, pp. 874–77; also in AGKK I, 3: 274–76. The memorandum was obviously written in answer to a request for opinion about the military advantages and disadvantages of possible retrocession to Austria of Bessarabian territory. More important for Hess than the precise boundary line in Bessarabia was the security of the Danube itself mentioned later. See also Unckel, pp. 243–44; Schroeder, *Austria, Great Britain*, pp. 314–15.

223. Protocol of the ministerial conference chaired by the Emperor, 11 February 1856 (AGKK I, 3: 370 No. 215): "Count Buol pointed out, that the right of freedom of navigation [for warships on the Danube] would be difficult to achieve."

224. Reproduced in AGKK I, 3: 105.

225. Reproduced in AGKK I, 3: 104–5.

226. See above p. 36 (concerning the fifth point); further Clarendon to Seymour, London, 6 December 1855 (HHSA, PA VIII 42 f. 86–87); F. Heinrich Geffcken, *Zur Geschichte des orientalischen Krieges 1853–1856*, pp. 201–3 (for the other points).

227. Despatch Buol to Esterházy (confidential), Vienna, 16 December 1855 (AGKK I, 3: 164–66); despatch Buol to Esterházy (secret), Vienna, 16 December 1855 (*ibid.*, pp. 166–67).

228. Cowley to Clarendon, 18 November 1855 (Temperley, "Austria," pp. 630–31). The source must again be appraised with caution (see above n. 214).

229. Lerchenfeld to King Max, Vienna, 16 December 1855 (BGSA, MA I 598 No. 32). See also Clarendon to Hudson, London, 20 December 1855 (Fonti, 98: 192): "As I can't believe that Count Buol or the Emperor look to it being accepted by the Czar, they must have made up their minds to Austria taking a more active part."

230. Ernest, 2: 286.

231. Metternich to Buol, Vienna, 29 March 1854 (Metternich, p. 156 No. 108). For the most recent literature on the history of Austrian finances in the nineteenth century, cf. Baumgart, "Probleme," pp. 80–81; the detailed analysis by Harm-Hinrich Brandt, *Der österreichische Neoabsolutismus: Staatsfinanzen und Politik 1848–1860* (especially 1: 338–78; 2: 687–723).

232. The budget of the Austrian monarchy in the years of the Crimean War presented the following picture:

	1854	1855	1856
Income (in florin)	245 million	263 million	273 million
Expenditures	386 million	402 million	335 million
a) ordinary military expenses	117 million	114 million	110 million

b) extraordinary   91 million   101 million   14 million
   military expenses

(Source: Official Austrian information as enclosures in the Badenese diplomatic correspondence from Vienna, GLA, Abt. 48, Nos. 2504 and 2507.)

233. Unckel, p. 223.

234. Friedjung, pp. 166–69.

235. Lerchenfeld to King Max, Vienna, 5 December 1855 (BGSA, MA I 598); Lerchenfeld to King Max, Vienna 13 December 1855 (*ibid.,* No. 25).

236. Despatch (draft) Buol to Hübner, Vienna, 29 December 1855 (AGKK I, 3: 200 No. 92). Buol spoke in the same sense to Bourqueney. Cf. Charles-Roux, pp. 58–59.

237. AGKK I, 3: 168–69, 171–73.

238. For example Eckhart, p. 201.

239. Montgelas to King Max, Berlin, 26 September 1855 (BGSA, MA I 597 No. 89).

240. Meysenbug to Hübner/Károlyi, Vienna, 27 September 1855 (HHSA, PA IX 51 f. 283); Wich von der Reuth to King Max, Vienna, 28 September 1855 (BGSA, MA I 597 No. 90); see also AGKK I, 3: 58–59, 69–70; Schroeder, *Austria, Great Britain,* pp. 312–13.

241. Schweizer to Rüdt, Paris, 28 September 1855 (GLA, Abt. 48, No. 2050 f. 579–81).

242. Jomini, p. 369.

243. Werther to Manteuffel, Petersburg, 24 October 1855 (Manteuffel, 3: 163–64); Bray to King Max, Petersburg, 27 November 1855 (BGSA, MA I 598 No. 8).

244. Montgelas to King Max (confidential; about conversation with King Frederick William), Berlin, 23 November 1855 (BGSA, MA I 598). See also Leopold von Gerlach's diary entry of 28 November 1855 (L. von Gerlach, 2: 358).

245. *Ibid.*; further *ibid.,* p. 360, diary entry of 1 December 1855.

246. *Moniteur* of 16 November 1855.

247. See above p. 14 and below pp. 70–71.

248. See Leopold von Gerlach's diary entry of 28 November 1855 (L. von Gerlach, 2: 358): "In the event of non-acceptance on Russia's side, H.M. envisions the capture of Petersburg by the Swedes and the French, the rebellion of the nationalities, etc., alliance of the Western powers with Austria, Sweden and Denmark."

249. See above p. 26.

250. Published by Borries, pp. 385–86.

251. Published by Geffcken, pp. 208–9.

252. There is hardly any documentation for such secret designs by Austria on Silesia. The importance of Silesia for Prusso-Austrian relations from Frederick the Great to the end of the First World War needs comprehensive investigation. Intriguing though the theme may be, the documentary evidence is of course hard to come by. Cf. above n. 96. See also Heinrich Ritter von Srbik, *Deutsche Einheit,* 2: 250.

253. Peter Hoffmann, *Die diplomatischen Beziehungen zwischen Württemberg und Bayern im Krimkrieg und bis zum Beginn der italienischen Krise (1853–1858)*, p. 111; Eckhart, p. 191.

254. Gise to King Max, Dresden, 16 October 1855 (BGSA, MA I 597 No. 109).

255. Vote of von der Pfordten to King Max, 18 October 1855 (*ibid.*, No. 114).

256. King Max's marginal notes on a note by von der Pfordten, Munich, 9 January 1856 (BGSA, MA I 598 No. 91): "I commend very strongly the intention of raising Bavaria to the highest level of importance in its relations with foreign states. The desire, however, to take part from the beginning in the councils of the great powers, seems to me, in the present circumstances, to go further than would be advisable."

257. Bismarck to Leopold von Gerlach, Frankfurt, 21 December 1855 (Bismarck, XIV, 1: 424).

258. Munich, 12 November 1855 (BGSA, MA I 597 No. 132).

259. Bismarck to King Frederick William, 21 December 1855 (Bismarck, 2: 84–85). See also the letter mentioned in n. 257.

260. Gise to King Max (confidential), Dresden, 8 November 1855 (BGSA, MA I 597).

261. Beust asserts in his memoirs (Friedrich Ferdinand, Count Beust, *Aus drei Viertel-Jahrhunderten,* 1: 202) that his corresponding report to Nesselrode could not be found in the Dresden archives (in a copy or as a draft). Harald Straube ("Sachsens Rolle in Krimkrieg," p. 108), who used the Dresden documents, although he certainly did not exhaust them, seems not to have discovered it.

262. Bray to King Max, Petersburg, 27 November 1855 (BGSA, MA I 598 No. 8); Bray to von der Pfordten, Petersburg, 28 November 1855 (*ibid.*, No. 9).

263. Published in Beust, 1: 205–6. The answer directed to Munich by Nesselrode (to Severin [copy], Petersburg, 23 December 1855. BGSA, MA I 598 No. 65) is limited to meaningless commonplaces.

264. Alexander to Prince M. D. Gorchakov, Moscow, 15 September 1855 ("Imperator Aleksandr Nikolaevič v ėpochu vojny 1855 goda," ed. M. I. Bogdanovič, p. 220).

265. To M. D. Gorchakov (*ibid.*, p. 325).

266. Bray to King Max, Petersburg, 27 November 1855 (BGSA, MA I 598 No. 8).

267. To M. D. Gorchakov ("Imperator Aleksandr," p. 322).

268. For the more recent literature about him and his relations with Princess Lieven see Baumgart, "Probleme," pp. 78–79. See also Princess Lieven's letters from the period of the Crimean War to Baron Meyendorff (Peter von Meyendorff, *Ein russischer Diplomat an den Höfen von Berlin und Wien,* 3, No. 516, 518, 521–23, 525). On the Gorchakov-Morny contacts see the new account in John Shelton Curtiss, *Russia's Crimean War,* pp. 480–81, 485–90.

269. Nades, 14 September 1855 ("Au temps de la guerre de Crimée. Correspondance inédite du Comte de Morny et de la Princesse de Lieven," ed. Geneviève Gille, p. 559).

270. Charles-Roux, p. 49. Jomini (p. 373) and Tatiščev (1: 162) ascribe it on the contrary to Morny.

271. [Charles Auguste Louis Joseph] Duke of Morny, *Une ambassade en Russie.*

272. Morny's notes, undated [end November 1855] (*ibid.,* pp. 17–25).

273. Gorchakov to Morny (via Sina/Eskeles), 21 November 1855 (*ibid.,* p. 10): "This is why it is permissible for me to recall that the height of Napoleon I's power was the period of his close alliance with Russia."

274. Jomini, p. 376.

275. Granville to Canning, 16 January 1856 (Fitzmaurice, 1: 143).

276. Charles-Roux, pp. 53–55. Cf. Curtiss, *Russia's Crimean War,* pp. 490–91, 494.

277. The comparison is not appropriate. The Sea of Azov is very shallow (average depth nine meters) and is not suited for use by sea-going vessels (except very shallow-bottomed small boats).

278. "Imperator Aleksandr," p. 599.

279. Post between Vienna and Petersburg demanded eight to ten days; the report could however have been transmitted in shortened form by the telegraph.

280. Published by Serge Goriainow, *Le Bosphore et les Dardanelles,* pp. 127–28. The report presumably originated from the Morny channel or was leaked to Gorchakov from the Vienna Foreign Ministry.

281. The Petersburg Cabinet was informed of this at approximately the same time by the despatch from Frederick William mentioned and by Count Bray's communications. Cf. above n. 244 and n. 258.

281a. According to the telegram sent by Gorchakov on 2 December (Goriainow, p. 128) this corresponds to the telegram transmitted at the same time or shortly before to Seebach, as Jomini gives it (p. 379). See also Bray to King Max, Petersburg, 3 January 1856 (BGSA, MA I 598 No. 104).

282. This is to be attributed to Jomini's presentation, which, although based on official Russian documents, displays a consistent lack of accurate dates. In the relevant passage, he says (pp. 376–77): "But already the attention of the Vienna Cabinet had been awakened. An indiscretion of M. de Beust had put him on the trail of the negotiations of Baron de Seebach [which cannot be confirmed from the Austrian documents]. Austria . . . saw herself threatened with exclusion. . . . The Vienna Cabinet profited with undeniable skill from the moment of hesitation, which, after the climax of the siege of Sevastopol, dominated official actions."

283. This is already known from Jomini; only historians did not take into consideration the inaccuracy and contradictoriness of his deductions. He writes, p. 380: "This conviction determined the imperial cabinet to *seize the initiative* in communicating to the Austrian government the conditions to which we were ready to agree. . . . In any case, this demarche could not block the vigorous impulse which the skill of Count Buol had been able to impart to his own negotiation." However, the Austrian peace initiative was already drafted, in principle and in most of the details, so there was no reason "to seize the initiative." Italics mine.

284. The latter interpretation is deduced from a letter of Walewski's of 18 November 1855 destined for the British government (Charles-Roux, p. 61), although it is not conclusively demonstrated by it: "The Emperor envisions the

offer made to us as a fortunate and unanticipated opportunity which we should seize eagerly, without allowing the Vienna Cabinet time to renege on an overture whose amplitude has perhaps not been weighed, and whose consequences may not have been probed." This passage again hints that Napoleon, by opening different peace channels, was letting several things develop at once and that he wanted to exercise pressure on *all* sides, including his British allies, in order to achieve a quick peace settlement.

285. Cf. n. 281a.

286. Telegram, Gorchakov to Nesselrode, Vienna, 25 November 1855 (Goriainow, p. 129).

287. The Tsar wrote in the margin of this communication from Gorchakov: "All this presages nothing good."

288. Leopold von Gerlach's diary entry of 14 December 1855 (L. von Gerlach, 2: 364): "Everywhere the desire for peace. Russia turns about suddenly and agrees to the neutralization of the Black Sea." See also Nesselrode to Severin (copy), Petersburg, 23 December 1855 (communicated to the Bavarian government on 31 December 1855. BGSA, MA I 598). See also *Aktenstücke zur orientalischen Frage,* ed. J. von Jasmund, 2: 314–15.

289. Despatch Buol to Hübner/Colloredo, Vienna, 11 December 1855 (AGKK I, 3: 157–58).

290. Queen Victoria to Napoleon, 26 November 1855 (Martin, 3: 529). See also the British proposal for revision concerning Point Three in Geffcken, pp. 202–3.

291. Thus Walewski's account to the Austrian government, which was thereby officially informed for the first time of the Seebach contacts. Hübner to Buol, Paris, 17 December 1855 (HHSA, PA IX 50 f. 261–62); despatch Buol to Esterházy, Vienna, 22 December 1855 (HHSA, PA X 42 f. 219–20); see also AGKK I, 3: 185–86.

292. Jomini's version (p. 380), which has passed into the literature and can neither be proved nor disproved by the documents used here, is the following: Walewski reproached the Russian regime for communicating its remarks to Vienna as well, and he used this circumstance as the pretext for breaking off contact.

293. Lettre particulière (copy), Buol to Hübner, Vienna, 1 February 1856 (AGKK I, 3: 330).

294. Clarendon to Palmerston, The Grove, 26 December 1855 (Di Nolfo, *Europa,* pp. 466–67).

295. See above p. 26.

296. See above p. 55.

297. F. de Martens, 15: 298–99. The italics in the quotation (which indirectly reflects the instructions) are my own.

298. Jomini, p. 380: "If France had really wanted it, she could have separated Austria and England." It is possible that the secret offers of alliance to France are to be traced back to the ideas of Gorchakov or other members of the Francophile party at the Petersburg court (for example Orlov) and that Alexander adopted them. This is suggested by, first, Gorchakov's telegram to Petersburg of 12 January 1856, in which he urged that the Austrian ultimatum be refused and that they "turn directly to Napoleon with proposals that would

satisfy France" (Jomini, p. 389n.; Tatiščev, 1: 170–71) and, second, Nesselrode's warning to Alexander of 11 February 1856 (Nesselrode, 11: 113) about making common cause with Napoleon, if he wanted to seize the left bank of the Rhine. This warning could only have been given if there were corresponding ideas in Alexander's circle which had to be fought.

299. Hübner to Buol, Paris, 22 December 1855 (AGKK I, 3: 185).

300. Jomini, pp. 381–82.

301. In the communications destined for London and Vienna about this part of the conversation, it was said that Napoleon had warned the Russian Cabinet against speculating on disagreement with the British ally (Clarendon to Palmerston, The Grove, 26 December 1855, Di Nolfo, *Europa,* p. 466; Hübner to Buol, Paris, 11 January 1856, AGKK I, 3: 231). Seebach expressed himself similarly to the Bavarian representative in Petersburg (Bray to King Max, Petersburg, 13 January 1856, BGSA, MA I 598 No. 137).

302. Hübner to Buol, Paris, 17 January 1856 (AGKK I, 3: 256).

303. Nothing can be established about this in the way of concrete detail, except that he had a series of lengthy audiences with the Tsar. Cf. Esterházy to Buol, Petersburg, 12 January 1856 (*ibid.,* p. 238).

304. Cf. Hübner to Buol, Paris, 17 January 1856 (*ibid.,* pp. 255–56).

305. Nesselrode to Gorchakov (copy; in the annex the formal counter-proposal), Petersburg, 5 January 1856 (HHSA, PA X 44 f. 21–26). German translation in *Aktenstücke,* 2: 315–18. See also Mosse, *The Rise and Fall,* p. 25.

306. Extract in the diary of Leopold von Gerlach under 10 January 1856 (L. von Gerlach, 2: 382). Cf. Geffcken, pp. 213–14.

307. Victoria, 3: 162–63.

308. Bourqueney to Walewski, 17 January 1855 (Charles-Roux, p. 63). Paul W. Schroeder (*Austria, Great Britain,* pp. 337–38) is of the opinion that Napoleon (as well as Britain) tried after the Austrian ultimatum to exclude Austria from further preparations for peace (including also the peace negotiations).

309. Queen Victoria to Clarendon, Windsor, 15 January 1856 (Victoria, 3: 163): "[The Queen's feelings] *cannot* be for peace now. . . . The Queen cannot yet bring herself to believe that the Russians are at all sincere, or that it will *now* end in peace." See also Palmerston to Queen Victoria, London, 17 January 1856 (*ibid.,* pp. 165–66).

310. *Ibid.,* p. 164.

311. Nesselrode to Gorchakov, Petersburg, 16 January 1856, 1 P.M. (arrival time 5:10 P.M., HHSA, PA X 44). See also Hübner's diary entry of 16 January 1856 (Hübner, 1: 382), and AGKK I, 3: 248 No. 130.

312. "Austria," p. 634. The essay does not redound to the great historian's honor. One notices throughout signs of a rough draft and general hastiness.

313. Sources: Meyendorff's notes, undated (Meyendorff, 3: 212–14 No. 526); Kiselev's diary entry (A. P. Zablockij-Desjatovskij, *Graf P. D. Kiselev i ego vremja,* 3: 3–5). In this chapter I adopt for the sake of clarity the expression "Crown Council" (not yet sufficiently researched) derived from Prussian constitutional history and applied to Russian circumstances. The Russian sources speak somewhat colorlessly of "Sitting, Discussion, Conference" among other things "presided over by the tsar." Cf. the short accounts in Schroeder, *Austria, Great Britain,* pp. 339–40; Curtiss, *Russia's Crimean War,* pp. 491–501.

314. Evgenij Viktorovič Tarle, *Krymskaja vojna,* 2: 503–4 (without a statement of sources).

315. See above pp. 66–67.

316. Telegram (copy) Buol to Esterházy, Vienna, 12 January 1856 (HHSA, PA X 43 f. 9–10); telegram (copy) Buol to Esterházy, Vienna, 14 January 1856 (*ibid.,* f. 11); AGKK I, 3: 232–33.

317. Nesselrode's memorandum of 15 January 1856 (Tatiščev, 1: 171–72); Meyendorff's notes of 15 January 1856 (Meyendorff, 3: 214–17 No. 527); Miljutin's memorandum for the war minister, n.d. (I. V. Bestužev, "Iz istorii Krymskoj vojny 1853–1856 gg.," pp. 206–8).

318. It was the same group as at the first Crown Council; the only addition was War Minister Prince Dolgorukov.

319. Cf. Tarle, 2: 507–9. About the aspect of the intellectual and "ideological" confrontation between the West and the East of Europe, which can only be touched on here but which is nonetheless very important in the Crimean War, see in general Alexander von Schelting, *Russland und Europa im russischen Geschichtsdenken,* pp. 186–205; for the more recent literature on this see Baumgart, "Probleme," pp. 388–94.

320. Alexander to M. D. Gorchakov, Petersburg, 23 December 1855 and 6 January 1856 ("Imperator Aleksandr," pp. 605, 608).

321. See above p. 14, Nordin to Stjerneld, Petersburg, 18 December 1855 (Hallendorff, *Konung Oscar,* pp. 103–5 No. 36). Text of the treaty in F. de Martens, 15: 628–31.

322. Nordin to Manderström, Petersburg, 25 December 1855 (Hallendorff, *Oscar,* pp. 353 to 355 No. 58). See also *ibid.,* pp. 125–27.

323. Nesselrode must have derived this report from news in the French press, which announced the war council, or from Seebach's communications.

324. For the more recent literature on Finland and Poland, see Baumgart, "Probleme," pp. 385–88.

325. Bray to King Max, Petersburg, 2 May 1854 (*Russland 1852–1871,* ed. Barbara Jelavich, p. 33).

326. See Table 5 in Walter McK. Pintner, "Inflation in Russia during the Crimean War Period," p. 85, with the sources given there.

327. Bestužev, "Krymskaja vojna," pp. 197–98.

328. Table 4 in Pintner, p. 85, and the estimates sent by the Austrian embassy from Petersburg to Vienna, also coming from official sources, do not agree (Esterházy to Buol, Petersburg, 29 January 1856, HHSA, PA X 43 f. 73–74, 76, 78).

329. S. G. Strumilin, *Očerki ėkonomičeskoj istorii Rossii,* pp. 478–79.

330. Bray to King Max, Petersburg, 19 April 1855 (*Russland, 1852–1871,* pp. 43–44); Bray to King Max, Petersburg, 18 April 1856 (*ibid.,* p. 51, 53). See also Pintner, pp. 86–87; William L. Blackwell, *The Beginnings of Russian Industrialization 1800–1860,* p. 186.

331. Bestužev, "Iz istorii," pp. 206–8.

332. Cf. Bestužev, "Krymskaja vojna," pp. 195–96 (with the sources given there). Further John Shelton Curtiss, *The Russian Army under Nicholas I, 1825–1855,* pp. 359–61.

333. Curtiss, *The Russian Army,* pp. 250–51. In the Russo-Turkish War of 1828 to 1829 half of the Russian army was carried off during 1829 through illness (malaria, dysentery, typhus) (*ibid.,* p. 248).

334. See also Bestužev, "Krymskaja vojna," pp. 196–97; Curtiss, *The Russian Army,* pp. 123–30; P. A. Zajončkovskij, *Voennye reformy 1860–1870 godov v Rossii,* p. 28.

335. Russia seems to have met a portion of her needs through imports from Germany. Memel was the transfer point for the secret trade with Prussia. Cf. Bray to King Max, Petersburg, 6 November 1854 (*Russland 1852–1871,* p. 36).

336. Martin, 3: 377.

337. Prince William of Prussia's notes about his stay in Petersburg, July 1855 (Jutta-Martina Schneider, "Christian Friedrich von Stockmar," p. 233).

338. Hompesch to King Max, Petersburg, 2 October 1855 (BGSA, MA I 597 No. 103).

339. Bray to King Max, Petersburg, 26 June 1852 (*Russland 1852–1871,* p. 21); Bray to King Max, Petersburg, 30 November 1852 (*ibid.,* pp. 28–29). For the significance of railroads for the conduct of war in the nineteenth and twentieth centuries, see my survey: Winfried Baumgart, "Eisenbahnen und Kriegführung in der Geschichte" (for the Crimean War, pp. 202–3, 208).

340. Bray to King Max, Petersburg, 6 November 1854 (*Russland 1852–1871,* p. 35).

341. Cf. Baumgart, "Probleme," pp. 87–88.

342. *The Politics of Autocracy,* ed. Alfred J. Rieber, pp. 24–26. On the army see also P. A. Zajončkovskij, pp. 3–67; Curtiss, *Russia's Crimean War,* pp. 530–48.

343. Bray to King Max, Petersburg, 6 November 1854 (*Russland 1852–1871,* p. 39).

II. *The Peace Negotiations*

THE PRELIMINARY PEACE

EVEN BEFORE IT WAS KNOWN that Russia had decided to accept the Austrian ultimatum, differences arose between the three allied cabinets, just as Nesselrode had suspected in pleading for peace. For a moment, the whole peace effort was in question.

As early as 6 December 1855—upon sending their amendments to the Franco-Austrian memorandum to Vienna—the British government announced to Buol that they expected their special conditions (nonfortification of the Aland Islands, admission of consuls to the Russian Black Sea ports, discussion at the conference of the status of the Caucasus) to be communicated to the Russian government.[1] Buol categorically refused. On 4 January 1856, Clarendon informed Count Colloredo, the Austrian envoy in London, that the three special conditions were just as important as the general provisions of the memorandum.[2] As he put it some days later, the peace negotiations would fail like the Vienna Conference if Britain were not guaranteed Russian acceptance of these demands before the preliminary peace and the armistice.[3] In Paris Lord Cowley said Britain would continue the war if her conditions were not fulfilled.[4]

The British ministers put forward this demand in fear of public opinion, especially as evidenced in the press. The Russian acceptance caused great disappointment.[5] People had expected Russia to refuse. *The Times* wrote that another campaign would be more advantageous than peace. Given allied armaments and resources, they could anticipate Russia's "total exhaustion and complete defeat."[6] Parliament would vote out the Cabinet, Cowley told Walewski, if it could not guarantee nonfortification of the Aland Islands. The navy at least considered this a point of honor.[7]

The "most English minister" sent a resounding telegram to Vienna: "England cannot consent to be told by any foreign government that England must sign without hesitations or conditions a national engagement. . . . England cannot recede from her position."[8] It was Palmerston's old tactic: using strong words and even threats of war to announce Britain's determination to defend her honor. Hamilton Seymour, the British ambassador in Vienna, and the French foreign minister were blamed. The former was accused of not having presented British demands effectively enough in Vienna;[9] Walewski, as usual, was considered dishonest, the leader of a "cabal of stock-jobbing politicians."[10] Of course, he was incapable of patriotism or any concern beyond the Paris Bourse.

Palmerston realized, however, that great politics could not be made with petty tricks, especially if France and Austria were as determined as he. Bitterly but sensibly, he wrote the Queen that Britain would put herself in the wrong if she continued the war after Russia had accepted. It was an indirect admission that continuing the war would mainly help Britain.

As for the British special conditions, the Austrian foreign minister believed that previous agreements precluded such demands by the belligerents except during the peace negotiations.[11] Point Five would be meaningless if it were accompanied by specific conditions. Austria was not bound to negotiate a definitive treaty; she was trying to get Russia to accept the preliminaries.[12] Moreover, the British demand for consuls in the Black Sea ports was covered in Point Three. The Aland question would certainly be settled in Britain's favor in the end, "but it must be negotiated and not brushed aside."[13] Buol did not present his arguments directly to London. He communicated them to the French Cabinet and deputed them "to bring [the British government] to reason."[14] He judged this the most effective way to achieve his goal.

Originally, Napoleon had been impressed by British firmness. He admitted that they had drawn up the ultimatum hastily; its flaws emerged "when examined by real men of business in England."[15] Buol's objections he dismissed as matters of form.[16] He feared a breach with Britain if they did not meet her at least halfway. When Britain demanded on 24 January that Russia be told that Britain and France regarded as essential conditions the nonfortification of the Aland Islands and discussion of the situation in the Caucasus (there was now no more talk of the consuls), Walewski did refuse to send a "second ultimatum" to Russia; but he agreed, along with Napoleon, to communicate both British special conditions to the Russian government and to pledge secretly that their realization would be a *conditio sine qua non*.[17] The Viennese Cabinet was not explicitly informed of this secret arrangement, but they knew Walewski would use the Seebach channel for appropriate clarifications in Petersburg.[18] Thus the misunderstanding—as Napoleon called it—between Paris and London was resolved.

The differences between the three allies on the way to peace and the form in which they were resolved foreshadow the positions adopted during the peace negotiations.

Austria was ready to stiffen the conditions, insofar as they derived from the original four points, reaching back to the beginning of the war. Britain's new demands seemed to answer Britain's special interests and to have little or no relevance to the Eastern Question or to maintaining the Ottoman Empire. The Aland Islands question especially seemed unrelated to this war aim; it suggested a possible future dimension for the war. It did not spring from any of the formal agreements such as the Anglo-French alliance treaty of 10 April 1854 or the December Treaty of the same year. The instructions of 11 February 1856, drawn up within the confines of the Eastern Question to guide the Austrian plenipotentiaries,[19] demonstrate the limits of Austria's interests earlier exemplified by the 14 November memorandum and the 16 December ultimatum. The fifth point was vaguely described as reserving belligerent rights to raise special conditions only to the extent that they "are directed towards the preservation of European interests and do not seriously hinder the restoration of peace."

Britain had throughout followed the allies' lead unwillingly. For Palmerston, most of the Cabinet, the Queen, the Prince Consort and the overwhelming majority of the public, the war had ended at least a year too soon. For the British, protecting the integrity of the Ottoman Empire was not an end in itself, but was one means of setting limits to Russia's expansionary drive. The chief aim was to weaken Russia as much as and however possible, whether that meant building up the Ottoman Empire, destroying Russian naval power on the Black Sea and in the Baltic, economic blockade, radicalizing non-Russian ethnic groups and subsequently dismembering the Russian Empire. So it appeared to Palmerston. The Queen summed it up in simpler and less specific language, which every Englander, whatever his political persuasion, might have echoed: "England's policy throughout has been the *same, singularly unselfish,* and *solely* actuated by the *desire* of *seeing Europe saved* from the *arrogant* and *dangerous pretensions* of that *barbarous power* Russia—and having *such safeguards* established for the *future,* which may insure us against a *repetition* of similar untoward events."[20] According to British ideas, the Crimean War was only indirectly a war to maintain the Ottoman Empire; more correctly understood, it was the first war between the rival world powers of the nineteenth century. Britain (or at least Palmerston) wanted to fight it through to the finish, since she had a powerful ally: that is, to restore the European balance interpreted in the British sense in order to be able to maintain and extend from strength the superiority outside Europe.

Napoleon grasped the long-term British goal, at least insofar as it concerned Europe, because it was only too close to his own and because he himself, in intimate exchanges with Palmerston, liked to redistribute European territory. But after one of Russia's outer defenses had been broken through joint efforts, he sought the chink in her armor in another direction, not the Caucasus, not the Gulf of Finland, where only Britain would profit, but in Poland, where a revolution—or as he put it to Britain, a restoration of the status of 1815—could be most effective in starting a remodelling of Europe. When the special interests of the two sides appeared in discussion and diverged, Napoleon, with typical adroitness, steered for peace by offering generous terms to the Russian enemy. Couldn't his goal, French hegemony on the continent through a series of national revolutions, be achieved more cheaply if Russia offered support? Austria, weakened and divided but still bound to Napoleon in a conservative alliance, could be used to reestablish peace quickly. Napoleon's power seemed to have peaked: he forced the British, bent on war, to follow his lead towards peace; he flirted with Russia, still hostile, but responsive; he used Austria's pacifism to embroil her with Russia, knowing that in Piedmont (in the phrase of the Prussian envoy in Turin) he held "a pistol pointed at Austria." His minister remarked right after the fall of Sevastopol: "Who could deny that France comes out of all this enlarged and Russia diminished? France *alone* will have profited in this struggle. Today she holds first place in Europe."[21] This comment was repeated widely in Napoleon's circle. Princess Lieven wrote Baron Meyendorff from Paris a couple of weeks later: "I am struck by the general deference to the Emperor Napoleon. This war has carried him pretty high, him and France; it has not enhanced England."[22] Already contemporaries sensed the shift of power from the East, personified in Nicholas, the "policeman of Europe," and his awesome military machine, "Europe's fire brigade," to the West, to Napoleon, the world's arbiter.

Symbolic of this shift was the choice of Paris for peace negotiations. The decision had been made as early as the end of January 1856. The *Constitutionnel* commented: "Paris becoming the center of negotiations for peace in the Orient, is France becoming the pivot of the diplomacy of the Governments of Europe";[23] although this judgment betrayed national self-congratulation, it appropriately rendered a widespread impression. This sentiment of patriotic pride appears immediately after Sevastopol, a fact explained partly by the victory on the Black Sea and partly by the failure of previous collective peace efforts initiated in Vienna.[24] Moreover, in 1855, Paris, since Louis XIV the intellectual and cultural center of Europe, was the scene of a glittering international exhibition—another symbol of French creativity, turning towards peace in the middle of war.

In London the selection of Paris for negotiations was at first unpopular, since people there obviously grasped its implications; they proposed a neutral city—Brussels, Frankfurt, or better yet, Mainz. Vienna was rejected—a sign of British bitterness against the Austrian Cabinet, held responsible for the premature initiative.[25] Then, early in January, Nesselrode dexterously brought up Paris,[26] and the business was as good as done.

For Buol, too, the choice of the French capital suggested that Vienna's role was played out. Metternich had declared at the start of the eastern crisis, thinking in the perspectives of 1815: "Vienna is and remains the best place for understanding";[27] but this was no longer true.

A more practical motive for choosing Paris was the fact that the plenipotentiaries believed that Napoleon would mediate. Each counted on blocking the intrigues of the others by appeal to the Emperor. Clarendon and Buol expected to frustrate Walewski's pro-Russian tendencies. Orlov reckoned on Napoleon's favor thanks to the signals transmitted by Seebach. Cavour must have believed that in Paris he would be able to sneak the Italian dilemma before the European forum. For this, Vienna would have been impossible. In fact, Napoleon did affect the negotiations significantly through frequent private audiences.

However, thanks to technical considerations, the next step towards peace was taken in Vienna. On 18 January, Nesselrode proposed to the Austrian government that the Five Points be signed in Vienna as a "Projet de Préliminaires" to formalize its character[28]—and that a short protocol be added to say that the governments concerned would name plenipotentiaries who would meet in Paris in no later than three weeks to draw up a formal preliminary treaty, an armistice, and the final peace settlement. This method of proceeding was approved by everyone, particularly because it seemed to save time. On 1 February 1856 such a "conference protocol" was initialled in Vienna by the ambassadors of the two western powers and Russia, the Ottoman minister, and Buol.[29]

Historians have been surprisingly unconcerned with the device of the preliminary peace as a peacemaking instrument. In the history of European peace treaties, a typical sequence evolved which can be observed as late as the middle of the nineteenth century.[30] The first step is peace soundings during the war itself; these overtures could lead to a second stage with a binding preliminary treaty indicating the bases of the final peace settlement. An armistice marking the third stage would lead to the final peace treaty, the fourth stage, coming from extended negotiations.

This early form, typical of the Thirty Years' War and the eighteenth-century cabinet wars, is still applicable to the Crimean War. In subsequent nineteenth- and early-twentieth-century wars, stages two and three have been reversed. An example is the armistice of Versailles (1871). In contrast to earlier purely military armistice treaties, this one assumed a new character because it included political and territorial provisions anticipating the definitive peace. There are of course many exceptions. Each peace settlement must be examined in context rather than being measured against a fictitious norm of international law.

At the end of the Crimean War, there was no formal preliminary peace, although one had been called for in the Vienna "conference protocol" of 1 February 1856. In a private meeting on 21 February, the French and British plenipotentiaries and Austria agreed to transform the Vienna protocol into a preliminary peace by simply adding it to the first peace conference protocol.[31] Walewski, chosen president of the conference at the first session, on 25 February, duly proposed this measure, which was unanimously adopted.[32]

Their motive can be explained as the desire to gain time by avoiding the negotiation and ratification of a preliminary peace. The French especially wanted the peace negotiations to proceed as quickly as possible: Napoleon must have suspected Britain's sincerity in concluding peace.[33] Doubtless he sought to achieve a fait accompli from which there could be no going back. His own attitude during the congress, and that of his mouthpiece, Walewski, demonstrates this. In Austrian reports, there is repeated mention of "calculated haste," of the "constant scarcely comprehensible pressure" from Walewski.[34]

Another important reason for Napoleon's haste was the catastrophic health of the French expeditionary force in the Crimea, which made continuation of the war almost impossible. In the first winter, the British army had been decimated by the effects of climate and illness (far more than by enemy action), while the French escaped because of their well-organized hospital system; but in the second winter, the situation was reversed. The French army was afflicted with such ravaging illness (scurvy, typhus, tuberculosis) that the sanitary services collapsed. In April 1856, some 5,000 British soldiers were on sick leave (out of 63,000); among the French, 42,000 (out of 150,000 soldiers). Among the British sick, 3 died each day; on the French side, 250. A quick peace permitting rapid withdrawal had become imperative.[35]

Like the preliminary peace, the armistice of 1856 has peculiarities, but there are parallels. After the Vienna protocol had been given "the force of formal peace preliminaries" in the first session,[36] it was agreed to let the commanders-in-chief in the Crimea negotiate an armistice running until 31 March. This order[37] would be transmitted by telegram. An armistice was duly concluded on 14 March at the Traktir Bridge,[38] although hostilities had actually ended on 29 February. It was only a partial armistice, however, since the naval blockade was excepted. The naval commanders were ordered not to operate against enemy territory, but they were permitted to proceed against convoys and troop transports in coastal waters.[39]

The British Admiralty and the peace delegation believed that extending the armistice to the sea would help the Russians, since they could use it to construct fortifications. The mild season permitted navigation on the Baltic. When Buol, speaking confidentially to Clarendon on 21 February, expressed the wish for a formal naval armistice, Clarendon pointed out that international law did not permit a maritime armistice during a blockade.[40] So they hit on the expedient of the order to the naval commanders already described.

The fact that the blockade was maintained and that the possibility of extending it when the weather might permit was specifically held open[41] symbolizes British distrust of Russian intentions and indicates that Britain wanted to be ready to continue the war. The relatively short duration of the land armistice demonstrates the French desire to conclude peace as quickly as possible. The shortness of the period could be made an incentive to Russia to negotiate in earnest.

The Negotiations

Territorial Questions
(Bessarabia, the Caucasus, the Aland Islands)

The first meeting was held on 25 February 1856.[42] The two sea powers were represented by their foreign ministers, Clarendon and Walewski, and also by a specially qualified ambassador, Cowley for England and Bourqueney for France. Buol and Hübner, the minister to Paris, acted for Austria. The Tsar had sent Orlov, his adjutant general, and Brunnov, the minister to the German Diet at Frankfurt. For the Ottoman Empire, Ali Pasha, the grand vizier, was present, the highest-ranking official among the delegates; the Ottoman minister in Paris, Mehemed Djemil, worked with him. From Turin came Minister President Cavour, with the Sardinian minister in Paris, Villamarina. Prussia was belatedly included on 18 March, represented by Otto von Manteuffel, the minister president, and Count Hatzfeldt, minister to Paris.

Theoretically, the causes of the war had been addressed through Russian acceptance of the Austrian ultimatum and through the Vienna protocol. Now the groundwork provided by the Five Points had to be transformed into specific stipulations. It seemed scarcely likely that the negotiations would collapse as long as everyone sincerely wanted peace. Britain was initially uneasy and suspicious. In contrast, the French and Austrians' desire for peace came close to mania. The

Russian delegation, too, under Nesselrode's instructions sought to bring home a peace.[43] The Ottoman Empire, existing by Europe's grace, depended on the three allies. Cavour's participation was marginal; his role consisted primarily of backstairs intrigue. Prussia was an unwelcome guest. In actuality, peace was made by the four great powers.

Despite Russian acceptance of the outlines of peace, it was to be expected that there would be difficult moments when one or another plenipotentiary would threaten war, if a major condition were not met. As Bismarck wrote sarcastically: "Before peace is achieved, each one will inevitably test what he can get, and, like a Jewish horse trader, seize the latch, as if he meant to leave."[44] An instance occurred shortly after the negotiations began.

On 26 February the plenipotentiaries of the western powers and Russia met at Orlov's suggestion to discuss in secret two problems which the Russians believed to be open, Bessarabia and Kars.[45] According to Russian instructions, the "boundary rectification" in Bessarabia was the most important question to be treated, since loss of this territory implied not only material disadvantage but also renunciation of "glorious traditions."[46] Russia had always wished to connect Kars and Bessarabia; Napoleon was privately prepared to agree and in January had urged Austria to go along.[47] Buol had won a free hand in the matter in the ministerial council of 11 February. Even without this, he had already assured Petersburg in private that the final boundary would be negotiable. As early as the end of February, Nesselrode reminded him of this promise.[48] On 20 February, when Buol had his first audience with Napoleon, the latter sought to persuade him to yield part of the Bessarabian territory, if Russia refused to cede Kars. Buol admitted this as an extreme possibility.[49] In principle, Clarendon too was ready, although he wrote London on 27 February: "We may in the next forty-eight hours find ourselves standing alone and having to decide the grave question of peace or war."[50]

So the allies had weakened their position almost before negotiations began. Certainly the capture of Kars had given the Russians a prime bargaining counter at the eleventh hour. But unneeded complications grew out of Austrian stupidity in demanding on military grounds large tracts of land in Bessarabia beyond the riparian territory necessary to insure freedom of shipping on the Danube. As early as 28 February, Buol informed Francis Joseph that "the Bessarabian boundary was the snag in the whole negotiation":[51] Russia would risk a rupture rather than give up Kars without full compensation, and the western powers would not leave Kars in Russian hands. Buol proposed restoring part of Bessarabia to Russia in return for Kars (thus lightening the conditions originally offered). If Russia refused, this could be regarded as rejection of the original conditions. It would then be "evident" that Russia was to blame for breaking off negotiations and Austria could proceed as envisioned in the Franco-Austrian memorandum, that is, breaking diplomatic relations with Russia and discussing "further steps" with her allies.

On 5 and 8 March, no less than three proposals were advanced by the opposing sides: the Russians went from a minimum concession to the maximum; the Austrians, in reverse, went from the maximum to the minimum. Franco-Russian cooperation was striking now and on 10 March, according to an extensive and neglected report filed by Orlov.[52] This collaboration went so far that one can accurately speak of two camps, in one France and Russia, in the other, Austria and Britain— unrelated to the wartime grouping. This division did not appear so crudely in the sessions, but it dominated negotiations behind the scenes, as far as the Bessarabian affair is concerned.

In the 6 March meeting, Brunnov, somewhat sarcastically, asked the Austrians to propose an exact line since the territorial cession had been demanded "at Austria's wish and in her interest." Buol replied sharply that Austria had posed this condition as trustee for the three allies, and refused. He insisted that the boundary running from Chotin south-easterly along the watershed between the Pruth and the Dnestr to Lake Sasyk had already been conceded in principle by Russia when she accepted the ultimatum. The session broke off without results because of the "advanced hour."[53]

Orlov now tried to get help from Napoleon. He showed the Emperor three boundary proposals, the third of which, offering the most extensive concessions, Napoleon promised to support. It was arranged with Walewski that in the following session the Russians would present the first and second projects to avoid "the appearance of previous arrangements" between Russia and France. After Britain and Austria had objected, the third project would be laid on the table, and Walewski would take it up.

So it went—up to a point. In the 8 March session, Brunnov read the first Russian proposal, according to which Russia would cede the Danube delta between the Sulina and Kilia arms. As expected, the Austrian and British plenipotentiaries demurred "with signs of surprise"; the same happened to the second, which also gave a small triangle between the Danube, the Pruth, and Lake Yalpukh. Then Buol unveiled his compromise, after Hübner had recalled the concessions implied in the ultimatum. Buol described it as "the Allies' last word." The Russians asked for time to seek fresh instructions.[54]

Essentially, the Austrian compromise and the Russian third project differed on just one point: according to Russia about half way along the boundary, there was a Bulgarian and a German colony on whose retention in Russian Bessarabia Tsar Alexander personally insisted. On 9 March, in another direct appeal, Orlov turned to Napoleon, who promised to support him. In the session, next day, the Austrian and British delegates agreed, after the Russians had made a couple of unimportant concessions at either end of the line. On 14 March, Orlov was able to announce his court's consent.[55]

Settlement of the Bessarabian question, the knottiest problem of the peace, cannot be seen as a British victory, as does Temperley, generally considered an authority on the Crimean War.[56] If one must make such a judgment, it should be described as a Russian triumph, achieved with French support, and as at least a partial defeat for Austria, mitigated by British stubbornness. On the whole, Orlov's official description is accurate: "Napoleon's direct intervention, I might say, decided the question in our favor. We had an opportunity to find out how weak, even humiliating, our adversaries' position has become."

Russia derived the following advantages from the boundary settlement. 1. Russia retained Bolgrad, the center of Bessarabia's Bulgarian colony. Orlov commented: "I suspect our enemies did not understand the significance of this concession." This may be new proof of the Russians' deliberate double game in the Bolgrad affair, which created such a dust storm later.[57] 2. In contrast to the original plan, the portion of Bessarabia which went to the Ottomans did not border on Bukovina. The Austrian military plan to extend the Bukovina fortifications straight to the Danube mouth had collapsed. Russia retained Chotin, the key fortress. 3. The boundary between Bessarabia and Moldavia on the upper Pruth (as far as Katimor) was unchanged. 4. The strategically important mountain ridges running southeast from Chotin remained Russian.

In other words, Russia secured retrocession of two-thirds of the Bessarabian territory given up in principle in the ultimatum and the preliminary peace! Without French support, more or less explicit in the sessions, and still stronger behind the scenes, a policy typical of the Paris peace negotiations and nowhere more obvious than here, such a result could never have been attained.

For Austria, or rather the Austrian military leaders, the outcome was plainly a defeat. It was heightened by Buol's refusal to propose the claim advanced on 11 February in the ministerial council (certainly originating with the military and Francis Joseph) for an Austrian right to garrison the lower Danube and for navigation rights there for Austrian warships.[58] Buol could point out that this demand was inopportune without openly opposing the Emperor and the leading generals: mooting this after the defeat in the Bessarabian question would have isolated Austria and hurt her further. Thus Buol from Paris

undermined suggestions from the military that served Austrian interests too nakedly, whereas in Vienna, apparently discouraged by his
isolation, he had depended on technical objections. In Paris, he could
argue that a peace negotiator must have room to negotiate, that is, to
concede points clearly unattainable.

Nonetheless, politically and above all commercially, the solution in
Bessarabia helped Austria by removing Russia from the Danube. Buol
and Hübner could point to this advantage with the Emperor to soften
the military setback. In a joint report,[59] they called it "the liberation of
that great Austrian artery, of that essentially German river . . . [which]
will be, in the sight of Austria, Germany, and Europe, a striking justification of Your Majesty's diplomacy." The Emperor, decisively influenced by his minister during the Crimean War, actually thanked Buol
for the fact that "in Bessarabia, in spite of much opposition, the main
point was won."[60]

In another territorial question, the allies, especially Britain, had to
accept defeat: this was the question "of the status of the area on the east
coast of the Black Sea." This related to the British special conditions
under Point Five, which had never been fully defined, even between
the allies. In the first confidential discussion, on 21 February, Clarendon, replying to Buol's request for clarification, unhelpfully remarked
that it would be difficult to specify British views. Russia must rectify the
frontier with the Ottoman Empire; the Kuban River might divide the
two. Cowley added that this did not mean that they were implicitly
recognizing Russian sovereignty over "Abkhasia, Mingrelia, Imeretia
and other trans-Caucasian provinces."[61]

Walewski made it his first order of business to whisper Clarendon's
remarks to the Russians: the Englanders intended to contest Russia's
right to the territory south of the Kuban, to make her recognize its
independence and neutrality or else to restore it to the Porte. Napoleon
had refused to agree.[62]

When the affair was discussed on 1 March during the third meeting,
Brunnov gave documentary proof of the justice of Russian claims to
the area. He depended especially on Article 4 of the Treaty of Adrianople and Article 1 of the 1834 Russo-Turkish Convention of St.
Petersburg. He did not forgo the pleasure of asking the Ottoman
grand vizier for confirmation. Ali Pasha agreed and asked that a mixed
Russo-Ottoman commission verify the boundary, since certain points
were contested. Orlov concurred, with the reservation that this would
not entail any territorial cession. At Walewski's request, British and
French members were added to the commission. Secretly he told the
Russians that the presence of a French commissioner would help them.

In the same sitting, Clarendon had to withdraw his demand that Russia renounce the right to reconstruct fortresses on the east bank of the Black Sea, since he found himself without French support.[63] So this negotiation also went in Russia's favor, and against Britain.

How much the Russians depended on France for victory was manifest in the matter of Kars. The outcome, although negative for Russia, again involved a Franco-Russian intrigue. On 28 February, Orlov was received by Napoleon at the Tuileries.[64] He explained to the Emperor that in accepting the Austrian ultimatum, Alexander had expected, on the basis of hints, that Kars would be recognized as an exchange for allied demands in Points One and Five.

Napoleon admitted that he had implied—through Seebach—that Kars could weigh against Bessarabia. But Britain and Austria had opposed this more vigorously than expected. In fact, it was only thanks to his bluntness that Britain had withdrawn extreme and humiliating demands, such as the destruction of Nikolaev and neutralization of the Sea of Azov along with the Black Sea. Napoleon hinted here at the January disagreements with Britain, during which he had indeed committed himself to make restitution of Kars a *sine qua non.*[65]

Orlov gathered that he would face unanimous opposition. He had hinted at breaking off negotiations in the discussion with the French and British on 26 February if Kars were not taken as compensation for Bessarabia, but he declared officially on 1 March, that Russia would forgo such a linkage. He added the hope that other points would be arranged in a generous fashion.[66] This renunciation, which surprised the Austrians and the British, came out of Napoleon's conversation with Orlov the day before.

Finally, one of the British special conditions was demilitarization of the Aland Islands. The fortifications there had been demolished during the war by the British navy.

In January, King Oscar I of Sweden had sent a secret memorandum to the British and French governments.[67] Basing his case on the ultimatum's fifth point, he posed conditions for the "security of the north": limitation of Russian naval power in the Baltic Sea and the White Sea, restoration of the Aland Islands to Sweden or their neutralization, defortification of the Aland Islands and the Finnish coast, west and north of Sveaborg. However, Paris and London were scarcely favorable, and so he fell back on the third condition alone. Baron Manderström, his special emissary, was charged with presenting it.[68]

The Russian plenipotentiaries had been instructed to declare that Russia did not plan to rebuild the fortifications.[69] The declaration should be made in an exchange of notes between Russia and the sea powers, that is, independently of the peace treaty.

When the British demand was presented on 1 March, Orlov communicated the Russian position and explained it ironically by the fact that people in Petersburg set no value on the main island's Bomarsund fortifications since the engineering was faulty. Again, he made Russian renunciation an occasion for urging speed on other topics and asked that it be put in a special convention between Russia and the sea powers. Here, too, his motive was ironic: when Bomarsund had been besieged, Austria was in "close union" with Russia; Sardinia had not yet declared war; and the matter did not concern the Ottoman Empire.[70]

Buol felt that Orlov intended to remove the European character of the concession in Point Five; later, when the text of the treaty was drawn up, he insisted that the special convention be mentioned in one of the articles so that it was joined to the peace instrument. Buol's expressed reason, in which the British joined, is significant from the perspective of international law: Buol felt that a separate convention would be a dangerous precedent which could create a separate legal status for northern Europe.[71] This fact, along with other matters to be discussed later, demonstrates that the Paris Congress saw itself as a decisionmaking body in international law. Russian scholars, to be sure, later maintained like the Russian representatives, that the force of the convention was limited to its three signatories.[72]

The demilitarization of the Aland Islands was the only subject of negotiation that was not directly connected with the Crimean War and its principal cause, the Eastern Question. If one considers the background of the "Crimean" War, the confrontation between the two world powers, Britain and Russia, it is the element in the Paris peace settlement that betrays its inconclusiveness most clearly. It shows that the Anglo-Russian contest was interrupted in the middle. The Aland Islands were in the geographical area where the struggle between the world rivals would have been fought out. In destroying the fortifications, Britain breached the first barrier of the northern gate to Russian power. Only the Aland Convention itself can be interpreted as a "significant gain for England."[73] In a larger perspective, it is a paradigm of the incomplete and equivocal nature of the war.

The Neutralization of the Black Sea

On her southern route for expansion, Russia was blocked more effectively—by water on the Black Sea and by land in the Danubian principalities.

The neutralization of the Black Sea, prescribed by the third point, demanded the most attention from the negotiators after the Bessara-

bian affair and the British special demands in Point Five, and it constituted the allies' most significant victory over Russia.

In a special instruction concerning the third point, the Petersburg
Cabinet had ordered Count Orlov to advance two reservations and to
see that they were included in the treaty.[74] One concerned Nikolaev,
which is not located on the Black Sea coast but twenty-two kilometers
inland on the Bug River. It should not come under the third point.
Second, the Sea of Azov should be excepted. Beyond this, the definition of the term *naval arsenals* should, if possible, not include forts and
fortifications. As for the prohibition on a Black Sea fleet, Orlov was to
mention that the two coastal states occupied different positions: Russia
extended over a great part of the coast and had a responsibility for
controlling the slave trade and military contraband in the East.

Nikolaev and the Sea of Azov had been discussed by the British even
before negotiations started. To Palmerston's distress, the Queen's ad-
vocates determined that the principle of demolition of arsenals could
not be applied to the Sea of Azov or to inland harbors such as Nikolaev
and Kherson.

On 4 March, the negotiations turned to the third point,[75] and Orlov
employed the following tactics.[76] In the Austrian ultimatum of 16
December 1855, the introduction to Point Three read: "The Black Sea
will be neutralized. Open to the merchant marine of every nation, its
waters will remain prohibited to naval vessels. As a corollary, no naval
arsenals will be established or maintained there." The Russian counterproject of 5 January 1856 was more precise: "As a corollary, no naval
arsenals will be established or maintained on the shores of the Black
Sea." According to the Russian interpretation, the new draft in no way
justified the inclusion of Nikolaev. Unfortunately, Austria had rejected
the counterproject. The draft third point read by Walewski at the
fourth negotiating session, drawn up with Russian help, repeated the
sense of the Russian January counterproject, and had the further
advantage for Russia of explaining the demilitarization suitably, that is,
without wounding Russian honor: "The Black Sea *being* declared neutral. . . . As a consequence, His Majesty the Emperor of Russia and His
Majesty the Sultan pledge neither to erect nor to maintain, *on these
shores,* any naval arsenals." Nikolaev was not affected.

Clarendon's reference to Nikolaev during the discussion allowed
Orlov to clarify the distinction:[77] his master could not with honor give a
formal pledge about a fortification in the interior of the empire. But he
was empowered to explain that Russia did not intend to build warships
beyond the number of police gunboats which would be specified for the
Black Sea. As proof of sincerity, his government would ask permission
for the two warships in process of completion at Nikolaev to pass the

Straits for the Baltic. This spontaneous explanation, intended for the protocol, impressed the other participants, and the impression was reinforced on 6 March when the same formula was applied to the harbor at Kherson and the Sea of Azov.[78]

In contrast to this speedy consensus on the core of the official allied program, a new crisis, just as violent as that over Bessarabia, exploded over a related question.

The number and type of police gunboats to be maintained on the Black Sea was to be prescribed by a special convention between Russia and the Porte annexed to the treaty. Right at the beginning, Britain made a claim to consultation in drafting the conditions. She was afraid that Russia would try to obtain the maximum possible number and tonnage of vessels and auxiliaries to provide the nucleus for a future war fleet. It soon became apparent that Russia interpreted "light warships" as meaning frigates as well as corvettes and wished to keep a sizable number of transport ships and hulks for the harbor police, sanitary and customs administrations.

It is not necessary to enter into the details of the Anglo-Russian confrontation over this point.[79] Basically the British suspected the efficacy of an imposed limitation and the Russians wanted to evade the provision however possible. Orlov generally explained away his rapid shifts by saying that he was no sailor and would have to seek expert advice; Clarendon threatened to break off the negotiations whenever Orlov and Walewski balked. In the end they agreed on six steamships with a maximum tonnage of eight hundred tons and four light steam or sailing vessels of a maximum of two hundred tons.[80]

With the regulation of Point Three, the allies had attained their main goal in fighting Russia. Vaguely phrased in the beginning as "revision of the Straits Convention in the interests of European security," it was now expressed in a concrete formula, which, to its initiators, must have provided the most effective method which could be devised for ending the Russian threat to Constantinople and restoring the European balance. The rule in force since the beginning of the nineteenth century, neutralization of the Turkish Straits, that is, no passage for warships in peacetime, was now applied to the whole Black Sea. Since this "ancient rule" of the Ottoman Empire rested on international guarantee and was confirmed by the great powers in the Paris Treaty,[81] the Black Sea too, which had been an Ottoman lake from 1453 to Peter the Great and which had then turned into a pawn between the Ottomans and Russia, became a European concern. Neutralization of the Black Sea through demilitarization soothed a 150-year-old Ottoman-Russian canker. Until 1871, the Black Sea remained pacified. Its neutralization is the only case in history of the pacification[82] of an entire sea. Attempts to close the

Baltic to warships—1780 to 1781, in connection with "armed neutrality" and again by the Russians after the First and Second World Wars—were unsuccessful.

The Danubian Principalities

The goal accomplished on water by neutralization of the Black Sea was to be accomplished on land by stipulations concerning the Danubian principalities and the Danube, both aimed at rolling back Russian influence from Constantinople.

In all important modern peace negotiations there have been questions that were not satisfactorily settled, where resolution was postponed because the negotiators' views were irreconcilable and could not be imposed by a draconian peace.

During the Paris negotiations the Danubian principalities presented such a problem. The peculiar feature was that the delay did not spring from differences between the wartime enemies, Russia and the sea powers, but from cleavages between the victors themselves. France's interpretation, in which Russia and Sardinia concurred for their own reasons, contrasted with that of Austria and the Ottoman Empire. Britain was less rigid. The only point on which the victors agreed was that Russia's protectorate must end; however, they disagreed about what should replace it. Ultimately, the whole affair became connected with the Italian question, to be discussed later, not just directly, since it played a part in Cavour's territorial exchange plans, but also indirectly, since Napoleon saw in the Danubian principalities (rather than northern Italy) the safest testing ground for his design to promote the principle of nationalities, and above all for a general redrawing of the European map.

According to the western powers' original arrangement with Austria in the autumn of 1855, the first point, concerning Moldavia and Wallachia, like the last point, was to be taken up by an ambassadorial conference in Constantinople. The idea was partly to simplify negotiations through prior discussion by experts on the subject—without Russian participation—and partly to de-Russify the principalities and to give Russia a "tangible defeat in her age-long policy," as Buol put it in an instruction of December 1855.[83] The decades of Russian protection had marked both provinces, particularly with respect to their constitution, based on the "Règlement organique" imposed by the Russian army during the occupation of 1828 to 1834.

It is superfluous to expatiate on the Constantinople discussions, since they did not in fact prepare the ground for the Paris negotiations. But the principle must be outlined—an alternative among the numerous contemporary plans for the provinces.

Of the three ambassadors, Lord Redcliffe and Prokesch-Osten[84] were especially committed to tightening the sagging bonds between the principalities and the Ottoman Empire through reforms, as one means of increasing the cohesion of the empire. These efforts, in which the Ottoman foreign minister, Fuad Pasha, concurred, were expressed in the project worked out on 11 February 1856, which laid down the basic organization of the principalities in thirty articles.[85] The Russo-Ottoman treaties relative to Moldavia and Wallachia and the Règlement organique emanating from them had been voided by the war. However, the Porte would renew the immunities and privileges granted to the provinces since Bayezid I and Mehmed II. In article 2 it was explicitly stated that Moldavia and Wallachia were integral parts of the Ottoman Empire under the Sultan's suzerainty. The next articles spelled out what was meant by suzerainty: the Porte would represent the principalities abroad; treaties concluded by the Porte would apply to the principalities; both principalities would pay annual tribute, the amount to be set later; in case of unrest, the Porte might intervene; the principalities' armed forces could be called upon to help defend the empire. In other words, a dependent relationship should be restored, which would leave the principalities very limited freedom in external matters. In an additional article, the Porte claimed the right to occupy the fortresses on the left bank of the Danube as far as the mouth of the Pruth and other fortified places on the Moldavian-Russian boundary after peace was concluded. These proposals by Redcliffe and Prokesch-Osten—Thouvenel signed because he had no contrary instructions—expressed their conviction that the Ottoman Empire could be rejuvenated.

On 9 March, when news reached Constantinople that the Paris Congress was working for union of the principalities, the rejection was unanimous. Napoleon had telegraphed his ambassador to urge the Porte to agree. From Prokesch-Osten's conversations about the French union project, the thrust of the arguments against it is clear.[86] It is a striking example of imperialist thinking, reacting vehemently to dangers to the empire.

To Prokesch, a united country on the lower Danube would be a second Switzerland for Austria, an instrument of aggression for Russia and a thorn in Ottoman flesh. The Rumanians would soon see Ottoman suzerainty as unjust and would demand independence, along with Bukovina, Rumanian Transylvania, and the Banat, taking the Balkan Mountains as the southern boundary. This example would spur Serbia, and these countries would look to Russia to help reach their goals. Austria would hurt to "the marrow of her bones." To the destructive principle of nationalities, Prokesch opposed the "loftier and conciliatory conception of the state." Happily, since 1849 nationalism had been mortified. One could not satisfy it at one point without arousing it elsewhere, in Italy, Poland, and Hungary, and preparing "an hour of incalculable struggles."

The dangers, as threatening to the Hapsburgs as to the Ottomans, were inherent in any form of union for the principalities; Prokesch-Osten etched them sharply. The same conclusions were reached in Vienna, although people there did not accept the same premises.

Francis Joseph busied himself with the principalities' future. He assumed that the bonds between the Porte and the principalities should not be tightened; on the contrary their independence should be increased, that is, their collective privileges must be reaffirmed, whether they had come spontaneously from the Sultan or from Russo-Ottoman treaties. He rejected the Ottoman claim to build fortresses in Moldavia and wanted the Porte's right of intervention to be limited. His maxim was Austria must oppose "all *Turkish* ambitions in those territories."[87]

The Emperor's motives must be deduced indirectly, but they can be established conclusively. There was the subconscious hereditary enmity against the Turkish aggressor going back to the days when the Hapsburgs were Christianity's first line of defense; but the main motive was the need for security. Austria could not allow any source of unrest on her borders to the south and southeast. The Ottoman garrisons in the Christian Balkans were such trouble spots, as had been proved in 1852 and 1853 in Montenegro or in the continuing dissension in Serbia. Ottoman troops, garrisoned in Belgrade and other places, faced popularly supported guerilla attacks. Policy concerning the Danubian principalities was strictly subordinate to Austrian security; this explains Francis Joseph's wish to limit Ottoman overlordship to previous agreements, his demand for a transitional arrangement such that the new kaimakams should not be placed beside the old hospodars chosen under the Règlement organique, and finally his opposition to the French union project, since its realization would tend to dissolve the bonds between Constantinople and the principalities and to create a country in need of Russian support. In short, Austria's interests demanded a vacuum in the southeast, a buffer zone, which no great power would dominate.

Logically this meant that Austria too must refrain from control. We surmise that Francis Joseph and quite certainly Buol were aware of this; but not ministers like Bruck, and certainly not military leaders such as Hess and Coronini; they were incapable of appreciating the utility of a power vacuum and saw security only in extending Austrian rule. These divergences have previously passed unnoticed[88] or to the extent that new sources have exposed them, other conclusions have been drawn.[89]

For Francis Joseph, there is some additional important evidence.[90]

Concerning Ottoman reorganization, which he related to Lord Redcliffe's efforts to introduce a British-style constitution, he asked: "Why overturn the authorities now existing in the principalities and assuring law and order, only to replace them with a new untried administration, open to every party pressure, and thereby wantonly expose these areas to the horrors of anarchy?"[91] Concerning the French project of union, he reflected: naturally Russia concurred in order to profit by allied disunity. But what would happen after union? Only independence or submission to Ottoman suzerainty.

Francis Joseph rejected the first, because it would contravene the principle of Ottoman integrity (necessary for Austria) and because a foreign prince would be needed to rule. Napoleon's idea of transferring the Duke of Modena, he considered dangerous; it might be the beginning of a rectification of the European map, with Austria footing the bill. The great powers would hardly accept another archduke. Furthermore, the country itself, if given a choice, would scarcely seek an archduke. Francis Joseph continued his reasoning against installation of a Hapsburg thus: "The first archduke I imagine there would remain a good Austrian always, but history teaches us that future generations soon deny the homeland." Any other prince would ally with Russia, the natural lodestone.

The second possibility, union under the Porte, Francis Joseph rejected too. In one sense, the country would be too strong, in another, too weak; too strong because they could easily escape from the Ottomans; too weak to preserve independence vis-à-vis Russia. "In either case there would then arise a Daco-Rumanian empire, which cannot be a matter of indifference to us in view of our many Rumanian subjects."

Francis Joseph's letters and instructions give his major arguments against any drastic change in the organization of the principalities. As for Buol, his confidential communications to the Emperor from Paris demonstrate clearly his opinion that Austria should not pursue territorial ambitions in the southeast. Buol's reflections suggest that he was a good politician, indeed a statesman, since like Francis Joseph, he not only grasped Austria's interests but also recognized the right of the European Concert of the great powers to be consulted.

On 8 March, when the French proposal for union was officially produced, the participants did not speak out decisively, and the Porte's attitude was not clear either, so that Buol had to reckon with a possible Ottoman capitulation; he therefore considered any sharp opposition futile. Indeed, he believed it would endanger Austria to be the only power opposed. If the Porte itself was not against, he hinted to the Emperor,[92] then Austria must subordinate her interests, however important, to the demands of Europe. For Austria then, the question would be to remove the danger from union, that is, union must be the capstone of political organization, not the starting point. Under these circumstances, Buol felt it would be least damaging to put an archduke in charge in the end. Only his choice must not spark territorial change in Italy, as the French planned.

Naturally, Buol could not say this himself during the session. But here too, since the other participants more or less supported the French union project, he did not unconditionally oppose.[93] He did reject Walewski's appeal to popular will as currently manifest. Such accents were "the work of intriguers." He did not deny that "honorable men" in the principalities might demand a union; but at least as many would vote for separation. The lower classes he considered too naive politically to participate effectively in a vote on a question they did not understand or really care about. The international commission, to be appointed by the congress to reform the principalities, might arrange for senates in Moldavia and Wallachia. If these bodies met and desired union, then the great powers should take up this demand in a conference and, if they judged it feasible, should sanction it.

It is not politic in the European Concert to oppose the intent of all the others when one can see that the minority view will be run over: far wiser to choose the least among evils and to hold one's influence in reserve, to derive the best outcome. Buol negotiated this way, even when the Emperor tried to hold him strictly to his instructions. He managed to obtain that nothing binding was decided about the principalities' future; certain principles were expressed without prejudicing future development.

Buol's attitude on this important question exemplifies his European outlook; his opposition to direct Austrian influence on the principalities is proved by his position on continued Austrian occupation. Obviously Buol could not absolutely renounce an indirect Austrian influence (above all commercial). This influence however should remain minimal and in balance with other powers.

The question of evacuating foreign troops from Ottoman territory was discussed after the peace treaty was signed on 4 April.[94] In front of the Russians a painful disagreement arose between the allies about the means of evacuating Anglo-French and Austrian troops. Walewski demanded that the Austrians set a date to complete evacuation of the principalities. Since they were near home, the Austrian troops could be withdrawn quicker than the British or French. Furthermore their presence would hinder domestic reorganization. Clarendon agreed that the presence of foreign troops might distort the people's vote concerning their political future. Buol and Hübner could not obstruct French and British demands; but they questioned their motives. After an unedifying discussion, it was decided that evacuation must proceed at the same rate everywhere, that is, six months would be allowed.

However, the reiterated principle that foreign troops were to leave the Ottoman Empire "as soon as possible," laid a moral obligation on Austria to withdraw her troops quicker because of the shorter distance.

Hübner's and Buol's reports to Vienna constitute a massive attack on the Austrian generals, who wished to continue occupation at least until the principalities had been reorganized, that is, for an unlimited time. The generals saw a pretext in the agreement of Boyadji-Köi of 14 June 1854, the basis for the Ottoman request for Austrian troops; the withdrawal of these troops, in contrast to the Anglo-French troops, was not fixed, but was to be arranged later. The generals had intended the occupation to be permanent. Coronini's correspondence exemplifies their combination of missionizing zeal and political naiveté and demonstrates how the generals immediately became intoxicated with prospects for expanding Austrian influence.[95] An analogy is the attitude of some German generals in 1918, like Lossow, Ludendorff, and Seeckt, who dreamed of conquering the Caucasus and moving against the British Empire in India.[96]

In his report Hübner alluded to the occupation's real goal: to defend the provinces against the Russians, to protect European Turkey, and to force Russia to accept peace preliminaries.[97] The task of the troops was primarily military; political goals were secondary. As soon as the military task was fulfilled, that is, as soon as the Russians left the portion of Bessarabia they had given up, the occupation could not be prolonged without becoming political. If Austria did not retire now, it would be forced to by pressure from all Europe.

In his confidential letter to the Emperor, Buol was more explicit.[98] The letter is one of a few documents which shows Buol's motives relatively clearly. After explaining the proposals for withdrawal, he expressed the wish that the military authorities would regard their political mission as ended. Austrian occupation had made an unfortunate impression on the principalities and on the world. The problem was not the attitude of the troops, but "the unhappy inclination of our generals to play politics, for which they lack the right perspective. Master of the Ordinance Hess had abused his position from the start; the opinions of Count Coronini were desperately partial; even Count Paar was not dexterous in this field." Although the Austrian troops had achieved their strategic goal, the political evil brought by the occupation was irreparable. Like Hübner, Buol pleaded for the quickest possible evacuation, so that Austrian diplomats could once again have a free hand. Certainly Austria could permit that "the future organization of the principalities be discussed without the protection of our bayonets." Now, with the war over, Buol saw an opportunity to cut back the military, to push the generals out of politics and to limit them to their own sphere.

The conflict between Buol and Hess is a classic example of the distorted balance between politics and the army in wartime, in which the generals misuse their increased power to determine the content of policies for which they are merely asked to furnish the means. This struggle, previously almost unnoted, is one of those situations in which the army, winning over the diplomats, steered the ship of state towards a wreck, in this instance, 1859.[99]

Our interpretation of Buol's policy is confirmed by Hübner's intimate testimony. In his diary, Hübner terms his chief's letter to the Emperor a brave step and speaks of the "silent struggle" between him and the military, which constantly hindered the negotiations.[100] In a later audience with the Emperor he complained about "the evil of the army dabbling in politics" which he blamed for Austrian isolation.[101] Decades later, in a speech in the Reichsrat, he indirectly justified his superior's policy towards the principalities, which he had not always understood, when he enunciated the following principle: Austria's interests demanded that no other great power rule the Balkan peninsula; they did not demand that she rule there herself.[102]

The discussion of the Danubian principalities at the peace negotiations was complicated by French plans to unify the two provinces. In Napoleon's program, the union project served two purposes. It afforded a starting point for remodelling Europe, and it offered Napoleon a first chance to assist the principle of nationalities to a victory.

In its first capacity, the plan went back to the beginning of the war. As early as 1854 the principalities were to be bartered for Austria's Italian possessions.[103] At the time of the peace negotiations, the plan took on detail: the Duke of Modena should be popularly chosen as king of the united principalities. The Duchess of Parma would be transferred to Modena and Parma would be given to Sardinia, to compensate her for military participation and to put her under obligation to France.[104]

In its second function, the union plan goes back to the Vienna Conference of 1855. Bourqueney described it as fulfilling popular wishes.[105] During the peace negotiations, the Rumanian nationalists in Paris influenced the French emperor through propaganda and through their lively behind-the-scenes activity in favor of union. They also provided conference members whom they expected to help, such as Walewski, Cavour, and Clarendon, with countless brochures and memoranda.

On 5 March, Napoleon wrote Walewski that he had reached a conclusion concerning the Danubian principalities: "It is evident to me that the principalities desire union and independence. United, they form a country as populous as Bavaria. They count for something in the European balance of power. Divided, they are nothing."[106] To some extent, this was an effort to meet the inhabitants' wishes; but it also represented a centuries-old French policy: to hold Hapsburg power in check through groupings of states in central and eastern Europe—the Rhenish Confederation, Sweden, Poland, the Ottoman Empire. The principle, applied to the united Danubian principalities, could now be turned against Russia as well. Napoleon continued: "Forming a separate kingdom, they are a real barrier against Russia, who will think twice before violating the territory of an independent sovereign. . . . In the interest properly understood of the independence of the Ottoman Empire, in the interest of the stability of Europe, it is necessary that the two principalities be united and independent." But the principle of Ottoman integrity, according to the Ottomans' interpretation, must run directly counter to this plan.

For Walewski, the Emperor's words were the signal to bring up the union plan on 8 March.[107] Austrian and Ottoman opposition did not presage a speedy great power consensus. Agreement was reached on just one point, to mention the privileges of the principalities and their relation to the Porte in general terms in the treaty and to let the details be worked out by a European commission sitting in Bucharest and by divans to be set up by the Porte on an ad hoc basis. Since the French wanted to finish the peacemaking job as quickly as possible, it was not feasible to deal with specific arrangements.[108]

Clarendon spoke out here, strangely enough, for union of the principalities. His vote is particularly astonishing since he had marshalled an array of counterarguments on 6 March in talking to Napoleon, who wanted to win him over for union.[109] He had noted the difficulty of finding a foreign prince. He would have to be either Catholic or Greek Orthodox. Furthermore, he would have to accept Ottoman suzerainty. If he were Catholic, he would have to reckon with bitter opposition from the Orthodox priests and the inhabitants and would lean on Russian help. If he were Greek Orthodox, he would fall under Russian influence from the start. One would create a second Greece, under conditions even less favorable for Europe. The Porte was right to oppose the project, for the foreign prince would soon reject the Ottomans and declare independence. The same process would be repeated in Serbia: "Turkey would thus be deprived of about six millions of her subjects, and her power and position in Europe would be at an end, and I do not see what answer could be given to the Sultan if he appealed to us as the defenders of the integrity of the Ottoman Empire against such an act of spoliation."

F. Heinrich Geffcken, the international legal scholar, depending primarily on English documents in presenting the negotiations, explains this discrepancy between the careful reasoning *against* and the vote in the session *for* by an error in the protocol:[110] the protocol records Clarendon's concurrence in Walewski's remarks *in general*, hence also in the union project, whereas Clarendon's agreement probably applied only to the *consideration* of the question. However, Clarendon's specific approval is recorded not only in the protocol, which he himself signed, but also in the Austrian report of the session.[111]

The contradiction cannot be explained away. Undoubtedly the British negotiator, like the others, sometimes used a double standard. In British historiography, the corruption in diplomatic morals so apparent during the 1850s and 1860s has been ascribed to Napoleon and his "gangster followers," Drouyn, Walewski, and so on,[112] yet the Paris negotiations offer many examples of "immoral" British attitudes which differ from the French only, if at all, in being less consistent.

It cannot be made out who Clarendon hoped to injure by his vote. Those who profited from it were Napoleon—and Cavour. This may be the solution. Cavour had used all his strength to win assent to the union project, for Parma would be a real gain for Sardinia. Cavour's influence on Clarendon emerges beyond question from the treatment of the Italian affair at the congress. In London a similar relationship developed between the Sardinian minister, d'Azeglio, and Palmerston. In fact, on 7 March, Palmerston wrote a letter to Clarendon in which he clearly although not blindly favored union: "If it was intended to have for the Principalities any Foreign Prince then of course they must be united. As far as England is concerned it would I should say be our interest and wish to increase the territories of Sardinia and Italy and the addition of Parma would be a great acquisition."[113] This letter may have influenced Clarendon's stand next day.[114] Cavour was rather pleased: Clarendon had supported the union, even if not emphatically. He must be stirred up.[115]

The discussion about the Danubian principalities had indeed accomplished the negative result that the Russian protectorate, as it was called in the preliminaries, was ended; but for the moment, only the signatories' collective guarantee of "privileges and immunities" replaced it. It is a very significant feature of the Paris negotiations that the principle of nationalities was considered for the first time in an international congress because two great powers recognized popular wishes. Opposing this is the principle of reason of state transcending nationality—best represented by Austria—the imperial principle of the multinational state that all the great powers had supported at the Vienna Congress.

Napoleon appealed explicitly to the Vienna Congress in justifying his standpoint. The great mistake at Vienna, he explained to the British foreign secretary, had been that the negotiators had acted only according to the interests of sovereigns, never according to the interests of subjects.[116] The current congress must not repeat the mistake.

Using the principle of nationalities, Napoleon intended to undermine the Vienna Congress's work. For his ally, Cavour, the principalities question merely provided a way of advancing his own state's interests. Cavour likewise alluded to the Vienna Congress, which must not be copied, to avoid large-scale violation of "human rights." However, in all this, he was only concerned with grabbing Austria's "wobbly scepter" over Italy and "orientalizing" it.[117]

In contrast, Buol did not specifically appeal to the Vienna Congress, so far as we can tell, but he explained that he could not recognize the principle of nationalities as a reason for remodelling "the existing political configuration of a country" (the Ottoman Empire).[118] In the discussion about the Danubian principalities, it was a question for Austria, as for the Ottoman Empire, of a law of survival. Indeed on 9 March Buol heard from Vienna: "His Imperial Majesty sees the question of the principalities as a question of life and death for his empire."[119]

The differences seemed unbridgeable. Could a satisfactory solution be found? The British statesman John Russell said no. "You must either throw over the Turks, or offend the inhabitants of the Principalities."[120]

Freedom of Navigation on the Danube

The Paris negotiations assumed a special character because they not only dealt with the causes of war between the belligerents but they also exposed cleavages between the victors to the advantage of the losers. This same situation had emerged at the Vienna Congress, but with a different effect: the defeated power reassumed its lost place in the concert. As result, the European political order reemerged highly homogeneous. In Paris, on the contrary, the bonds of the concert were weakened: to some extent, the individual members found new links which worked against the concert and revealed its heterogeneity. The handling of the principalities question provided the first clear evidence of this aspect of the negotiations. A second sign was the question of freedom of navigation on the Danube, outlined in the second point of the war aims program. But the discussion here finally led to consensus.

The principle of free shipping on international waterways, that is, rivers flowing through several states, had been recognized relatively late. Although it originated in Roman law, it had been lost since the Middle Ages. Countless tariff barriers hindered free exchange of goods. The French Revolution represented the first real break with absolute territorial sovereignty over the portions of international rivers located within existing political boundaries. The Vienna Congress adopted the idea of internationalizing river courses and in Articles 108–117 of the Final Act proclaimed free shipping on international rivers. However, the question here was not enactment of a principle but encouragement to the signatories to initiate arrangements. This was done for the Rhine and the Elbe.

The Danube was expressly excluded from this settlement, since the Ottomans, who ruled the lower Danube, were not represented. Russia had become a riverain of the Danube through the Treaty of Bucharest (1812); at the delta, however, the Russo-Ottoman boundary ran along the Kilia arm. Only in 1829 did Russia acquire the Sulina arm, important for shipping. With the new boundary along the St. George arm, the right bank of which remained Ottoman, Russia became mistress of the Danube delta as well as the lower Danube. To favor Odessa, Russia allowed the Sulina arm to silt up, so that in comparison with Ottoman times, commerce steadily declined. While the Ottomans had held open the Sulina channel to a depth of sixteen feet, the depth in 1844 was only about eleven feet, in 1850, nine feet, and at the outbreak of war, seven and a half. Russia created further obstacles to shipping by severe quarantine regulations and high freight charges. If a cargo was quarantined at the Sulina mouth, it could not remain there, but had to be shipped to Odessa. The freight charges between Galatz and the Bosporus were considerably higher than the fees for the longer route between Odessa and the Bosporus.

The first draft of the Four Points of 8 August 1854 stated that shipping at the Danube mouth must be free under the principles of the Vienna Final Act. In the Vienna Conference of spring 1855, these demands were made more specific. In the peace preliminaries, further changes were introduced because Russia, thanks to the cession in Bessarabia, was no longer a riparian state. Also the phraseology was altered from free shipping on the delta to the "Danube and its outlets."

On 6 March, Walewski read a draft for these provisions of the peace, which explicitly demanded free shipping on the entire course of the Danube, and further proposed a European commission and a commission of riparian states dependent on it. In this session and on 12 March, Buol rejected any extension of internationalization to the upper Danube.[121] However, in two extensive reports compiled with Hübner and in a simultaneous confidential letter to the Emperor, he urged that they accept the French demands, since they were also supported by the others.[122] The reports demonstrate again how thoroughly Buol's ideas were rooted in European rather than merely Austrian attitudes.

From the perspective of Austrian domestic policy and commercial interests, the new order was certainly problematical. Above all, the

Austrian steamship company's exclusive rights had been guaranteed by the government until 1880; there would have to be an indemnity, at state expense. The new European law would overlap with domestic law and would conflict with it. Nonetheless, in a long view, a free Danube must profit Austrian commerce, once the financial sacrifices of the transition were overcome.

Buol put it to the Emperor that the Austrian thesis, which he had presented previously, namely application of the Vienna Final Act to the lower Danube but not to the upper, was untenable from a European standpoint. The wording of the preliminaries clearly permitted the construction which Walewski and the other delegates advocated. Furthermore, the Austrian thesis contradicted the common goal of the war, to admit the Ottoman Empire into the European state system under the jurisdiction of European law—the preliminary for a formal collective guarantee of Ottoman integrity in general and for internationalization of the lower Danube in particular. Now the Ottoman Danube was to become European; but the German Danube must remain Bavarian and Austrian. Clarendon's reproach to the Austrian delegates was right: they wished Europe to open the delta to them, so that they alone could ply the river.

Already in the ministerial council on 11 February, Buol had spoken against Bruck's proposal that they let the works necessary to open the Danube mouth be carried out by the riparian states, not by the European commission. For reason, he had alluded to the sacrifices made by the belligerents to free the Danube. Now he restated this argument more effectively, as coming from Britain: Britain reproached Austria with wishing to transform the freedom of the Danube, won largely by western military efforts, into an Austrian monopoly.

In his private letter to the Emperor, Buol was even more frank. Maintaining the Austrian position would elicit a "universal cry of indignation." It could jeopardize the peace entirely or lead to reprisals: since Austria would not permit freedom on the upper Danube, she should not enjoy it at the delta. It could even result in Austria's exclusion from settlement of the Danube question. Austria would be in a "very false political position" vis-à-vis Europe and would betray the "general political principles" guiding her foreign policy. Buol naturally did not omit the prospect—to help the Emperor decide—that Austria would dominate the riparian commission, once it had received full powers from the temporary European commission.

In light of Buol's ideas, Francis Joseph gave up the original Austrian view.[123] Boul announced on 18 March that Austria would not object to extending the Vienna Final Act to the upper Danube, providing that relevant domestic regulations were taken into account.[124]

The peace treaty (Articles 15–19) prescribed establishment of both

Danube commissions. Within two years, the European Danube Commission should see to dredging the delta from Isaccea downstream. On this commission France, Austria, Britain, Prussia, Russia, Sardinia, and the Ottoman Empire would be represented by one delegate each. The second, a "permanent riverain commission," consisting of one representative each from Austria, Bavaria, Turkey, Württemberg, and the three Danubian principalities (including Serbia), should work out a code regulating shipping and policing of the river; after the European Danube Commission had finished its work, this new commission should replace it.

The Status of Ottoman Christians

Russia had made no demands during the discussion of the second point of the preliminaries; but relative to the fourth point claims arose which again illuminate the occasion for the war, which had receded more and more: the status of Christians in the Ottoman Empire.[125]

Directly before the negotiations began, on 17 February 1856, the Sultan emitted a solemn decree, the Hatt-ı Hümayun, which explicitly assured the legal position of his Christian subjects. He hoped to preclude discussion of the touchy problem before a European forum, since this might lead to intervention in Ottoman domestic affairs and an attack on his sovereignty. However, the great powers insisted on mentioning the Hatt in the treaty. Now the conflict was how. The Sultan considered the spontaneity of his solemn act to be impaired if it were even mentioned. The Russians wanted to give it a form which would allow their right of intervention in favor of fellow-believers, previously deduced from the Treaty of Kuchuk Kainarji. This alleged right had served as the motive for the war. Could not the peace provide some fruits?

First the Russians tried to introduce a passage into the preamble about "the powers' solicitude for the fate of the Christians of Turkey." Clarendon pointed out that it had not been a war of religion, and the grand vizier explained that he would oppose any such reference by refusing to sign. The Russians next tried to mention the Hatt right after the treaty provisions which announced Ottoman admission to the European Concert in order to suggest a connection between the two clauses. Apparently thanks to Napoleon, this succeeded. As a formula, they proposed that the great powers should "take formal notice" (*prendre acte*) of the Hatt.[126]

The Porte was in an uproar over the news from Paris[127]—during the summer of 1855, telegraphic communications had been established with western Europe. Not only did they consider the spontaneity of the Sultan's act compromised by the new draft; they also believed that despite their assurances the powers were forging a treaty right of

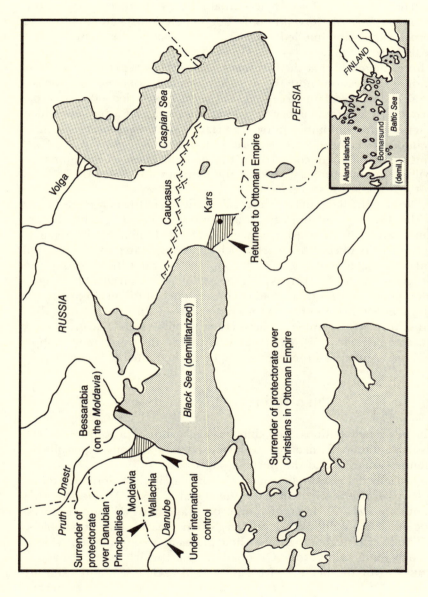

5. Russian Losses under the Paris Peace Treaty, 1856

intervention; in other words, they wanted to introduce into international law a principle which would destroy Ottoman independence. In the council of the Porte, it was unanimously decided to reject the phrase *prendre acte*. It could not be adequately translated anyhow: the French expression implied a bilateral commitment; this sense was lost in Turkish.

Buol suggested that the formula *prendre acte* be replaced by the less binding expression "note the great importance" (*constater la haute valeur*). The proposal was accepted.[128] The Russians tried again to transform the war into a victory by asking acceptance of a passage which described the communication of the Hatt to the great powers as a "new pledge of the improvement of the fate of the Christians in the East, joint object of their concern, in the general interests of humanity, civilization and compassion." But the demand was rejected.[129]

It was the last disagreement.

The goal the Russians only partially achieved in the peace was hailed by the Tsar in a solemn act. In a manifesto coinciding with the announcement of the peace treaty on 31 March 1856 at St. Petersburg, Alexander invoked Providence which had brought to pass the "original and principal aim of the war": "From now on, the future destiny and the rights of all Christians in the Orient are assured. The Sultan solemnly recognizes them, and in consequence of this act of justice the Ottoman Empire enters into the community of European states! Russians! Your efforts and your sacrifices were not in vain. The great work is accomplished. . . ."[130] In his subjects' minds, the other, more important consequences of the war were to be pushed into the background.

NEGOTIATING TECHNIQUES

The peace negotiations also exhibit special technical procedures, which distinguish them from other modern peace negotiations, especially the Vienna Congress and the Berlin Congress.

Officially the sessions began on 25 February in the Salon des Ambassadeurs of the foreign ministry, the "Quai d'Orsay."[131] On the walls hung life-size portraits of Emperor Napoleon III and Empress Eugénie. On a shelf, like a local deity, stood a marble bust of Napoleon I. The twelve negotiators took their places at a round green table in French alphabetical order. Originally, an *order* which seated the representatives of the belligerents across from each other had been envisioned,[132] but it was not employed, since Austria, a nonbelligerent, participated. According to custom, at Count Buol's request, Count Walewski, son of Napoleon I, was chosen *president* as the chief representative of the host country. Benedetti, director of the political section of the Foreign Ministry, was named *recording secretary*. The diplomats agreed to meet in strictest secrecy. The sessions were to be held every other afternoon, but this arrangement was not faithfully adhered to.

As customary with peace conferences and congresses, a good part of the work, including some of the most important, was accomplished outside the official sittings through *confidential conversations*. For example, a confidential meeting was held on 21 February between the plenipotentiaries of the sea powers and Austria to adopt a common line.[133] They agreed not to discuss any topic with the Russians in any form outside of the sessions.

Shortly thereafter, this agreement was broken by Clarendon and Walewski, and it was not maintained thereafter. On the twenty-sixth, ostensibly at the Russians' wish, the representatives of the two western powers met with them confidentially to discuss Russian ideas about using Kars as compensation for Bessarabia. "From the point of view of the mutual agreement . . . ," Buol and Hübner wrote, "it was an irregularity, from the point of view of diplomacy, a mistake."[134]

The introduction of such a gentleman's agreement demonstrates the Austrians' attempt to build a united front against the Russians and to prevent their own isolation; its scuttling by the sea powers reveals the victors' disunity. Their differences surfaced often enough in the official sessions—to the Russians' advantage and the Sardinians' satisfaction—for example, in the discussion concerning the Danubian principalities on 8 March or the situation in Italy on 8 April. The latter session was perhaps the moment when the Crimean coalition, formed to contain Russia, collapsed resoundingly over an issue completely unrelated to the Eastern Question. Austria was put in the prisoner's dock, with Lord Clarendon the prosecutor.

On 15 March the Austrians again met confidentially with the plenipotentiaries of the western powers.[135] The question was the establishment of a European commission in Bucharest to collect information about developments in the Danubian principalities and to report to the Paris ambassadorial conference, which would function as the executive arm implementing the treaty. Clarendon proposed that a Sardinian representative be added to the commission. Buol reminded his colleague of the gentleman's agreement of 21 February against involving Sardinia in the implementation of treaty conditions relative to the principalities.[136] If Clarendon persisted, he threatened to bring up this understanding in the official session. He pointed out that Austria had not asked to sit on the commission to regulate the Russo-Ottoman boundary in Asia. By analogy, Sardinia should not feel injured by exclusion from the Bucharest Commission.

The Austrian position was accepted, and it was agreed instead to reserve for Sardinia a seat on the commission revising the Straits

Convention of 1841. Buol and Hübner wrote Vienna: "We put too much faith in Lord Clarendon's word not to consider Sardinia as decisively excluded from the commission on the principalities." Nonetheless, a few weeks later, Clarendon insisted that a Sardinian representative be granted a seat and a vote on the Bucharest Commission.[137]

The establishment of *committees and commissions* is customary in peace conferences to facilitate negotiation or to supervise execution of the treaty provisions. Besides the three commissions named, the following committees also met during the negotiations: a committee to draft stipulations relative to the Danubian principalities (including Serbia), comprising Buol, Bourqueney, and Ali Pasha; a committee to draw up the terms of the entire treaty, consisting of Ali Pasha and the second plenipotentiaries of Austria, France, Britain, Russia, and Sardinia; and a committee to formulate the preamble which included all the second plenipotentiaries including Prussia's. Committees were also set up to draft the special conventions annexed to the peace treaty using representatives of the powers directly concerned: these conventions were the Russo-Ottoman Convention about warships on the Black Sea, and the Aland Islands Convention.[138]

Just as the Austrians had tried on 21 February to prescribe procedure for the three allied powers, the Russians endeavored to bend the negotiating process in their favor. The meeting with the representatives of the sea powers on 26 February about the affair of Kars and Bessarabia was a preliminary attempt. A few days later, Nesselrode instructed his representatives "to reach an understanding about all points of conflict . . . with the plenipotentiaries of England and France.[139] Changes in the peace terms could only be achieved if the sea powers concurred. "The question about war and peace will be decided between them and us. Consequently the negotiations must be conducted between us three." On the whole, this strategy was not successful, but on important points, such as the Bessarabian and Aland Islands questions, they [the negotiators] did tend to follow this principle.

A peculiar feature of the Paris negotiations was the *audiences* which Napoleon granted certain individuals. They were the most significant negotiating techniques; the official sessions often became secondary. This was how Napoleon honored his promise to the Russians transmitted through Seebach at the beginning of January that he would try to soften the peace conditions and to move closer to the Russians.[140] When Brunnov came to Paris, he was advised that the Russians should turn directly to Napoleon in case of disagreement. Napoleon expressly gave the chief Russian plenipotentiary the right to speak with him at any time.[141] On many occasions, Orlov could happily announce to Petersburg results won by direct appeal to the Emperor. Audiences were also employed by other representatives, but the Russians used them to the greatest advantage. In this way, Napoleon himself was able to play the decisive role in the peace negotiations. Although he remained in the background, he dominated the congress. Unfortunately, the sources available concerning his audiences are not very rich.

In contrast, the twenty-four conferences (really twenty-three[142]) held between 25 February and 16 April can be reconstructed quite accurately. Naturally, the official *protocols* are an important source. However, they are not as "complete and exhaustive" as Temperley supposed.[143] If one based an account of the negotiations solely on them, one could indeed list the topics of discussion and fill in the broad outlines but the portrait would be colorless. The sharp opposition crackling between the powers would disappear; the disagreements behind the scenes, so typical of the congress, would not emerge. Cavour's role would be reduced to his brief intervention on 8 April. The ups and downs of his tireless pleading for Italy outside the conference room would remain hidden. Actually his reports are a most revealing source, not only for the Italian question but for important Near Eastern matters, quite apart from the atmosphere, which is conveyed in a masterful though one-sided way.

The protocols drafted by Benedetti are only a précis of discussions lasting many hours. They are formal and polished; they omit the polemics. When harsh or unedifying remarks were made, the representatives usually agreed explicitly to omit them from the protocol. In other instances, Benedetti deliberately skipped them. There was no trace in the protocol of Clarendon's dig at the stubborn Russians over the Bessarabian question—they were returning two-thirds of the territory Russia had pledged to cede and were asking as compensation only a couple of "pools of water and insalubrious swamps."[144]

A speaker's express desire to suppress this or that comment was not always heeded. For instance, Walewski as president rejected Buol's wish to drop the "exchange of ideas" about Italian affairs on 8 April as unconnected with the goal of the negotiations.[145] It was indicated in the protocol that the congress expected an amnesty to be granted by the King of Naples. Although Buol dissociated himself from this, the protocol stated "that the majority of the plenipotentiaries did not dispute the efficacity of measures of clemency. . . ."[146] On the other hand, Cavour's remarks about the hardships inflicted by Austria on the Legations were softened, so that they did not constitute a formal protest, as Cavour had intended. This 8 April protocol is the only one that distorts the discussions; but the fact that the discussion was held was not glossed over, as Buol had wished.

The protocols were not supposed to be confidential, as Temperley asserts. In the twenty-third session, the plenipotentiaries secretly decided that the protocols could be published after ratifications were exchanged. But they agreed that it would be desirable that "disagreements, which had arisen during the Congress sessions and which might have been reported by the plenipotentiaries to their courts," not be made public. However, no formal pledge was exacted.[147] Obviously, the British representatives did not want to make promises which would exclude a blue book.[148]

PEACE CONFERENCE OR PEACE CONGRESS?

Were the Paris negotiations a peace conference or a peace congress? This question is more than a mere technicality. Previously, it has not been considered; the negotiations have been called conference or congress interchangeably.

The testimony of the representatives gathered at Paris should be crucial. However there is a preliminary problem: did people in the nineteenth century distinguish between conferences and congresses? In point of fact, there seems to be no conceptual difference either in international law or in diplomatic usage—the latter, the interpretation adopted by practitioners, is more relevant than scholarly dicta. At best, certain features can be described which characterize one more than the other.

Congress is the older term for international gatherings aimed at negotiating a peace treaty. The term *conference* was commonly used in the nineteenth century for less solemn diplomatic meetings serving to settle a specific dispute. However, contrary to some French authors (Genet, Sibert),[149] the term *congress* cannot be reserved for meetings which adjudicated important political questions with special authority. In the early nineteenth century, important meetings might be called conferences, like the London Conference (1827–1832) to resolve the Greek and Belgian questions. On the other hand, the meetings of the four sovereigns between 1818 and 1822 can hardly be defined as congresses, although at least the last three are so known. In their letter of invitation to the conference of Aix-la-Chapelle, the four powers explicitly stated that they did not wish to hold a congress.[150] Metternich, who sometimes described himself as the inventor of these "ministerial meetings" and as "an old legislator in the domain of world affairs,"[151] never called the Aix-la-Chapelle meeting a congress; but his language changed with subsequent meetings. It would be clearer to term these meetings conferences, to differentiate them from the three nineteenth-century peace congresses.

The plenipotentiaries who met in Paris originally styled their sessions conferences, because they were to settle a narrowly defined conflict, the Eastern Question. Napoleon's idea of a princely congress, noised about after Sevastopol through various channels to handle many or even all unsettled European problems, was not realized, since none of the sovereigns warmed up to it. Yet Napoleon did not drop the thought. He was never one to give up a grandiose plan; it was just a matter of proper timing. If he had persisted, the peace effort would have been held back. For pressing reasons, this could not be allowed. But the idea could be associated with the current negotiations; after the conclusion of peace, legally ending the state of war with Russia and permitting repatriation of the dying army, the negotiations could continue according to Napoleon's intent—to revise the Vienna settlement, the preceding major act of international law. There could scarcely be a better occasion: the ministers of the great powers had gathered to end a great war. The work of peace would be perfected, if other disputes could be settled immediately thereafter. In this respect, the peace negotiations, still termed a conference, could be given the more pretentious title, congress. Once again Napoleon used the press and his confidential conversations to publicize the idea of revising the treaties of 1815 through a congress.

On 24 February the *Moniteur* declared that the peace "congress" would open next day at one o'clock. Earlier, on 22 February, the semiofficial *Pays* had published an article by the editor in chief, Joseph Cohen, titled "Le droit public de l'Europe." Public law and the European balance of power, it said, had rested since the beginning of the century on diplomatic procedures and principles, such as the 1815 treaties, the Holy Alliance, and the Triple Alliance between Austria, Russia, and Prussia. What was their base today? Since the demise of the two alliances had been celebrated in France some months earlier, Cohen did not linger on them. What remained of the treaties of 1815? Europe had changed territorially, institutionally, and dynastically.[152] With great power assent, Belgium, after a revolution, had separated from the Netherlands; Greece had been set up as an independent state by France, Britain, and Russia; Poland had been wiped off the map. The Ottoman Empire, systematically disregarded in 1815, was entering the European family. On the continent, France, Prussia, and various second-rank states had introduced representative governments. The Bourbon monarchy guaranteed by the victors had ceased to exist; a new dynasty reigned in Spain; the Danish succession had been redefined.

And now the cat popped out of the bag: "Last but not least, the Napoleonic dynasty, proscribed forever by the 1815 treaties, has reascended the imperial throne, with the unanimous mandate of the French people." Europe, that is the Vienna signatories, had not protested. Why shouldn't the powers assembled in Paris define after peace was signed "what had changed in forty years, and what in the future must lead them along the road of progress?" There were two kinds of policy: the policy of foresight and the policy of repression. Europe must adopt the first "in order to . . . prevent the evils which can spring from a defective and badly defined system, instead of having to rectify them one day by that terrible means we call war."

These sentences accurately expressed Napoleon's thinking. They were repeated in various forms in newspapers and pamphlets. To the Second Empire, the Paris peace negotiations, ending the two-year eastern war, were a congress from the start, even though the real "congress" had not begun.

In audiences with the plenipotentiaries, Napoleon emphasized the same idea. He spoke frankly to Count Buol and Count Orlov. "Don't you think," he asked Buol on 20 February, "that some other topics [besides the Orient] could usefully be settled by a congress, of course after the conclusion of peace? Was nothing to be done for the Poles?"[153] The status of Italy also called for new agreements. This echoed the question flung at the astonished and delighted Cavour some weeks before: "What can we do for Italy?"

The Emperor must have been nervous about the Austrian's reaction. Buol warned him off, but not in the harsh manner usually attributed to him. Poland's legal position was especially delicate. He could not see that something could be accomplished here by a "European transaction." The solution should be left to Emperor Alexander. He did not deny that there were grievances concerning Italy, that is, specifically the long-drawn-out occupation of the Papal States. Revolutionary pressures, administrative deficiencies such as the lack of a good police force, and financial disarray all created difficulties. But as with Poland, he considered that "submitting the Roman situation to a European council" would not put things right. Austria was prepared to discuss directly with France "how the matter could be given a practical solution in cooperation with the Holy Father."

Austria was well aware that something had to be done. But only those directly concerned should consult. The decision of a European congress might assume an imperative character inadmissible for a great power.

The Austrian delegates tried to keep the negotiations within their "natural limits."[154] When Walewski, on Napoleon's instruction, introduced the principalities question "frankly and vigorously,"[155] Buol called this motion a "new element," irrelevant to the congress's task. He recognized the real goal of the union project, namely to pave the way for other territorial changes and "to spin out of it an occasion for a European congress."[156] But he consoled himself that Napoleon, "with his clear judgment," must already see that this was not feasible. As long as the Porte refused, there should be nothing to fear. Francis Joseph had insisted that he must not discuss questions that went beyond the Five Points. "His Imperial Majesty does not wish," according to a telegram of 6 April, "that the Paris conference consider other questions than those directly related to the Eastern Question."[157]

Napoleon also tried out his pet idea on the British and Russian chief delegates. As early as the beginning of March, however, Queen Victoria announced her refusal.[158]

The Petersburg Cabinet was more receptive. Count Orlov was first received by Napoleon on 23 February.[159] He assured the Emperor that he was no diplomat and would have to be straightforward. Napoleon seemed happy to meet a congenial individual. After exchanging several remarks about peace terms, he turned to the 1815 treaty and the need for revision. Orlov tried to warn him off; this puzzle was outside his instructions. Napoleon did not give up: it was just a conversation, and he continued to talk of "poor Italy" and "poor Poland." Poland was suffering for its own mistakes, replied Orlov; the people had forfeited their rights through revolution. However, his sovereign would profit by his coronation, scheduled for the summer of 1856, to mitigate the Poles' lot.

Orlov wrote Petersburg that the idea of a congress to revise the Vienna Treaty preoccupied the Emperor to the virtual exclusion of other considerations. In Petersburg Napoleon's wish to alter the situation in Italy and Poland was not taken as the real motive for the confidential conversation with Orlov; instead people emphasized Napoleon's drive to solidify his dynasty at home and abroad by ending the proscription of the Bonaparte line written into the Vienna Treaty. Before his departure in April, Orlov, along with the other representatives, was asked to sign a declaration invalidating the Vienna terms concerning Napoleon's family.[160]

In general Napoleon's congress plans won little sympathy. Publicly the Paris Peace Conference "styled" itself a peace congress without ever making a formal decision on the subject. The protocol of the first session, on 25 February, uses the word *conference* for the first and last time to refer to the activities of the peace delegation. Subsequent protocols read *congress*.

On 5 March, Buol wrote Francis Joseph that both in the protocols and in semiofficial talk, the word *congress* had "pushed aside" the word *conference*.[161] This did not altogether correspond to "accepted usage," but he believed that he ought not to object because the only motive seemed to be "to give the negotiations the greatest possible importance in the eyes of the public and of history." Besides this, Napoleon, in using the word, intended to transform the negotiations into a "clearing house," where all European questions could be treated, even if only little by little.

Both reasons for using the term *congress* can be confirmed by the sources, the first through information intended for the public, the second through unpublished sources. The press just referred to the Congress of Paris. On 16 March, Empress Eugénie gave birth to a son, the "congress child," and the plenipotentiaries came to the Tuileries to offer good wishes; the *Moniteur* next day printed the congratulatory address with the comment: "Europe was represented on this solemn occasion, by the most eminent personages of their countries, all Prime Ministers or Foreign Secretaries and enjoying the highest confidence of their sovereigns."

Given this testimony about the actors' intentions, historians should not hesitate to describe the Paris negotiations the way contemporaries did, as a congress, even if the gathering does not fit one of the two main contemporary definitions, that is to say, a group drafting a very broad agenda.

The documents tell us which general European problems beyond the Eastern Question and the Italian and Polish situations were possible subjects for a congress in the broad sense. Confidentially Napoleon himself referred to the question of Cracow,[162] which was indeed directly related to the Vienna Treaty. He spoke of measures against the revolutionary press, especially in Belgium, and against granting asylum to refugees in Switzerland.[163] If the agenda were extended, Prussia wanted consideration of the Neufchâtel question and the Sound Dues.[164] Prussia was concerned not only with abolition of the shipping duties levied by Denmark since 1429 and discussed in 1856 at Copenhagen,[165] but was also interested in closing the access to the Baltic, parallel to the system for the Ottoman Straits, in view of the threat to her own coasts, which had become acute during the war because of the British navy. Austria and Russia were not eager to see new questions introduced. In the Austrian government, only the finance minister, Bruck, favored a new item: construction of a canal across the Isthmus of Suez.[166] Sweden wanted to bring forward the grievances already mentioned, but was finally obliged to limit herself to the Aland Islands question, which interested no one else except the British. Spain, after trying in vain to participate in the negotiations, wanted to bring the quarrel with the United States over Cuba before the congress.[167] Cavour's thinking circled tirelessly around the situation in Italy. And Britain?

Britain played a double game. Palmerston considered it the "great aim" of the peace negotiations "to provide fresh securities for the future peace of Europe."[168] The original goal had been to settle the questions connected with the Crimean War; but now that the great power representatives were assembled to discuss questions of general European interest they should not separate without debating the explosive situation in Italy. As a point of departure, there was the fact that many territories in Europe were occupied by foreign troops and should be evacuated now that the war was over: Ottoman and Greek territory—and Italian territory. Through this back door, demands for withdrawal of Austrian troops from the Papal States could be laid before the congress.

Palmerston's argument was just as farfetched as the one Napoleon adopted to persuade Austria that it was necessary to discuss the status of Italy; he emphasized the revolutionary press in Belgium and above all Switzerland's position as a refuge for revolutionaries. When Napoleon tried out his reasoning on Clarendon, the latter characterized it in writing to Palmerston as "wild . . . views,"[169] which simply gave an excuse to force the other powers to discuss Italy. He explained unceremoniously that Britian would not cooperate in "gagging" the press and would not allow "expressions of opinion" about freedom of the press and the right of asylum to appear in the protocol. Yet when Palmerston suggested that the Eastern and the Italian questions be linked by the analogous stationing of troops, he decided "to do something for Italy and for Greece and for Bomba's victims [the revolutionaries condemned by King Ferdinand] and place an opinion on record about Poland" and concluded, in spite of the likelihood of general opposition on these matters, "I am determined however to stir in them all."

Since Napoleon was in a hurry to finish, he dropped the congress idea. 1 April was to be the day for signing the treaty. Orlov supposedly remarked that people would take this date as a bad joke.[170] So 30 March was chosen—a date now that must have looked like a poor joke to Orlov. It was the forty-second anniversary of the Russian and Prussian victory over Napoleon I, the day when Montmartre was taken. Orlov had been in Nesselrode's retinue, entering Paris in triumph. Now he was the one to confirm the second Alexander's defeat in Paris.[171]

The congress's work did not end with the treaty signing. They still had to discuss evacuating foreign troops from Ottoman territory. On 2 April Walewski asked Buol whether the "Greek and Roman situations" as well might not be brought before the congress.[172] Buol admitted that the evacuation of Greece was related to the Eastern Question, but the occupation of the Papal States decidedly was not, since it rested on special treaties. Should the situation in other states be discussed, he would state his view that these matters lay outside the scope of the congress; he could not take them up in the absence of those most closely involved.

On 8 April, when conditions in Rome and Naples finally did come before the congress, Buol made his threatened declaration. Aside from the legal ambiguities he alluded to, the congress was hampered by

Russia's negative response—Orlov pleaded lack of instructions—and had to be satisfied with expressing a "wish" in the protocol. As will be shown, the famous but overrated discussion of the Italian question originated in British pressure. Without this British intervention, Count Cavour would have gone away empty-handed like Prince Adam Czartoryski.

Originally, after Sevastopol, Napoleon had supported the Polish leader's demand for restoration of Congress Poland because at that point Poland had top priority in his broadened war aims program. As the negotiations approached, Czartoryski reduced his goal mainly to preserving the Polish people from Russification—that is, full freedom of conscience, use of Polish in the courts, and a native educational system with instruction in the mother tongue.[173] Napoleon adopted these demands because their presentation at the congress could offer the opportunity for revision of the Vienna Treaty. Then he sounded out Count Orlov and the latter gave him to understand that Russia's rule in Poland was not based on the Vienna Treaty but on conquest after the 1830 revolution; so Napoleon let the Polish question alone. At the end of March, Clarendon's readiness to initiate it must have embarrassed Napoleon. After Sevastopol it was he who had urged doing something for Poland and the British who had demurred. Meanwhile, bringing about a Franco-Russian rapprochement had seized his attention; the Polish situation had receded. How could Britain's sudden move be averted?

On 7 April Napoleon remarked to Clarendon that he would have to speak to Orlov again and would like to know what he should say concerning Poland.[174] Clarendon, just as well briefed on Poland by Czartoryski as on Italy by Cavour, repeated the Prince's concerns and suggested that Orlov might give appropriate assurances, either on his own or by request.

Napoleon met Orlov that evening. We do not know exactly what was said. Apparently Orlov reiterated his position of 23 February and referred to Emperor Alexander's declaration planned for the coronation. Buol regretted after 8 April that "the other questions" could not have been resolved the same way.[175] Unlike the Italian question, the Polish question was sacrificed to the Franco-Russian rapprochement and never came before the congress.

Napoleon's fertile plan had not been realized. The mandate of the congress should have been broadened after the peace treaty was signed, but Russian and especially Austrian opposition was too great. The 8 April session was more like farce than like the opening of a congress to resolve the open questions of European diplomacy.

Napoleon must have seen this, for a recently published letter from Clarendon to Queen Victoria reveals that at heart he was disappointed by the famous twenty-second session.[176] For the first time he confided to one of the plenipotentiaries, Clarendon, that he had anticipated a general European restructuring. Since this hope had been frustrated, he wanted to know whether Britain would object to such a congress later on.

Clarendon's flourish on 8 April had been primarily for home consumption; he now feigned alarm. He reproached Napoleon. Restructuring: that would mean the Rhine boundary for France, which Prussia could not accept; it would mean restoration of Poland, which Russia did not want to hear about; driving Austria out of Italy, which she would never abide; reforming the German Confederation, which Austria wanted to master; dissolution of the smaller German states as compensation for Austria and Prussia. Clarendon obviously wanted to paint the deeds of the famous uncle to scare the nephew about the notorious consequences. "Lord Clarendon begged the Emperor to consider what interests and passions and hopes and fears would be excited by such a congress and the extreme difficulty of carrying out any decisions that it might come to except by coercion which might lead to general war."

Here Clarendon touched the sore point: how should decisions once made be implemented? By force? A look at the Eastern Question since 1853 was enough. Meetings of the five great powers in Vienna in 1855 had not sufficed to prevent a military solution, although the agenda of the conference had been limited and thus in theory it should have been successful. Napoleon did seem to understand the necessity of previous agreements; he conceded that it would be stupid to call such a congress, unless three or four of the great powers had decided beforehand on the changes proposed.

At the same time, Napoleon talked to the Prussian minister president about his congress idea.[177] Again it is clear that Napoleon had hoped that an all-embracing congress would evolve from the peace negotiations. In his farewell audience with Clarendon on 17 April, he told the British minister that he had renounced the congress plan because he could now assess the obstacles.[178] He asked, however, whether it would not be desirable, if a serious question emerged such as the Italian problem, to invite the powers concerned to send plenipotentiaries to Paris or some other meeting place. This procedure would bring a quicker resolution than a continual exchange of notes. With railway connections it could easily be put in practice.

This proposal was certainly realistic. Clarendon broadened it relative to Italy: if matters did not improve within three months, such a conference should be called with the nuncio participating, "in order to learn Europe's opinion concerning the Papal regime."

Napoleon's congress plan had failed. In fact the Paris Congress only solved the existing Near Eastern conflict and that for a limited period. It did not avert future conflicts—a goal which also preoccupied public opinion,[179] especially in view of the appalling military struggle. Subsequently, Napoleon did not lose sight of the plan which he believed he had almost brought off during the Crimean War. But he was no more successful later.

The congress plan's history has yet to be written. In 1839, Napoleon had expressed the prototype in his *Napoleonic Ideas*; he contrasted it with making war and called it the only humane method of reconstructing Europe and assuring peace.

However, in the reduced form of the Paris ambassadorial conference, proposed by Napoleon to Clarendon, the plan was actually implemented. For ten years after 1857, a conference met intermittently and occupied itself with the Danubian principalities. It was a direct result of the Paris Congress.

SARDINIA'S POSITION

Sardinia's role in the war and Cavour's activities at the congress have been more thoroughly explored than any other detail of Crimean War history. Early Italian nationalist historiography about the Risorgimento, generally hagiographic in tone, believed that Cavour, the ingenious architect of unity, had conceived his masterpiece very early, had laid the foundations in the Crimean War, and subsequently filled it in piece by piece. This adulatory attitude has continued almost unbroken far into the twentieth century. Scholarly examination began to bear fruit only in the 1930s. In a fundamental study, Adolfo Omodeo offered a revisionist assessment of Cavour's domestic accomplishments. He rejected the tendency to present Cavour as a kind of deity, gifted with the facility of genius, who overcame all the difficulties which had defeated other pioneers of the Risorgimento. For Cavour's foreign policy, the studies of Paul Matter and Franco Valsecchi parallel Omodeo's interpretation.[180]

The legend dating back to the Risorgimento of Cavour as a "miracle-worker," a legend which measured events by their conclusion, has been discredited today. Sardinia's entry into the Crimean War on the western side was not an example of "clairvoyant perception" according to a conscious plan leading to Italian unification; it was an improvisation, which did indeed look at the future, but never obscured the view of what was currently attainable. Also, Sardinian participation did not come about on Cavour's initiative but through western pressure: in the winter of 1854/55 the western powers were searching desperately for soldiers to replenish their armies, decimated by sickness and cold. In fact, the western powers did not turn to Sardinia first but to the Kingdom of Naples. Only when it was apparent that King Ferdinand would be neutral did they plead urgently with Turin; finally, after Cavour hesitated and Dabormida posed high conditions, they sent an ultimatum demanding unconditional entry.

Since we agree by and large with recent Italian interpretations concerning Sardinia's role in the war, and since Ennio Di Nolfo's recent book following Valsecchi has summarized for now all the important details about the relation of the Italian question to European history in 1855 and 1856, we can simply invoke some aspects of the Italian question essential to the Paris Congress and here and there emphasize somewhat different points from Di Nolfo.

For Sardinia, the December Treaty between Austria and the western powers was almost catastrophic: with one stroke it annihilated all hope of driving Austria out of Italy, especially to the extent those hopes focused on Napoleon. In the same month a previously neglected Franco-Austrian convention was signed,[181] by which Austria pinned down French support for the territorial status quo in Italy. The convention did not eliminate Austrian mistrust of Napoleon; but it soothed matters "for the duration of the eastern crisis" (it would be in force during the war). Buol saw it as reinsurance; it lessened the danger of revolutionary movements during the conflict, but did not do away with it altogether. For Cavour it meant an enforced truce with Austria.

In November 1854, the western powers had instructed their plenipotentiaries in Turin, Hudson and the Duke of Gramont, to hint about sending Sardinian troops to the Orient.[182] The Turin government set two conditions: the western powers must promise to urge Austria to end sequestration (property seizure affecting Austrian refugees from Lombardo-Venetia, now living in Sardinia) and to permit "discussion of Italian affairs" at the peace negotiations.[183] Both conditions were refused.[184]

Clarendon's expressed grounds for rejection are especially important in view of his standpoint on the Italian question during the Paris Congress. If Sardinia were pursuing political ends by her demands, he wrote Hudson, and if she wanted to imply that she stood on the same foot as the great powers, who traditionally regulated European affairs and meant to have an equal voice in the congress with Britain, France, and Austria, just because she had provided fifteen thousand men, and not free at that, then her demands were inadmissible.[185] If the war continued and other small states provided contingents, they might claim parity with Sardinia. In the end, the congress would be like the Frankfurt Diet. Of course Sardinia would be consulted about everything involving her interests; obviously, she would sign the peace. But she should not expect to be asked about questions that did not concern her.

In Turin, Hudson and Gramont exploited the King's bellicose attitude to force unconditional accession to the British-French-Ottoman treaty of 10 April 1854. After a governmental crisis, in which Dabormida was sacrificed and Cavour became foreign minister, Sardinia declared herself ready to agree without conditions. However in June 1855, Cavour tried again to have Sardinia's status defined by the western powers with regard to peacemaking. He demanded recognition of Sardinia's right to participate directly in the negotiations, "as well as in discussions which may arise from questions to be considered, according to her material and moral interests."[186] The British government in association with the French confirmed the Italian right to participate in all discussions which could involve Sardinia's "special interests," and assured Cavour that the Sardinian plenipotentiary would be informed about "all overtures or projects of general interest" which he was not asked to discuss directly.[187]

Cavour knew how to make useful connections in Paris and London at the end of 1855, during his sovereign's state visits, and how to explain Sardinian grievances without importunity. On 7 December, at Compiègne, Napoleon gave him the famous but overrated hint: "Write confidentially to Walewski about what you think I could do for Piedmont and Italy."[188] This was not the germ of the later Plombières pact; but it did offer encouragement to offset the disappointment over the war's premature end. Cavour had hoped, with some justification, that the eastern war would be transformed into a general European war providing at the conclusion a suitable occasion for recognizing Sardinia's wishes. Massimo d'Azeglio, the former minister president, who expected to be the plenipotentiary, worked up a comprehensive memorandum on the strength of Napoleon's cue; he offered a grandiose plan of reorganization for the entire Apennine peninsula. Cavour, with his flair for the possible and attainable, refused to send this memorandum to Paris and London and substituted four concise points: amelioration of Austrian rule in Lombardo-Venetia; reform of the government in the Kingdom of Naples; withdrawal of Austrian troops from the Legations and cession of these territories to Modena or to Tuscany, in other words, secularization of the Papal States; abolition of the sequestrations.[189]

As a precaution Walewski had told the Sardinian government that it would be premature "to create new complications in the Eastern Question by raising the Italian."[190] As the negotiations approached, he tried to delimit Sardinia's role exactly. His arguments against Turin's claims to equal participation, seconded by Palmerston, rested on the June agreement and had precedent in international law, especially at the Vienna Congress. From the perspective of relations between France and Britain, the discussion about Sardinia between the end of January and the end of February 1856 is illuminating, because of the divergent points of departure and because of the motives leading France and Britain to adopt different attitudes. These motives offer a yardstick for judging contemporary support for Cavour's cause at the congress, and in our opinion have not been distinguished clearly enough.

Walewski started with a lofty concept of great power status. He reminded the government in Turin that it was a principle of European public law, that in peace negotiations like those now opening, each power be given an importance corresponding to its role in European questions.[191] In other words, the place of each power in the negotiations is determined by its rank as a power. Rank, so Gramont told Cibrario, confers rights but also duties.[192] Power status must be accurately reflected by the impact on negotiations. First-rank powers must control the affairs of Europe.

The immediate calculation behind this argument was to limit the agenda of the negotiations to the causes of the Crimean War, rather than introducing new, complicating questions. Here there was undeniably a difference between the attitude of the minister and that of Napoleon. They agreed on wishing a speedy peace. They separated when Napoleon wished to begin his comprehensive congress. Beyond this, Walewski was interested in a conservative alliance with Austria, laying aside the Italian question. Napoleon's opinion was not well defined at the beginning of 1856.

Britain's standpoint, or rather Palmerston's, was mainly pragmatic. Clarendon, whose "Italianism" was still considered mild by the Sardinian representative in London at the beginning of February,[193] maintained to Palmerston[194] that British interests would not be served by treating Sardinia as a great power in violation of the facts; he referred to the June Treaty, which had adequately set out Sardinia's role. But Palmerston soon convinced him of Sardinia's potential usefulness as a British satellite as she now suggested. Besides his sympathy with liberal Sardinia, Palmerston's bitterness about the interrupted war came into play. He especially resented Austria, which could be coerced by open friendliness between Britain and Sardinia.[195] In mid-February, Clarendon's language already approached Palmerston's. He declared to the French that Sardinia, which had fought for the European cause, not selfish interests, should logically discuss subjects of general European concern.[196]

The right of a *belligerent* to full participation in the peace negotiations now weighed more heavily with Clarendon than the unwritten rules of the "système européen des grandes puissances." In fact, topics of Sardinian and of European concern could not be sharply differentiated. As a naval power, Sardinia was just as interested in the third point, about the neutralization of the Black Sea, as in the second point, demanding freedom of shipping on the Danube. And one could even construe an essential Sardinian interest in the internal organization of the Danubian principalities, given Palmerston's and Napoleon's plans for a territorial exchange.

In the confidential discussion already mentioned between Clarendon, Walewski, and Buol on 21 February, Sardinia's position was considered.[197] Buol advanced the grounds for diminished participation which Walewski had used earlier: he appealed to precedent, especially the Vienna Congress, where great powers alone regulated European questions. If Sardinia participated on the same footing as the other powers, she would immediately gain the status of a first-rank power, in the position so to speak of Prussia. These newly won rights would imply new duties, which Sardinia would hardly be able to fulfill.

These were all Metternichian arguments, a way of thinking about the balance of power in Europe which was still a matter of course. Walewski, who belonged to this school, did not participate, because Napoleon planned to open the Italian question through an exchange with the Danubian principalities. Clarendon found Buol's tone towards Sardinia "respectful and bienveillant"—although Buol is said to have been arrogant and irritable at the congress—and considered him essentially correct. Clarendon demanded participation in all the sessions. Beyond this he would trust Count Cavour's moderation. In case a subject completely strange to Sardinia was to be discussed—the Aland Islands question was perhaps the only example—the Sardinian delegation would spontaneously withdraw, just as he, Buol, would not speak up about the terms of the armistice.

On the basis of this pragmatic gentleman's agreement, the congress proceeded. No declaration of principles was ever made. To soothe the Austrians, Palmerston appealed to a precedent of the Vienna Congress.[198] At that time, Portugal, whose troops were paid by the British like the Sardinians now, had participated in discussions without deriving any future right to be included in great power negotiations concerning questions not directly affecting her.

The conclusion was justifiable, but not the premises. Portugal had only participated in the insignificant eight power discussions. The big questions were decided by the committee of four or five powers.

Up to the signing of the peace, the official sessions were exclusively occupied with the problems of the war. Behind the scenes, however, the

Italian situation was discussed intensively, but more as a matter of form than of content. The most difficult question was: how might it be introduced given Austrian opposition and Russian indifference? The delegates would plead lack of instructions and might refuse to ask for them, since the preliminaries were the only valid basis for discussion. The nuncio and the diplomatic representatives of Naples and Tuscany had expressed to Buol their fear that the Italian problem might be laid before the congress. Nothing could be decided without participation of the Italian states. Therefore one must reckon with official protests from the Curia and other Italian states.[199]

Napoleon had oulined his position before the congress began. He expressed it frankly to the chief delegates of the three great powers and to Count Cavour:[200] if there were a general redrawing of the map of Italy, he would very much like to enlarge Piedmont, but at this point, he could not touch the Papal States; it was also impossible to encroach on Austria's Italian possessions. "The only way," he added, "would be to send the Duke of Modena and the Duchess of Parma to Wallachia and Moldavia and to give Parma and Modena to your King."

In Napoleon's eyes the union of the Danubian principalities was an indispensable precondition for this exchange plan. And this could not be accomplished during the negotiations. Napoleon's readiness "to do something for Italy" pivoted on the union. The Catholic clergy in France, "one of the three instruments for governing his Empire,"[201] must not be antagonized by action against the Papal States. To promote relations with the Catholic Church, Napoleon considered asking the Pope to be godfather to his newborn child. Last but not least, good relations with Austria were essential, which precluded roughing her up in Italy.

Clarendon had come to Paris determined not to go away "without having spoken Italian."[202] During the congress, he became very fond of Cavour. Early in the negotiations, he gave him to understand that the Italian matter should be introduced, as soon as the main questions had been resolved. Cavour himself realized that his concern was incidental to the negotiations and wished that it be discussed only when the "great questions over war and peace"[203] were settled. This reasonable and perceptive attitude impressed Clarendon deeply. "He is an excellent fellow," he wrote Palmerston, "and the more I see of him, the more I like him."[204] The awareness that he was dealing with a man of equal political ability and the perception that Napoleon was wavering, the more the unpleasantness implicit in the Italian problem appeared, strengthened Clarendon's desire to astonish Europe with a dramatic stroke.

It is important to emphasize this distinction between French and British attitudes towards Italy in order to judge the 8 April sitting correctly. The more Napoleon dragged, the more Clarendon insisted on speaking the word *Italy* before the European forum. This difference, known in essentials for some decades through Cavour's published papers, emerges still more sharply in Clarendon's recently published letters from the congress to Palmerston. It can now be said with more certainty that without British pressure, Cavour's activities would have left no trace in the protocols and there would have been less food for the Cavour legend.

Cavour played two roles at the congress: he was chief plenipotentiary of a belligerent state on the same footing as the great power representatives and he was a conspirator par excellence. Officially he was limited to brief appearances in the Salon des Ambassadeurs of the Quai d'Orsay; his unofficial activity was pushed uninterruptedly in the salons and at the Tuileries.

Cavour's papers provide abundant and incomparably piquant details about this. Cavour tried to bribe the Ottoman grand vizier, and when Ali Pasha was incorruptible, regretted that the Serail was too far from Paris. He did not hesitate to influence Napoleon through his personal physician, Dr. Conneau, and Palmerston through Lady Palmerston. With some members, especially Orlov, he sought to play the same game with female beauties, brought with him from Italy. He tried to disgrace Walewski, then president of the congress, who was not enamored of his projects, by using the French ambassador to London, Persigny, Walewski's enemy and Napoleon's confidant. In his restless imagination, he made and unmade kings and married princes and princesses. All this to advance bit by bit Sardinia's ardently desired territorial aggrandisement, which Napoleon and Palmerston approved throughout.

The practical result was precisely nothing. A contemporary characterized this labor of Sisyphus ironically: "Imagine a gambler, on his arrival at Baden, finding the casino closed for the season."[205] Cavour himself summed it up more elegantly the day after the treaty was signed: "Peace is signed. The play is over and the curtain falls without having brought a resolution materially favorable to us. This result is sad."[206]

However Clarendon and Palmerston made sure that the last word had not been spoken. At the end of February, Palmerston let Cavour know that he would be happy to see "an increase in territory for the House of Savoy as result of the conference."[207] The cession of Lombardy or the duchies of Parma and Modena or even all of them seemed most desirable. As compensation for Austria he hit upon the Papal States and the transfer of an archduke to the united Danubian principalities.[208] To be sure, he did not underrate the inconsistency of the transaction in the principalities with the principle of Ottoman integrity:[209] a sick man, told that his leg would be cut off to do him good, might well be refractory. But he assumed that the sick man would be powerless before the doctors, once they were unanimous. To d'Azeglio, the envoy, who wanted the prime minister's opinion about "total removal" of Austria from Italy, Palmerston explained that the European balance would not be disturbed if Austria received the Danubian principalities, to which one might add Serbia and Bosnia.

Cavour meanwhile developed the idea of making the Prince of Carignan, who was to marry the Duchess of Parma, king of the Danubian principalities.[210] However, when no agreement was reached about the union project, Palmerston hit upon the alternative of setting the Prince on the Greek throne, whose legitimate occupant, the Wittelsbach Otto, had been a thorn in his flesh since the beginning of the Crimean War because of his pro-Russianism. He wrote to Clarendon: "The very idea of such a change does one's heart good. The mere thinking of it is refreshing."[211] Would it not be possible to have the British and French troops returning from the Crimea make a stop in Greece and effect the change? Naturally the step would have to be discussed in Paris.[212]

Palmerston's daring plans, a coup, fantastic exchanges of territory, the creation and deposition of kings, and so on, all to be put through without the Cabinet's participation, and above all his major aim, the decomposition of Russia, find a parallel only in Ludendorff's grotesque eastern plans at the end of the First World War or, if you will, in Himmler's "general eastern plan" from the Second World War. They outstripped everything which Napoleon had turned in his head before and during the congress. Previously, Napoleon had been considered the great advocate of change in the European map. However, at the end of the Crimean War it was Palmerston who pursued such activities most intensively—if only in fantasy.

In mid-March, Clarendon was so deeply impressed by Cavour's complaints and so little persuaded of Napoleon's steadfastness that he decided to seize the initiative "about the state of Italy which was a scandal to Europe and which a European Congress was bound to consider."[213] On 19 March, he reminded the Emperor of his original intention of introducing the Italian question. As we now know from Clarendon's recently published secret letters to Palmerston, Napoleon insisted that he had not changed his views.[214] But the more he reflected, he said, the greater the difficulties seemed. Only force could persuade Austria and the Pope to concur in reform. He did not want to go to war with Austria, or to proceed against the Pope, since this would enrage the French clergy. Clarendon challenged the Emperor to speak up to Buol and to tell him that at the end of a war undertaken for the balance of power, an Austrian army could no longer be tolerated in the

Legations. Napoleon agreed to instruct his minister to speak in this sense to Buol. Some days later, Clarendon asked the Emperor not to entrust this important task solely to Walewski, but to enlighten Buol personally.

When Clarendon found his hopes disappointed, he himself spoke to Buol. He found him surprisingly cooperative.[215] However, Buol characterized as utopian Clarendon's ideas of urging the Pope to reform the administration of the Papal States after withdrawal of foreign troops. Clarendon then announced that the subject would come before the congress. He feared that Napoleon would renege and that he would have to step forward alone. This would achieve no practical result, but Britain's views would be publicly stated. In a declaration he proposed that the congress should declare "that for full restoration of the political balance in Europe and for the preservation of peace from every danger it is necessary that the occupation of the Roman states by the troops of His Majesty the Emperor of France and the troops of His Majesty the Emperor of Austria should cease as soon as possible (or better: before the end of the year)."[216] The congress must further state that to maintain law and order an administration separate from the spiritual power must be introduced and a national guard formed.

With this project, Clarendon showed himself more Italian than Cavour. As we now know for the first time, the latter asked the British minister to change his statement.[217] If it were published, he would be open to reproach for having demanded less than the British government. Also Napoleon's anxieties should not go unheeded.

In the 8 April session then, the later famous declaration about Italy was presented by Walewski and Clarendon. To judge its dimensions adequately it must be considered from two viewpoints: that of the Napoleonic idea of a congress and that of Italy's history in the next five years.

Especially if one goes beyond the official protocol to the delegates' confidential reports, the session of 8 April must appear a perversion of Napoleon's congress plan or at least a miserable manifestation of his peacekeeping ideal. It was the only attempt by the great powers in that century, when settling the debts after a sacrificial war, to remove the causes for future conflicts by eliminating the danger from the revolutionary idea of the nation state and thus to preserve the peace for at least a generation; but it failed in the 8 April session and in the following related session of 14 April.[218] It failed because the task, covering conflicts from Cracow to Cuba, from the White Sea to Suez, was simply too vast; because each of the great powers had a different intention and a different notion of its feasibility.

Napoleon might have been firmly convinced that war is unworthy, and that conflicts should be eliminated in a great forum; but at the same time, he pursued real political goals, namely a remodelling of Europe in favor of France. Clarendon feared the revolutionary effect of restructuring the heart of Europe. Buol, as Metternich's pupil, supported a congress only insofar as it remained within the confines of the Eastern Question, which was complicated enough, especially since Austria would probably suffer most and profit least. Russia was fully occupied with the consequences, above all domestic, of losing the war. Frederick William was only interested in a congress if there were a chance for full restitution of his beloved Neufchâtel. Finally, Cavour was thinking monomaniacally about Sardinia and Italy.

From Walewski's words on 8 April, when he raised the discussion to a new plane, Napoleon's original intention emerges again: although the congress had met just to settle the Eastern Question, it might be reproached with missing the opportunity "to elucidate certain questions, affirm certain principles, express intentions, always and only in the intention of assuring, for the future, the tranquillity of the world, by dissipating, before they became menacing, the clouds one can see still lowering on the political horizon."[219] To start, Walewski had explicitly characterized the discussion as an "exchange of ideas." After speaking of the occupation of Greece, he announced the French government's provisional readiness to withdraw from Rome, and added a "wish" for "consolidation of the Roman government." This formula avoided insult to the Pope. Walewski's language about Naples was more explicit: the government there must be enlightened about its "false path"; he would find it useful to send "a warning"; moreover, there should be amnesty for those "who had gone astray" (that is, condemned revolutionaries).

Clarendon based his remarks on the need to eliminate conflicts which could disturb Europe's political balance. He asked the Pope to implement "secularization of the government" of the Papal States and the King of Naples the "freeing of political prisoners."[220]

Buol denied the congress any right to intervene in the domestic affairs of a foreign state. In his report to Vienna, he described Clarendon's challenge as "instigated with an eye to his Parliamentary position and probably influenced by Count Cavour, who, failing material advantages for his country, would be glad to bring home some seeming victories for his policy."[221] Neither insinuation was completely wrong. Clarendon had written Palmerston a week before that public opinion in Britain could be bought off with such declarations.[222] The "public opinion of England" was the invisible British negotiator at the congress, a fact all too easily overlooked.[223] Clarendon's own judgment on the 8 April session reveals dissatisfaction and irritation. "We have made bad work of it today with the Italian question," he wrote Palmerston.[224] He saw his statement merely as "a point de départ for future remonstrance which is all we shall have done for Italy!"

Napoleon immediately reproached Clarendon, as appears from Clarendon's letter to Queen Victoria, recently published, for making a declaration in this form.[225] He had always predicted nothing good would come from broaching the Italian question at the congress. Even if the criticism applies to him too, it does show that Napoleon, thinking of the Pope[226] and of relations with Austria, wanted to let the Italian question ride after the union of the Danubian principalities had fallen through.

Cavour, moreover, was bitterly disappointed by the entire course of the congress, including the 8 April session. The declarations he accurately described as "sterile wishes."[227] The weeks of planning had brought no tangible result. None of the goals he had formulated before the congress had been achieved, although he had considered them very modest, and they had steadily lowered during the meeting. He had anticipated support from the French and British, but Napoleon, originally enthusiastic about enlarging Sardinia if affairs developed in southeastern Europe, had become more and more evasive; at the end he was even inclined to remove the Italian question from the congress agenda. Walewski had always opposed Cavour's plans with antipathy. Clarendon displayed more sympathy thanks to growing admiration for a like-minded associate, and to strong anti-Papal sentiment mixed with Protestant moralism and the need to express accumulated irritation against neutral and pacific Austria; but in the end, his actual support did not go beyond platonic affection and a few strong words.

However, even though there was no concrete result, Cavour's own belief that he had sowed seeds for the future held a measure of truth. His activities, as he wrote Cibrario, had at least won Sardinia the friendship and sympathy of several powers.[228] From this might come the "germs of future achievements." In such expressions, a nationalistic historiography has discerned the prophetic insight of the sagacious master and has prefigured Plombières, the inevitable war with Austria, and the subsequent unification movement. Sardinia's participation in the Crimean War and Cavour's role at the congress supposedly cleared the path for the great work of unification.

Such a way of looking at things is methodologically unsound. Certainly Cavour had demonstrated to Europe that there was an "Italian question," and its solution was bound up with peace. And he had, in Di Nolfo's word, "diplomatized" the question,[229] that is, associated it with international politics;[230] at the same time, however, he had to give up close ties with the revolution (Mazzini). But the crucial figure for the solution of the Italian question was Napoleon, and in 1856 he was far from risking an Italian war of liberation, even if Cavour suspected at the congress as the conclusion of weeks of thought that the only effective answer would be "the cannon."[231] Napoleon's revisionism right after the war was not directed to the Apennines but to the Balkans and the Danube. Here was the point of least resistance where his great plan could be pushed forward. Here, not in Italy, a war almost broke out in 1858 between Austria and France which might have involved other powers, a fact almost unknown and needing investigation. When war did break out in 1859 in northern Italy, Napoleon did not intervene to repay Sardinia for her assistance but because the moment seemed favorable for revising the 1815 system and helping the principle of nationalities to victory.

The Crimean War did not expedite Italian unification; it actually retarded it. From 1848/49, the Austro-Sardinian quarrel was as sharp as after 1856 and was being monitored by Napoleon. During the Crimean War, it was put on ice, as is demonstrated by the Austro-French Convention of 22 December 1854, and also by the British efforts to keep the Austro-Sardinian conflict as subdued as possible.[232] Only after Orsini's assassination attempt of January 1858 was Napoleon obviously determined to settle the Austro-Sardinian affair, through war if necessary. The Crimean War has no direct connection with this.

ADMITTING PRUSSIA

Prussia's position at the Paris Congress offers more contrasts with the position of Sardinia than analogies. That Germany was unified under Prussian leadership, without Prussian participation in the Crimean War, indirectly supports our thesis that Sardinia's entry was not a prerequisite for unifying Italy. Just as Sardinia's policy must be judged insofar as possible without an eye on 1858 to 1861, so Prussia's role guided by Frederick William IV and Manteuffel should not be measured with yardsticks derived from Prusso-German history between 1862 and 1870.

The judgment that Frederick William IV's policy in 1853 to 1856 was "a policy of sentimentality," "wavering," "unsteady," "irresolute," and so on is just as hardy as the notion about Buol, who certainly did not conduct "a policy of sentimentality" but nonetheless culpably led Austria into isolation. And yet Prussia's approach was dominated by *Realpolitik* and was the only reasonable one according to *Prussian* interests, since, like Austria, it aimed at self-preservation, through staying aloof from the match between the block of western powers and the eastern colossus. Joining the West would have forced Prussia, weak politically and militarily, to become a satellite and would have exposed the long eastern boundary to Russian invasion. Going over to Russia would have made it the Russian battering ram against France and would have exposed the coasts to British bombardment. Neutrality was different in degree compared with Austria because Prussia had a different stake in the causes of the war. Unlike Austria, Prussia was not directly involved in the Balkans and the Black Sea.

Prussia's policy of "declared," "active" neutrality, which, as Peter Rassow has recently shown, was Frederick William's own policy not Bismarck's,[233] assured survival, negated French predominance in the West, and—joined with Austria's nonintervention—precluded war on German soil. Because of her status as a nonbelligerent, Prussia's participation in the peace negotiations was not inevitable; it was also not obvious—a peculiar feature of contemporary international relations—because of her position as one of the five great powers, that is, because of membership in the European Concert. According to the other four great powers, or at least according to the two western powers and Austria, Prussia had excluded herself from the concert by her lack of commitment.[234] She had signed neither the Four Points of 8 August 1854 nor the December Treaty. The corollary was clear, even to Prussia herself, especially after she was not admitted to the Vienna Conference in the spring of 1855 despite her sometimes undignified efforts: Prussia now regarded herself as outside the concert. At the beginning of 1856, when the question arose of associating Prussia with the peacemaking, people spoke of Prussia's reentry (*rentrée*) into the European Concert (*concert européen*). This concern with the European Concert can be read most clearly in Austria. The return to the concert, so the Austrians argued, gave Prussia renewed weight in international politics but renewed her duties too.

Prussia's invitation must be seen as a matter of general diplomacy and also as a question of restoring legal relationships. Up to now this has not been done.[235] Since the participants interpreted this relationship differently and also pursued their own interests, Prussia was invited belatedly.

As early as the Franco-Austrian memorandum of 14 November 1855, the allies' modus procedendi towards Prussia was specified: when peace conditions were sent to Petersburg, Austria should ask Prussia for support.[236] "The degree of support which the court at Berlin would lend them might merit a role in the general negotiations." So the condition for Prussian admission was vaguely formulated assuming Russia accepted the ultimatum. If Russia refused, the allies agreed to consult about new measures against Russia, and Prussia should be admitted to these deliberations, "as soon as she, too, has broken relations with Russia." In his autograph letter of 16 December 1855 to King Frederick William, Francis Joseph sketched the first condition plainly;

the second was explained to Prussia during Edwin von Manteuffel's mission to Vienna at the beginning of January 1856.[237] The Prussian government was not inclined to fulfill the last condition immediately, but they did not tell Vienna right away. Since Russia accepted the ultimatum, it became irrelevant.

In the following weeks, the Prussian government's position became clearer. Manteuffel, agreeing with the King, warned against showing "a *longing* . . . to return to the concert,"[238] and adopted a firm stand against Britain's hostility and Austria's second condition so that Buol's description of the Prussian minister president as coming before the congress like a "poor amnestied sinner"[239] is completely inappropriate. Manteuffel was also in complete agreement with Bismarck, his emissary to the Frankfurt Diet.[240] At the end of January, he let it be known in Paris that he could not fulfill the condition that Prussia first adhere to the December Treaty.[241] He was ready to adopt the Five Points, but would make no further commitment: the Russians had been kind to Prussia and there was no reason to offend them now. To do so would needlessly endanger the object of Prussian policy during the last two years. Prussia did not refuse accession, Manteuffel wrote on 16 February to King Leopold,[242] if European interests demanded it; however, he saw no reason "to pay for entry, least of all by slighting our mighty eastern neighbor, whom we have handled carefully in the past. They may conclude peace without us, if they want to; we will not lose a man from our army or a penny from our treasury." He also had no cause to fear the isolation held up to him, for Prussia was already being wooed secretly.

This assertion was bold. Manteuffel was alluding to a Franco-Russian alliance, which Prussia might join as a third. But in fact such offers were not made; rather it was he who attempted to raise them in Paris, in the awareness of good relations with Russia and in the expectation of a Franco-Russian rapprochement. "We have 500,000 bayonets to back up our policy," he declared to the French chargé d'affaires, Baron Malaret,[243] "one is never isolated with such an imposing force. . . . Moreover we must not lose sight of the probability of an alliance between that Power and France, an alliance in which we certainly hope to be a partner."

Prussia never formally asked the belligerents for a role in the peace negotiations. However, at the end of January, she did declare her readiness to Vienna to sign preliminaries;[244] it was a way of trying to join the conferences. On 18 January, Buol had let it be known in London and Paris following Emperor Francis Joseph's wish that according to the Austrian interpretation, Prussia had fulfilled the conditions of the Franco-Austrian memorandum by interceding in Petersburg in support of the ultimatum; the moment had come to invite her to join the negotiations.[245] London's answer was negative:[246] Prussia had not effectively supported the ultimatum in Petersburg. She should not be rewarded for a diplomacy which had brought her such great commercial advantages. In the peace negotiations, she would act as Russia's advocate. The conclusion of the peace treaty would be the moment to invite her to accede.

From Paris came the rebuke that Prussia should first accept the commitments the allies had made among themselves.[247] Napoleon, who at the end of January distinctly disagreed with Britain over the special conditions of the fifth point, did not want to add a new controversy over Prussian admission. When Buol on 30 January transmitted Prussia's offer to sign the preliminaries to Paris and London, Napoleon seemed more accommodating after Hübner had also presented this reflection: if Prussia were excluded from the peace negotiations, Napoleon would throw her into Russia's arms.[248] He would reunite two members of the Northern Alliance and consolidate Russian influence in Berlin. The major result of the war for France had been to destroy this alliance, which had isolated France for decades; it would be put in doubt.

According to Hübner, the ghost of the Holy Alliance made a "great impression" on the Emperor. Napoleon agreed to consult London. Prussia would, however, have to support the British special conditions during negotiations and if negotiations failed, would have to adopt the same position as Austria.

The second condition, already known in Berlin, came to Prussia through the German Diet as well. In Frankfurt, on 7 February, the presidial representative, Count Rechberg, moved that the German Confederation should announce before Europe "that Germany as a whole, in agreement with Austria, *accepts the conditions and is prepared to uphold them,* so that the coming negotiations may firmly and lastingly build a general peace."[249] The motion was carried with the provision that the confederation should keep a "free hand with reference to special conditions to be brought forward by the belligerent powers."[250]

During the lengthy dispute over admission to the peace negotiations, Prussia faced the demand that she align with Austria. In case the alliance treaty were unconditionally accepted, this could mean that Austria would be the sole representative of German and Prussian interests—and also that Prussia would commit herself to the western powers to declare war on Russia in case negotiations failed. She could not accept either precondition: the first, because it was irreconcilable with her policy towards the German Confederation; the second, because she would admit in advance that Russia was guilty.

In Paris, even before the congress opened, Buol worked for Prussia's unconditional admission at his Emperor's request. He insisted that

Prussia must be admitted as a signatory of the Straits Convention, modification of which was envisioned in the third point. Clarendon and Napoleon acknowledged this. But then, on Clarendon's initiative, the negotiations were so arranged that before discussion of the third point, all other questions would be resolved, so that Prussia's admission would appear as pure formality, not full-fledged cooperation. For Prussia this was scarcely flattering. Her position at the congress was in fact subordinate to Sardinia's. Francis Joseph considered the result of his efforts "a sort of gentle slap."[251] Yet Buol personally must have rejoiced that Prussia, who tried to compete with Austria by every means for hegemony in Germany, was mortified at an international conference through British endeavors.

In the 10 March session, when the crucial questions had already been resolved, Walewski moved Prussia's admission. Manteuffel and Hatzfeldt were introduced in the 18 March session: according to Hübner, "in the middle of a deep silence and without their appearance occasioning any demonstration from either side."[252] Naturally, Prussia's role in this late phase of the congress was strictly limited. In fact Prussia was less significant than Sardinia and the Ottoman Empire.

Drafting the preamble, traditionally the place to assign the share of individual treaty partners in the negotiations and to establish their legal position, brought a controversy which again demonstrates British irritation with Prussia.[253] When Prussia was invited, Clarendon had assumed she would not join in the general negotiations but would merely come in for the decision about the Straits Convention of 1841. Walewski's letter, which Clarendon stupidly had not contested, was drawn up in such a way that Prussia could deduce a right to full participation, possibly even retroactively.[254] The first draft of the preamble drawn up by the Drafting Committee under Bourqueney and presented on 18 March again contained a phrase which might suggest that Prussia had taken part in the negotiations from the start.[255] A rather ludicrous dispute ensued; Clarendon baptized Walewski "Mr. Punch"[256] and both the Prussians and the British threatened to leave. Clarendon was able to change Walewski's mind after an audience with Napoleon, and on the twenty-fourth, after Clarendon, Walewski, and Buol had reached agreement, a text was given Prussia as an ultimatum which although mildly worded did confirm her extraordinary status.[257] Manteuffel, putting a good face on it, accepted. However, in subsequent sessions, he and Hatzfeldt participated fully, without objection from Clarendon. After all the only opportunity to have done this successfully had been in the letter of invitation. A draft preamble from Palmerston conceding Prussia only "assent to the treaty resulting from the solemn agreement of the other powers" arrived too late.[258]

Even if the Prussian plenipotentiaries did not materially influence subsequent negotiations, just the fact of their presence and their signing the peace treaty of 30 March formally confirmed Prussia's return to the European Concert.

For Prussia, however, the only important result of her Crimean War policy was not this formal act but maintenance of good relations with her mighty eastern neighbor. The awareness of having salvaged from the once-dominant Holy Alliance a good mutual relationship which might be binding in the future comes through again and again at the end of the Crimean War and in subsequent years both in Berlin and in Petersburg. Frederick William IV saw the conclusion of peace as a prerequisite for "restoration of our old and indeed blessed Triple Alliance."[259] Even though this expectation shows that he was thinking anachronistically and it was not shared in Petersburg, yet there too they celebrated continuation of the "dual entente." "Be confident, dear uncle," Alexander wrote the Prussian king, "I will be eternally grateful to you for the fine attitude which you maintained in Prussia during this whole crisis and which was so useful to us. May God reward you."[260] And Nesselrode believed that the entente between Prussia and Russia was unquestionably the keystone to developing Russia's relations with France. To Count Orlov, still in Paris, he wrote on 17 April: "Finally we must not forget that among the great powers, Prussia was the only one not hostile to us. Direct interests tie her to Russia, and we think that our relations with France, whatever shape they take, will only be useful if based on this entente."[261]

If one compares this testimony from 1856 with corresponding evidence from 1866 to 1870, one can agree at least in part with Ranke's judgment that "Frederick William IV's policy of neutrality formed the conditions [more accurately, one of the conditions] of the great result later accomplished."[262]

THE CONSTANTINOPLE CONFERENCE

In Constantinople, even before the Paris peace negotiations opened, a conference was held between the diplomatic representatives of the three allies and the two Ottoman ministers, Ali Pasha and Fuad Pasha, concerning the fourth point. In the literature on the Paris Congress it has either been overlooked or else only marginally noted. This is unjustifiable, since it took up one of the causes of the war, Russia's claim to protect the Orthodox population of the Ottoman Empire, and since it removed this problem through measures which involved transforming the basis of the empire.

The initiative to discuss the fourth point originated with the French minister Thouvenel, at the beginning of September 1855.[263] It was accepted by the Council of the Porte as well as by the three allied cabinets. Behind this lay the intention to exclude Russia from settlement of the fourth point. The process of drawing up and guaranteeing Christian religious rights within the empire involved more than just implementation of the fourth point. It was a question of political as well as religious equality of Christians and Moslems in the Ottoman Empire, and therefore implied renunciation of an important structural element in the imperial administration: the division of the population into two classes.

The Ottoman Empire consisted of a politically and socially privileged ruling class and a lower class without political and social rights. The first were the Moslems. They alone could bear arms and hold government positions. Their status was based on strict interpretation of the Koran. The second class was non-Moslem (Christians, Jews, and so on), the raya. Indeed within their communities (millets) the latter enjoyed varying degrees of autonomy, but they were excluded from military service in sign of subjection; they were limited in practicing their religion, were not permitted to testify in the courts (if suit were brought against a Moslem) and had to pay most of the taxes through a head tax (haraç). The principle of ethnic identity played no part in this class structure. Only in the nineteenth century was nationalism introduced from the outside, and together with European interference (claims to commercial privileges, protection of the Christian religious communities, and so on) and numerous inner flaws, it constituted the greatest danger to the empire's existence.

Since the end of the eighteenth century, perceptive Ottomans had recognized the need for fundamental reform. Under Sultan Mahmud (1808–1839) the first important decrees were issued ordering adoption of western military, administrative and financial institutions. The great reform edict of Gülhane 1839 stated for the first time the principle that all subjects were equal without religious discrimination. This was to counteract the centrifugal forces, strengthened by nationalism, which had won a first great victory in Greek independence.[264] It was hoped that emancipation of the previously underprivileged lower class would forge a stronger allegiance to the state and create a common imperial consciousness, "Ottomanism" or Osmanlılık. The greatest obstacle was Moslem opposition to political and social equivalence of "believers" with "unbelievers," who, according to Mohammed's law, did not even exist; paradoxically also, the millets objected because the Christians feared losing the protection of their respective foreign powers (Russia for the Orthodox, France for the Catholics) and because they, too, began to nurture national consciousness.

The Crimean War strengthened European influences on the Ottoman Empire. The allied powers which sent troops to the Balkans and the Crimea to protect Ottoman integrity continuously argued through their diplomats the necessity for inner regeneration through adoption of western cultural achievements. Significantly, Thouvenel introduced his proposal concerning the fourth point at the end of a conversation with Fuad Pasha about improving administrative institutions particularly by constructing telegraph lines. Improvement of the transportation system through train service was essential: railroad building began at that time, but during the war brought no practical result because of the enormous geographical and financial difficulties. It could be the prerequisite for governmental efficiency in the far-flung provinces, that is, for centralization, a main point of the reform program.

High-ranking Ottoman statesmen of the pre-Crimean War and Crimean War period, especially the great reformers Reshid Pasha and Fuad Pasha, believed that rational reorganization according to western models offered the sole chance of survival. The imperial edict (Hatt-ı Şerif) of Gülhane had been proclaimed in the hour of need, against Mehmed Ali's Egyptian army, and it was designed to win European intervention by emphasizing the willingness to reform. Yet, behind the vaguely known wartime discussions of the reform project in the Council of the Porte there existed a firm conviction that reforms must be executed in good faith and the opposition must be broken to demonstrate abroad the empire's survival capacity and to awaken a corresponding awareness in the interior. For this a transformation lasting several decades was necessary. The Crimean War powerfully pushed it on.[265]

After noncommittal preliminaries in November and December 1855, a series of intensive discussions occurred, beginning in January 1856, after transmission of the Austrian ultimatum to Petersburg, between Stratford de Redcliffe, Thouvenel, and Prokesch-Osten on the one side and Ali Pasha and Fuad Pasha on the other, about the way to settle the fourth point. In the first session, on 9 January[266] at the home of the grand vizier, the following problems were adduced: by Lord Redcliffe, non-Moslems' difficulties in acquiring and selling real property; by Thouvenel, the faulty composition of the Medjlis (meclis) or provincial and city councils and their insufficient control by the Porte; by Prokesch-Osten, the raya's religious freedom, limited in practice by many regulations, which could lead to situations where, for example, the simplest repair to a church or synagogue required express permission from the Porte. Ali Pasha admitted the justice of such complaints. Passing to the form of the projected stipulations, he expressed his expectation that they would not be mentioned in the peace treaty. They should be promulgated through a Hatt of the Sultan officially communicated to the powers. To Redcliffe's demand for word-by-word reproduction in the peace treaty, he declared with French and Austrian agreement that for the subjects of the empire, the reform must emanate from the Sultan, unless the Porte conceded what she had denied Russia in 1853 in the quarrel causing the war. The official communication of the Hatt to the powers already implied a right of supervision.

The three European representatives put together the proposals made in the first and following sessions as a draft of twenty-one paragraphs, which they laid before the Porte.[267] The majority of the demands were accepted without further discussion, but in certain cases they were amended. Differences of interpretation arose over two points: recognition of foreigners' right to acquire property and real estate and assessment of some consequences of religious freedom.

The first point involved principles regarded by the European representatives as a consequence of Ottoman inclusion in the jurisdiction of European international law, which especially since the French Revolution contained highly developed alien rights. The Ottoman ministers recognized the value of such stipulations for the material progress of the empire, but they demanded—in principle, not unreasonably—that they must originate in bilateral negotiations. It was a complicated matter, which could not be resolved quickly. It also involved the Europeans' legal position, which was already regulated in part by the capitulations (consular jurisdiction!). The matter was finally adopted in the draft agreement in the spirit of Ottoman objections.

The second difficulty originated with Lord Stratford's demand on behalf of his government, which seemed likely to impede promulgation of the reform edict, if it did not block it entirely. On 25 January Stratford transmitted a note dated 23 December 1855 in which he requested that the Sultan permit conversion to Christianity through a dispensation to his Moslem subjects.[268] The grand vizier, talking to Prokesch-Osten, called such a dispensation equivalent to abdication by the Sultan.[269] Prokesch supposed one of the motives was the proselytism of British missionary societies.[270] Even today, the grounds for Redcliffe's astonishing step cannot be determined in detail. Prokesch considered the British demand a flagrant contradiction to the joint goal of consolidating the Ottoman Empire. He asked his British colleague rhetorically whether if the Porte sought reciprocity, the Queen would permit her British subjects to convert to Catholicism or to Islam. Prokesch not unjustly assumed that no country in contemporary Europe permitted even as much religious tolerance as the Porte. The grand vizier's comment succinctly expressed Ottoman impotence with regard to her European protectors' demands: "This is how they treat the Ottoman Empire, which for forty years they have been saying they

wanted to save!"[271] After much pressure,[272] they succeeded in persuading Lord Stratford to renounce his demand, since Article 5 of the
joint draft already provided it in essentials. However, he made it a
condition that the Porte recognize his interpretation as stated in a note
he drew up—and afterwards modified several times.

Meanwhile, on 23 January the draft of the twenty-one articles was
accepted by the Grand Council of the Porte with some changes; it was
discussed a last time in the conference on 29 January. It was promulgated on 18 February, as an imperial edict entitled Hatt-ı Hümayun,
after some days' delay over Lord Redcliffe's battle of notes with the
Porte concerning the interpretation of Article 5 but right in time for
the opening of the Paris peace negotiations.[273]

With the emission of the Hatt-ı Hümayun and its "being placed on
record" by the Paris Congress,[274] three-quarters of a century of Russian
intervention in Ottoman internal affairs under the pretext of protecting the Greek Orthodox was ended. Laying aside the intentions behind
the Hatt, Russia could have agreed to everything except Articles 2 and
3.[275] In Article 2, the Sultan recognized just the *spiritual* privileges of
the Christian churches. Article 3 announced suppression of the *secular*
and judicial power of the Christian patriarchs over their fellow believers. Religious taxes of whatever sort should be abolished and replaced
by regular stipends for the clergy. The temporal administration of
church property should be transferred to a council consisting of clergy
and laity. Through such restructuring of the constitution of the church,
modelled on the principle of the separation of church and state,[276]
Russian power over the Patriarchate of Constantinople was to be
broken.

The catalogue of the remaining reforms is wide-ranging. Article 4
established equality of all cults and races. The old ruling principle of
the Ottoman Empire, the distinction between Moslems and non-
Moslems, was abolished in favor of the European idea of the state;
according to Prokesch, this should make possible "the tranquil symbiosis of different religions and races under the Moslem sovereign" in
order to maintain the empire.[277]

The following article drew the inescapable conclusion from this; in
fact it permitted changes from the Moslem faith even though it was
negatively expressed: "no one can be forced to change religion."
Thereby a fundamental Koranic law stating that renegades must suffer
death was eradicated. Whether this far-reaching commitment con-
tracted by the Sultan as spiritual head of Islam (Caliph, halife) would
help to consolidate the empire must remain doubtful; the Christian
missionary societies could now pursue their activities unhindered
among Moslems as well as Christians, and would introduce new elements of weakness into the empire. Later developments, such as the

sharp Moslem-Christian confrontation in Damascus 1860, bloodily verified fears that Prokesch for one expressed as early as 1856.

Some of the following articles confirmed civil equality between Christians and Moslems. Article 6 admitted Christians to all administrative positions. Article 8 provided mixed courts for disputes affecting Christians and Moslems. Articles 9 and 10 envisioned codification of commercial and criminal law; Article 13 proposed a new recruiting law concerning Christians. Further articles concerned reform of the police, provincial and municipal governments, tax collection, financial administration, founding of banks, improvement of instruction and the system of transportation.

Prokesch-Osten, who collaborated in drafting the reform edict, judged the Hatt thus: "The Sublime Porte has never promulgated a more thorough-going and radical act in the sense of restructuring that Empire. It could not be avoided any longer since the Ottomans' traditional existence has become incompatible with the demands of civilized Europe and with the position assigned by the Powers to that Empire in the European family. These reforms will either lead to reorganization of the Empire on principles similar to those of civilized States or to destruction of Moslem power."[278]

This ambiguity is echoed in scholarly judgments of the reform era, the so-called Tanzimat from 1839 to 1876,[279] in which the Hatt-ı Hümayun represented the most important step. Apart from criticism directed by contemporaries at the reform work, the Tanzimat is today considered either as a time when the attempted Europeanization of the Ottoman Empire failed or as a necessary transition indispensable to later efforts of the empire at the beginning of the twentieth century and of the republic after the First World War.

However, the nineteenth- and twentieth-century reforms must be understood as a whole, with Mahmud II at the beginning as the pioneer and Kemal Atatürk at the end as the achiever. In the nineteenth century, the Ottoman Empire faced the alternatives of extinction or of survival by accepting European ideas and civilized institutions. When Ottoman leaders chose the second path, they took on the almost impossible task of synthesizing Islamic and western culture. The coexistence of Islamic and European institutions especially in legal practice and education may have been a fatal dualism, but it was unavoidable once the choice was made. It must not be forgotten that the reforms introduced a process of secularization that blunted the originally harsh confrontation between Islam and Christianity. The state's energy—a fundamental, positive element in the reform—was forcefully exercised. While there was no noteworthy progress in the financial area—the public debt abroad led in 1875 to state bankruptcy—some integration was achieved in provincial administration, as has recently been shown by the example of Syria.[280] Rising nationalism did have a destructive effect in the European Balkans. But was the idea of Ottomanism unrealistic from the start? At least Ottoman statesmen had to try. Furthermore, one must not forget that without European intervention, neither Greek nor Rumanian nor Bulgarian independence would have been won in the nineteenth century. Although growing national consciousness existed there, in two other areas, Bosnia and Albania, ethnic consciousness was sharply overshadowed by a supranational imperial consciousness that derived from the widespread Islamization of earlier centuries. The separation of these areas from the empire (in 1878 and 1912) scarcely involved a striving for independence, but was brought about by the European great powers alone.

It is a legend scarcely taken seriously today that Kemal Atatürk was a revolutionary without predecessors. The history of modern Turkey is incomprehensible without the Europeanization of the Tanzimat. The Crimean War accelerated the process. The many destructive tendencies of the reform must be attributed in good part to the European powers, who pledged themselves in the peace treaty to renounce intervention, but who in fact interfered more strongly in the following decades than Russia had ever done.

THE CONGRESS AND INTERNATIONAL LAW

The Declaration of Maritime Law

The Paris Peace Treaty was the most important document of the *Ius publicum Europaeum* since the Final Act of the Vienna Congress.

However, we will not discuss the peace treaty as a significant source of international law, but will focus on the Paris Declaration of Maritime Law, signed by the congress participants on 16 April 1856, with the express goal of codifying the law of naval warfare. The earlier cherished reputation as the first modern codification of the laws of war does not entirely belong to the declaration; even before 1856 certain conditions of the law of maritime war had been taken up in peace treaties, as in Article 16 of the Paris Peace Treaty of 1763, and there had been proclamations about methods of economic warfare, such as blockade and contraband, as in the League of Armed Neutrality of 1780 to 1783. But it was the first general agreement about naval war valid even beyond the jurisdiction of European international law; in the following period, only the United States, Spain, and some South American countries remained aloof.

Walewski's interpretation of the declaration, as president of the congress, is interesting evidence of the Paris Congress's self-image. In the Austrian report it is said that Walewski, concluding his declaration on 8 April about Greece, Italy, and the Belgian press, expressed the wish that the congress might end its work with an act that people would greet unanimously throughout the world: "through a declaration, which would solemnly confirm the great principles of the law of naval warfare *that* correspond *to the spirit of the century and the progress of civilization.*"[281] According to the official protocol, Walewski said word for word: "The Congress of Westphalia sanctioned liberty of conscience,[282] the Congress of Vienna, abolition of the slave trade and freedom of river shipping. It would be worthy of the Congress of Paris to conclude overly lengthy disputes by laying the basis for a uniform maritime law in time of war."[283] Subsequently, Walewski enunciated four principles: abolition of privateering; no seizure of enemy goods under neutral flags (except war contraband); no seizure of neutral goods under enemy flags (except contraband); effectiveness of blockades.

According to the first principle, there could be no armed ships that were not warships. The right of privateering had previously allowed arming of merchant ships to capture enemy and neutral ships. Through letters of marque, issued by the home government, the proceedings of privateers had been legally covered. In fact, the European great powers had not drawn up any letters of marque since 1815, not even during the Crimean War. Point one of the declaration therefore formalized renunciation of a method of maritime war that had long since lost its meaning.

Principles two and three, which are complementary, favored neutral commerce by severely limiting the right of booty. Stopping and searching ships as well as the fate of the goods dispatched was now regulated according to the principle "free ships, free goods." Enemy goods, if under neutral flags, and neutral goods if under enemy flags were no longer liable to capture. Only war contraband was excluded. The Paris Declaration did not however define the term *contraband* precisely.

The fourth principle, already incorporated into the Treaty of Armed Neutrality and also recognized in British prize laws of the Napoleonic period, is particularly noteworthy because it hindered posing boundless *claims,* that is, it declared invalid the paper blockades often imposed in earlier centuries, and provided for establishment of blockades in reality, that is, the *actual* ("effective") investment of enemy coasts.

The immediate origin of the Paris Declaration cannot as yet be reconstructed in detail. According to the Russian scholar of international law, F. von Martens, Walewski had originally envisioned a statement with a single article concerning abolition of privateering.[284] Orlov, in whom Walewski confided, found this "a bit meager" and proposed some ideas about neutral shipping. Clarendon supposedly refused at first to go beyond the one article; but he finally let Walewski persuade him to include the other fundamental principles which Britain and France had proposed at the beginning of the war concerning procedures towards neutral shipping—that is, the principle of "free ships, free goods" and the principle of the effectiveness of blockades.[285] However, Orlov now discovered a passage humiliating to Russia: the abolition of privateering and the freedom of neutral commerce would be proclaimed "in conformity with the principles applied during the *present* war." This would suggest that measures taken during the Crimean War by the two enemies were to become permanent. He proposed to omit the section relating to the war. Otherwise it would be more appropriate to repeat Catherine II's proclamation of 1780.

Obviously they yielded to Orlov's wish, for no reference to the war is to be found either in Walewski's remarks on the subject in the 8 April session or in the final text.[286]

Concerning British motives in emitting the joint declaration at the beginning of the war and in concurring in the Paris Declaration, scholars were long uncertain, until H. W. Malkin in 1927 and Olive Anderson in 1960 investigated the British documents. Malkin demonstrated convincingly that the British government's statement abolishing privateering was to be attributed specifically to the wish to avoid disputes with neutrals such as the Scandinavian and German states and, above all, the United States. Britain also feared that the neutrals, in case Britain issued letters of marque, would help Russian privateers. A further reason was the effort to cooperate with the practices of her French ally. Britain originally intended to exclude neutrals from Russian coastal trade; but the French government refused to concur— thinking of a future war with Britain, when it might entrust its coastal trade to neutrals. Britain finally agreed, and they arrived at the identical declaration of 28 March 1854.[287] Significantly, Russia's overseas trade would not be fully interrupted by the British navy; for enemy goods in neutral ships would be unmolested.

Olive Anderson has shown a further motive for the British stand in not drawing up letters of marque or disturbing neutral commerce with Russia. Sir James Graham, First Lord of the Admiralty, next to Clarendon and the Admiralty's legal adviser, Stephen Lushington, the father of the idea, had decided that Russia's maritime commerce should not be suppressed. The bases of British power had changed since the Napoleonic wars: Britain as the greatest commercial and industrial nation was vitally interested in maintaining the flow of merchandise. On the other hand, neutrals would have to follow their duties strictly, and the British naval and economic war against Russia could be fought

out effectively with the remaining weapons of maritime war, blockade
and seizure of contraband.

The war bore out the justice of Graham's reflections. British imports
were never seriously disturbed, but Russia's foreign commerce was
profoundly affected through a strict blockade on the Black Sea and
Baltic coasts, although the damage could be at least partially repaired
by increased exchange of goods overland. At the end of the war, it
seemed appropriate that the principle of "freedom of the seas" should
be declared valid for the future, especially since according to British
reasoning, it would be combined with prohibition of privateering, in
order to repay the United States in her own coin. The United States
had tried during the war to isolate Britain by proposing to the smaller
naval powers an exchange of notes over recognition of the principle,
"free ships, free goods." Now Clarendon argued during the peace
negotiations that if concessions relating to the rights of neutrals in
maritime war could be joined to abolition of privateering, the United
States—favoring the first but rejecting the second—would be isolated.[288]

In April 1856, Anglo-American relations were so tense because of
various disputes (enlistment of American citizens in Canada for the
British Foreign Legion, strengthening of the British fleet in the North
Atlantic to capture Russian privateers, protection of Spanish Cuba
from American annexation, property disputes in Central America)
that war seemed imminent; tactical naval considerations therefore
played a greater role than ever. The United States never acceded to the
Declaration of Paris. In futile negotiations they demanded renunciation of the law of booty in naval war as a whole, that is, protection of
private property on the ocean, which was not affected by the declaration; they also pointed to the disadvantages for states with less important navies through abolition of privateering.[289]

Along with the Aland Convention, changed in the twentieth century
but not essentially affected, the Declaration of Paris is the only part of
the settlement still in force. Certainly its applicability to the great
maritime conflicts of the First and Second World Wars has proved
limited. Only the abolition of privateering remains unconditionally
effective. The definition of war contraband, omitted at Paris, was
specified by the London Conference on maritime law of 1908 to 1909,
but the conference's declaration was not ratified. The extension of the
definition in the world wars[290] and the application of the basic principles of "hostile infection"[291] and "continuous voyage"[292] have created
legal uncertainty and have rendered the Paris Declaration largely
inoperative on these points. Also, the principle of the effectiveness of
blockades was not observed in long-distance blockades (for example,

where areas on the high seas are closed and controlled with U-boats); to this extent the principle concerning short-range blockades has been destroyed.

International Arbitration

Besides the well-known attempt to codify the law of maritime war, the Paris Congress made a timid attempt, blocked at an early stage, to codify the law of peace or as it is called today, the law of prevention of war. It assumes a special significance in connection with the development of peacekeeping ideas because it is the first effort undertaken by the five great powers, the decisive political foci, to keep the peace through institutionalized conflict resolution. A short examination of the origins of this effort and the intentions of the participants will reveal it as a purely platonic declaration, although the outside world did not judge it so harshly.

In the last congress session but one, on 14 April, Clarendon referred to Article 8[293] of the peace treaty, which established the principle that in case of conflict, the Porte and one or more of the treaty partners should seek mediation from uninvolved treaty partners before recourse to force. Clarendon proposed that the present moment at the end of a war whose horror was still fresh would be the natural occasion to lend general applicability to the principle laid down in Article 8. This would erect a barrier to solving a conflict by force and would afford the participants an opportunity "to explain themselves and to reach agreement." The congress might draw up a resolution to this effect.

Most of the participants immediately announced reservations. Clarendon had already made the qualification that the resolution should not affect the "independence of the individual governments," and later described each power as "the sole judge of the demands of its honor and its interests." Governmental authority should not be limited, but rather a possibility should be created for calling into play another expedient of compromise in the event of conflict before recourse to force. Buol declared that he could not enter into any absolute commitment in his government's name which would limit Austrian independence. Walewski spoke in the same sense, but concluded that it was not a question of giving a pledge, but only of expressing a wish, which would not limit an independent power's normal freedom of action. When Cavour tried to turn to concrete applications and asked whether Clarendon's proposal would be valid for military intervention by a great power against de facto governments—as an example he named Austria's 1821 intervention in the Kingdom of Naples—Buol replied that the congress should avoid "irritating questions at its close," and reminded Cavour that that intervention was not an isolated Austrian action but the implementation of a great power agreement at the Conference of Laibach.

The resolution finally adopted merely referred to the congress's "wish" that states in conflict should appeal to the "good offices of a friendly power before resort to force." The obligation entailed remained far less than Article 8 of the peace treaty, which called for mediation in case of conflict between the Porte and another power, primarily Russia.

Temperley has commented on Clarendon's proposal in his short discussion of the Paris Congress.[294] In the 1920s the Paris Resolution of 14 April 1856 was often taken as a prototype of the League of Nations. Temperley points out that the plenipotentiaries did not take the proposal so seriously, and describes Clarendon's "source of inspiration" as mysterious. Other sources now available confirm Temperley's judgment but also offer a plausible explanation for the origins of Clarendon's initiative.

Buol wrote to the Emperor on 15 April: "the session tomorrow ought certainly to be the last, and it is high time to end our work. Impractical ideas are springing up. . . ."[295] Hübner's report assigned the British proposal no "practical value."[296] Clarendon suggested his plan to the other congress participants no later than 6 April. Napoleon's reaction is the more telling because it sheds light on his congress idea, which indeed is not identical to Clarendon's proposal but likewise started with *peaceful* solution of conflict. Clarendon wrote Palmerston that Napoleon agreed that the congress should come out in favor of mediation before a declaration of war; but he opposed any engagement which might fetter a government when its honor or its interest did "not brook delay. . . ."[297] According to his own testimony, Clarendon introduced his mediation proposal, like the other subjects discussed after 30 March—Greece, Italy, "Bomba's victims," Poland—not because of its intrinsic merit, but "[to] satisfy public opinion in England."[298]

The proposal, in the form Clarendon communicated to the Cabinet on 30 March, only mentioned arbitration. The idea of international arbitration was not new. Setting aside ancient Greek, Hellenic, and medieval practices, which cannot be regarded as precursors because of the different forms of government at that time, its origins could be ascribed to the beginning of the modern state system. With the formation and contiguous existence of national states recognizing reciprocal legal relations, a perception of interdependence emerged. From this the prototypes of modern arbitration can be discovered in scholars', international lawyers', and statesmen's plans for an organization of peace and a federation of states.[299] Such a plan had already appeared in connection with an earlier peace settlement. The Abbé de Saint

Pierre, secretary to the French delegation at the Peace Congress of Utrecht, had proposed a federation of all European states (except the Ottoman Empire) and a complicated procedure for ending disputes, which called for a court of arbitration in the last instance. He adopted similar earlier ideas, especially those of Henry IV, but the direct impulse came from the preceding war and the peace ending it.

In contrast to such intellectual constructs, appeal to arbitration in an international framework was first envisaged in the Jay Treaty, concluded in 1794 between Great Britain and the United States.[300] Proceeding from this pioneering treaty, the idea was extended and applied especially in Anglo-American legal jurisdiction.[301] So the history of international law provided a background for Clarendon's proposal.

What motivated Clarendon to drop the original concept of arbitration in favor of mediation cannot yet be determined, but it is not hard to guess. The realization of a plan, which would apply not only to signatories of the Paris Peace Treaty but to the whole community of states, would have demanded comprehensive codifying and organizing. The congress would have been obliged to hold many additional sessions. The participants were not agreed on this, except for Cavour (to the extent it could be connected with his dearest wish) and Clarendon himself. Clarendon expected much opposition on this question and on others, as his 31 March letter to Palmerston shows, and his fears were confirmed by the sessions of 4, 8, and 14 April. Probably he was quickly convinced by his colleagues in London or his associates in Paris to give up the complex expedient of arbitration in favor of less complicated mediation. The congress's "wish" on 14 April for conflict resolution by the "good offices" of an uninvolved party remained within the framework of traditional methods of settling disputes: in contrast to the judicial system necessary for arbitration, its exercise would not demand any new institutions, and general agreement could be expected.

Besides the background in international law for Clarendon's proposal, there is another chain of motives in intellectual history, which illuminate his "source of inspiration" even more sharply.

Clarendon himself had referred to the necessity of appeasing British "public opinion" without explaining what he meant. According to the official protocol, Walewski conjured up the "trends of our time" in concurring. Buol and Cavour reported explicitly on this. Buol attributed Clarendon's proposal to the wish "to do something nice for the friends of peace, who had addressed petitions to the members of the Congress."[302] Cavour wrote to Turin that Clarendon's proposal was supposed "to pay tribute to the pacifist spirit of certain religious sects in England."[303]

The phrase, "friends of peace," referred to the English "Peace Society," founded in 1816 in London by Quakers. According to its own organ *The Herald of Peace*,[304] the Peace Society sent three members to Paris in order to have an arbitration clause inserted into the treaty settlement by the British plenipotentiaries. Clarendon's mediation proposal can be traced directly to their activity.

The actions of the English Peace Society, which have not yet been investigated in detail for this period, must be seen in the context of a pacifist movement embracing all Europe and North America. The many peace societies founded in the first decades of the nineteenth century in the Anglo-Saxon world and in continental Europe are only one form of the nineteenth-century pacifist movement. They have their intellectual roots in the Enlightenment and go back in direct line to humanism. In Britain a view about peace based on rational economic grounds had developed along with the free trade doctrine of Adam Smith. Its adherents, like Jeremy Bentham, John Stuart Mill, and Richard Cobden, started from the tenets of utilitarianism and constructed a peace postulate based on economics: war is the worst human misfortune because it impedes the goal of the greatest possible happiness. Arms limitation became a dominant problem in the mid-nineteenth century due to the Industrial Revolution. This demand and the longing for equal treatment of everyone, including politically weak nations, set Cobden sharply against Palmerston's gunboat diplomacy and his principle of the European balance of power.

With the founding of different national peace societies, a rich literature was produced, mostly prize essays, about peacekeeping and international congresses.[305] In his 1842 essay, "War and Peace," William Jay, president of the American Federal Court of Justice, proposed that an arbitration clause should be included in all future treaties. Once this had taken hold, an international court of justice could be established. One year later the first of a series of peace congresses was held, and the previous literary ideas were summarized as resolutions. For example, the four resolutions of the 1848 Brussels Congress demanded abolition of war, international arbitration, an international congress to codify international law, and general disarmament. The British prime minister, Lord Russell, to whom the resolution was submitted, reacted favorably to arbitration. On 12 June 1849 a motion based on petitions from the English Peace Society was introduced into Parliament by Cobden; it called for arbitration treaties between Britain and other countries. It was the first time such a proposition had been presented to Parliament.

At the beginning of the Crimean War, the peace propaganda of Cobden, Bright, and the Peace Society was overwhelmed by popular anti-Russian feeling and enthusiasm for war. But the war inspired the

work of Francisque Bouvet, international law professor and admirer of
Napoleon: *Introduction à l'établissement d'un droit public européen;* it appeared first in 1855 and was reissued in 1856. It suggested a congress of
scholars to codify international law, examine international treaties, and
guarantee their maintenance. Also in an 1855 pamphlet, Bonn professor Peter Kaufmann proposed founding an academy of international
law, to concern itself with further evolution of international law and
also with settlement of disputes.[306]

These demands for international arbitration, congresses, and codification of international law, posed again and again in previous years,
demonstrate that the Paris Congress merely expressed a prevailing
opinion, in including a wish for peaceful resolution of disputes, although not in the form of an international court but merely through
diplomatic mediation in circumstances qualified by the reference to
honor and interests. In Britain, Gladstone explained that now for the
first time war would be officially proscribed by the civilized powers.[307]

Nonetheless, contemporary statesmen generally judged the resolution very harshly. Participants' opinions have been mentioned. The
resolution was not a suitable instrument for implementing Napoleon's
program. Napoleon believed that only a major congress would be
practicable for this; with it, he hoped to accomplish what in our century
is called "peaceful change," that is, to resolve the tension between
stability and movement without war and to eliminate trouble spots
through peaceful recasting of existing relationships.

For Buol, representing a status quo power, the postulate of mediation was superfluous, since mediation was a traditional and obviously
appropriate method for prevention or resolution of military conflict,
and his policy before and during the war had attempted repeatedly to
settle the dispute this way.

For Cavour, representing a forward-moving power, and supposing
himself in alliance with benevolent Britain and revisionist France, a
peaceful arrangement with hateful Austria seemed fruitless. While he,
like Clarendon, made a gesture to a utopian "religious sect," within
himself he was firmly resolved to declare war on Austria as soon as
possible. "War doesn't frighten me," he explained to Clarendon while
the congress was sitting. "We are determined to wage it to the limit, *to the
knife.*"[308]

Even disregarding Bismarck, who agreed with Cavour,[309] Prussian
politicians assigned no value to the Paris Resolution. Leopold von
Gerlach attributed military conflicts to causes which could not be removed: "Peace will bring many anxieties," he wrote Manteuffel on 15
April, "from which the proposed arbitration will not free us. War does
not come from tangled legal relationships, but from passions."[310]

In spite of such generally dominant scepticism, behind which in the end stood approval of war as a means of conflict resolution, the Paris Resolution had a certain influence. Subsequent nineteenth-century wars were preceded by mediation attempts; we do not yet know whether this came in part from the Paris Resolution. There were occasional references to it after 1856 in the press.[311] The organized peace movement expanded with further peace leagues, many national and international peace congresses, and literary and legal discussions. To be sure, the Berlin Congress did not discuss international arbitration or other peacekeeping methods, since the participating powers had agreed on French initiative before the meeting to consider only subjects arising directly from the Russo-Turkish War and since Bismarck watched carefully to see that points not on the agenda, such as socialism or international disarmament, should not be treated. Yet public discussion of peacekeeping possibilities won a first great victory two decades later, when Tsar Nicholas II invited the governments of the world to the Hague Peace Conference, which concluded with an "agreement for peaceful resolution of international conflicts." The Paris Resolution of 1856 and the first Hague Peace Conference of 1899 are directly related by way of the Brussels Conference of 1874. This is clear in comparing the wording of the Paris protocol and the Russian letter of invitation[312] and is also reflected in the agreement.

Notes

Full citations appear in the bibliography.

II. The Peace Negotiations

1. See above n. 226 (part one). See also Paul W. Schroeder, *Austria, Great Britain, and the Crimean War*, pp. 332–38, 347–50.

2. Colloredo to Buol, London, 4 January 1856 (*Akten zur Geschichte des Krimkriegs*, ed. Winfried Baumgart, I, 3: 216–17. Hereinafter cited as AGKK).

3. Colloredo to Buol, London, 16 January 1856 (HHSA, PA VIII 42 f. 31).

4. Hübner to Buol (secret), Paris, 19 January 1856 (AGKK I, 3: 269).

5. See Greville's diary entry of 22 January 1856 ([Charles Cavendish Fulke] Greville, *The Greville Memoirs 1814–1860*, 7: 193): "The Press has succeeded in inoculating the public with such an eager desire for war that there appears a general regret at the notion of making peace." For the more recent literature on public opinion during the Crimean War, see Winfried Baumgart, "Probleme der Krimkriegsforschung," pp. 388–94.

6. Cited by François Charles-Roux, *Alexandre II, Gortchakoff et Napoléon III*, p. 78. Further journalistic opinions *ibid.*, pp. 78–79.

7. See n. 4.

8. Palmerston to Seymour, 25 January 1856 (Harold Temperley, "Austria, England, and the Ultimatum to Russia 16. Dec. 1855," p. 635).

9. *Ibid.*

10. Palmerston to Queen Victoria, London, 17 January 1856 (Victoria, *The Letters of Queen Victoria,* 3: 166). See also n. 4.

11. Despatch (draft) Buol to Hübner, Vienna, 9 January 1856 (HHSA, PA IX 54 f. 7–9).

12. Telegram (copy) Buol to Hübner/Colloredo, Vienna, 20 January 1856 (AGKK I, 3: 271, 273).

13. Telegram (copy) Buol to Hübner/Colloredo, Vienna, 22 January 1856 (HHSA, PA IX 54 f. 63).

14. Lettre particulière Buol to Hübner, Vienna, 18 January 1856 (AGKK I, 3: 264–65).

15. Granville to Canning, 21 February 1856 (Edmond Fitzmaurice, *The Life of Granville George Leveson Gower,* 1: 167). See also Hübner to Buol, Paris, 27 January 1856 (AGKK I, 3: 307).

16. Hübner to Buol (secret), Paris, 19 January 1856 (AGKK, I, 3: 207, 267).

17. Telegram Hübner to Buol, Paris, 24 January 1856 (HHSA, PA IX 52 f. 86); Granville to Canning, London, 26 January (Fitzmaurice, 1: 146).

18. On 19 January Walewski first informed Hübner that he wanted to send the communication through the Russian representative at the German Diet in Frankfurt, Brunnov: Hübner to Buol, Paris, 19 January 1856 (HHSA, PA IX 52 f. 68). See also lettre particulière Buol to Hübner, Vienna, 1 February 1856 (AGKK I, 3: 330 No. 189).

19. The text is now printed in AGKK I, 3: 365–68. It is analyzed by Bernhard Unckel, *Österreich und der Krimkrieg,* pp. 244–46. I cannot altogether agree with Unckel's judgment, that the instruction is "at all points" the handiwork of the Emperor and more than any other document, testifies "to how great an extent Austrian policy in the period of the Crimean War was his, the Emperor's, own policy." Technically, the instruction was drafted by Buol, as is proved by the protocol of the ministerial council of 11 February (*ibid.,* p. 369). As for the content, a passage like that which speaks of "improvements in the spirit of the age" in the adminstration of the Danubian principalities could only come from Buol, who did not hide from himself the necessity of remedying abuses in the provinces.

20. Queen Victoria to King Leopold, Windsor, 29 January 1856 (Victoria, 3: 169). Italics original.

21. Walewski to Napoleon, Paris, 11 September 1855 ([Alexandre-Florian-Joseph Colonna, Count Walewski], "Les Papiers inédits du Comte Walewski," p. 488).

22. Paris, 9 November 1855 (Peter von Meyendorff, *Ein russischer Diplomat an den Höfen von Berlin und Wien,* 3: 211 No. 525).

23. Cited by F. Heinrich Geffcken, *Zur Geschichte des orientalischen Krieges 1853–1856,* p. 219.

24. See about this Arnim to Manteuffel, Vienna, 19 September 1855 (Otto Freiherr von Manteuffel, *Preussens auswärtige Politik 1850 bis 1858,* 3: 161); Granville to Clarendon, Paris, 7 October 1855 (Fitzmaurice, 1: 123); Bismarck to Leopold von Gerlach (about conversation with King William of Württem-

berg), Frankfurt, 21 December 1855 ([Prince Otto von] Bismarck, *Die gesammelten Werke,* XIV, 1: 424–25): "Abroad the distrust aroused against Austria may be the point on which even the belligerents are at one; for example the western powers and Russia are equally determined *not* to negotiate *in Vienna.*" Italics original.

25. Granville to Canning, 17 January 1856 (Fitzmaurice, 1: 144); Bismarck to Manteuffel, Frankfurt, 25 January 1856 (Bismarck, 2: 99 No. 110); Clarendon to Hudson, London, 20 December 1855 (*Le Relazioni diplomatiche fra la Gran Bretagna e il Regno di Sardegna,* series III: 1848–1860, ed. Federico Curato, 98: 193. Hereinafter cited as Fonti): "Whenever negotiations are recommended we of course do *not* intend that they shall be held at Vienna; some small neutral town must be selected for the purpose." Italics original.

26. See above n. 306 (part one).

27. Metternich to Buol, 18 November 1853 ([Klemens Wenzel Nepomuk Lothar von] Metternich, *Briefe des Staatskanzlers Fürsten Metternich-Winneburg an den österreichischen Minister des Allerhöchsten Hauses und des Äussern, Grafen Buol-Schauenstein aus den Jahren 1852–1859,* p. 148 No. 101, supplement to No. 100). The second English plenipotentiary, Lord Cowley, later deplored the choice of Paris because of the diversions which the French capital offers: "the thing to have done would have been to have them [the conferences] in some dull German town, where there would have been no amusements and occupations, and no intrigues, and where they would have applied themselves vigorously to their work in order to get it done as quickly as possible." (Greville's diary entry of 1 March 1856, Greville, 7: 209.)

28. Nesselrode to Gorchakov (copy), Petersburg, 18 January 1856 (HHSA, PA X 44 f. 33–34).

29. Text: *Recueil des traités de la France,* ed. [Alexandre Jean Henri] de Clerq, 7: 21–22. About the exclusion of the Sardinian chargé in Vienna from signing the protocol see Ennio Di Nolfo, *Europa e Italia nel 1855–1856,* pp. 201–6.

30. Hausmann's sketch traces the institution of the preliminary peace only back to the end of the seventeenth century (Preliminary Treaty of Berlin between Denmark and Holland of 6 July 1688). However, it can be traced back at least to the prelude to the peace of Westphalia (for example the Preliminary Treaty of Hamburg of 1641). In the first half of the eighteenth century, the conclusion of a preliminary peace became the rule. On the procedures related to two peace settlements of the twentieth century, see Winfried Baumgart, "Brest-Litovsk und Versailles," pp. 601–3 (or pp. 62–63).

31. Buol/Hübner to Francis Joseph, Paris, 24 February 1856 (AGKK I, 3: 410).

32. Buol/Hübner to Francis Joseph, Paris, 26 February 1856 (*ibid.,* p. 438).

33. See above pp. 67–68. See also Queen Victoria to King Leopold, Windsor, 29 January 1856 (Victoria, 3: 169).

34. Buol/Hübner to Francis Joseph, Paris, 23 March 1856 (AGKK I, 3: 538); Buol to Francis Joseph, Paris, 9 March 1856 (*ibid.,* p. 489).

35. Prince Albert to Stockmar, London, 13 April 1856 (Theodore Martin, *The Life of His Royal Highness the Prince Consort,* 3: 481; see also *ibid.,* p. 482). At the end of February 1856, 22,000 sick notices were sent in from the French army: Greville's diary entry of 5 March 1856 (Greville, 7: 212); Clarendon to

Stratford de Redcliffe, 25 April 1856 (Stanley Lane-Poole, *The Life of the Right Honourable Stratford Canning Viscount Stratford de Redcliffe*, 2: 436).

36. See n. 32; further De Clerq, 7: 23.

37. Suspension of hostilities is not identical with armistice. The use of the relevant terms in the official protocol of the first session (De Clerq, 7: 23–24) is ambiguous. Also the armistice concluded between Bismarck and Favre on 28 January 1871 is inaccurately headed "Convention between France and Germany concerning the suspension of hostilities"; however, in the individual articles, the word *armistice* appears correctly.

38. Text: De Clerq, 7: 56–58. On pp. 58–59 an agreement of 26 March 1856 on prolongation is also given.

39. De Clerq, 7: 24, 56.

40. Clarendon obviously referred to the axiom going back to Cicero, "there is no middle ground between peace and war," which has played a significant role in modern international law, for example, in Grotius, Pufendorf, and Vattel.

41. The protocol of the first session reads (De Clerq, 7: 24): "The Plenipotentiaries decide, furthermore, that the armistice will be without effect on blockades which have been established *or will be established.*" Italics mine.

42. A more accurate analysis must await a later, more comprehensive presentation, for which extensive archival researches are projected. In the previous literature, the course of the negotiations has best been summarized in Geffcken, pp. 222–92; Charles-Roux, pp. 81–108; Harold Temperley, "The Treaty of Paris of 1856 and its Execution;" Schroeder, *Austria, Great Britain*, pp. 357–67; John Shelton Curtiss, *Russia's Crimean War*, pp. 502–29. Characterization of the individual delegates is in Di Nolfo, *Europa*, pp. 226–51.

43. 11 February 1856 ("K istorii Parižskogo mira 1856 g.," ed. M. Ja. Bessmertnaja, p. 16). The Russian Foreign Ministry papers dealing with the Paris Peace Congress, which were published in Russian translation in the *Krasnyj Archiv* shortly before the beginning of the Second World War, have not yet been assessed. They will be extensively exploited here. Curtiss (*Russia's Crimean War*, pp. 502–29) used only unpublished Russian documents.

44. Bismarck to Leopold von Gerlach, Frankfurt, 26 February 1856 (Bismarck, XIV, 1: 434).

45. Nesselrode to Orlov, 29 February 1856 ("K istorii Parižskogo mira," p. 24). See also Geffcken, p. 227; Temperley, "Paris," p. 404 (there wrongly dated 27 February).

46. "K istorii Parižskogo mira," p. 15.

47. Hübner to Buol (secret; concerning conversation with Napoleon), Paris, 19 January 1856 (AGKK I, 3: 268); Hübner to Buol (about conversation with Walewski), Paris, 19 January 1856 (HHSA, PA IX 52 f. 67–69).

48. Nesselrode to Orlov, 29 February 1856 ("K istorii Parižskogo mira," p. 24).

49. Buol to Francis Joseph, Paris, 24 February 1856 (AGKK I, 3: 415).

50. Temperley, "Paris," p. 404.

51. Buol to Francis Joseph, Paris, 28 February 1856 (AGKK I, 3: 448–50).

52. Orlov to Nesselrode, 11 March 1856 ("K istorii Parižskogo mira," pp. 39–43).

53. Buol/Hübner to Francis Joseph, Paris, 7 March 1856 (AGKK I, 3: 480–81).

54. See n. 52; further Buol/Hübner to Francis Joseph, Paris 9 March 1856 (*ibid.*, pp. 484–86).

55. See n. 52; further Buol/Hübner to Francis Joseph, Paris, 12 March 1856 (*ibid.*, pp. 502–3); De Clerq, 7: 38 (protocol of the 14 March session).

56. Temperley, "Paris," p. 406; Temperley, "Austria," p. 637.

57. See below p. 195.

58. See also Unckel, pp. 261–62 (with a differently slanted interpretation).

59. Buol/Hübner to Francis Joseph, Paris, 9 March 1856 (AGKK I, 3: 488). According to Hübner's testimony ([Joseph Alexandre von] Hübner, Count Hübner, *Neuf ans de souvenirs d'un ambassadeur d'Autriche à Paris sous le Second Empire 1851–1859*, 1: 396, diary entry of 22 February 1856; p. 413, diary entry of 6 April 1856), the joint reports were drafted by him, Hübner, but bore the signatures of both. In addition, Buol regularly sent his own letters to the Emperor.

60. Francis Joseph to Buol, Vienna, 13 March 1856 (AGKK I, 3: 509).

61. Buol/Hübner to Francis Joseph, Paris, 24 February 1856 (*ibid.*, p. 412).

62. Orlov to Nesselrode, 11 March 1856 ("K istorii Parizskogo mira," p. 32).

63. *Ibid.*, pp. 32–33. Further Cavour to Cibrario, 2 March 1856 ([Camillo Benso] Cavour, *Cavour e l'Inghilterra*, 7: 239–40); the official protocol of the third session of 1 March 1856 (De Clerq, 7: 27); also Curtiss, *Russia's Crimean War*, pp. 509–10.

64. Orlov to Nesselrode, 2 March 1856 ("K istorii Parizskogo mira," p. 30).

65. See above p. 102.

66. Buol/Hübner to Francis Joseph, Paris, 2 March 1856 (AGKK I, 3: 464).

67. 18 January 1856 (Carl Hallendorff, *Konung Oscar I's politik under Krimkriget*, pp. 118–19 No. 50); see also King Oscar to Napoleon, 18 January 1856 (*ibid.*, pp. 119–20 No. 51).

68. King Oscar's special instructions for Manderström, Stockholm, 12 February 1856 (*ibid.*, pp. 135–39). Of course Manderström acted behind the scenes; Sweden was not a participant in the negotiations.

69. Nesselrode to Orlov, 29 February 1856 ("K istorii Parizskogo mira," p. 26).

70. Buol/Hübner to Francis Joseph, Paris, 2 March 1856 (AGKK I, 3: 462); Clarendon to Palmerston, Paris, 2 March 1856 (Fonti, 98: 245).

71. Buol/Hübner to Francis Joseph, Paris, 29 March 1856 (AGKK I, 3: 557–58).

72. *Recueil des traités et conventions conclus par la Russie avec les puissances étrangères*, 15: 288–90; hereinafter cited as F. de Martens. See also Geffcken, p. 258.

73. Temperley, "Paris," p. 396.

74. Reproduced in Evgenij Viktorovič Tarle, *Krymskaja vojna*, 2: 512–13.

75. Protocol of the session in De Clerq, 7: 28–29. Italics mine.

76. Orlov to Nesselrode, 11 March 1856 ("K istorii Parizskogo mira," pp. 34–45).

77. See n. 75 and n. 76; further Buol/Hübner to Francis Joseph, Paris, 5 March 1856 (AGKK I, 3:474–75).

78. De Clerq, 7: 29–30.
79. See Temperley, "Paris," pp. 407–8; Geffcken, pp. 237–41 (both based on British documents).
80. See the annex to Protocol No. 10 (De Clerq, 7: 41); further *ibid.*, p. 71, the text of the Russo-Turkish Convention of 30 March 1856.
81. See the special convention appended to the main treaty concerning closure of the Straits dated 30 March 1856 (De Clerq, 7: 69–70).
82. For the distinctions between the terms *pacification, demilitarization,* and *neutralization,* see *Wörterbuch des Völkerrechts*, ed. Karl Strupp, 1: 165.
83. Buol to Hübner/Colloredo, Vienna, 3 December 1855 (AGKK I, 3:151). See also Schroeder, *Austria, Great Britain,* pp. 343–46, 351–53.
84. Prokesch-Osten was, strictly speaking, not ambassador, but internuncio at the Sublime Porte.
85. "Projet concernant le 1er point de garantie arrêté entre les Représentans des trois Puissances et ceux de la S. Porte dans la réunion du 11 Février" (HHSA, PA XII 56 f. 256–66). See also AGKK I, 3: 372.
86. Note (copy) by Prokesch-Osten for Thouvenel, 10 March 1856 (AGKK I, 3: 500; partially published by L. Thouvenel, *Trois années de la question d'Orient,* pp. 6–7); Prokesch-Osten to Buol, Constantinople, 13 March 1856 (AGKK I, 3: 511–24).
87. Werner to Buol, Vienna, 25 February 1856 (AGKK I, 3: 418–22, 424–27). Italics original.
88. Recently Schroeder has challenged the legend that during the war Buol sought to achieve Austrian dominion over the principalities in some form or other (see on this point Baumgart, "Probleme," p. 248). I agree in essentials with his case, and extend it to the period of the Paris peace negotiations. See also my introduction in AGKK I, 3: 30–35; Winfried Baumgart, "Die Aktenedition zur Geschichte des Krimkriegs."
89. In Unckel's important work, no difference in principle is seen between Buol on the one side and Hess on the other, but only a difference in tactics. Buol's compliance in Paris is described as resignation; the demands he brought forward during the negotiations are attributed to lack of realism. See Unckel, pp. 260–61, 267–68.
90. Baumgart, "Aktenedition"; also Unckel, pp. 252–53.
91. Werner to Buol, Vienna, 25 February 1856 (AGKK I, 3: 421); Francis Joseph to Buol, Vienna, 13 March 1856 (*ibid.,* p. 509–10).
92. Buol to Francis Joseph, Paris, 9 March 1856 (*ibid.,* p. 490).
93. Buol/Hübner to Francis Joseph, Paris, 9 March 1856 (*ibid.,* pp. 486–87).
94. See the protocol in De Clerq, 7: 74–75. For the following, Buol/Hübner to Francis Joseph, Paris, 6 April 1856 (AGKK I, 3: 570–74).
95. Published in *Corespondența lui Coronini din Principate,* ed. Ion I. Nistor. See also Unckel, pp. 250–51.
96. See Winfried Baumgart, "Das Kaspi-Unternehmen."
97. See n. 94.
98. Buol to Francis Joseph, Paris, 6 April 1856 (AGKK I, 3: 576–78). See also Unckel, pp. 267–68 (with a different interpretation, which emerges from a different approach).

99. See for this point in general Gordon A. Craig, *War, Politics, and Diplomacy*, p. 16.

100. Entry of 6 April 1856 (Hübner, 1: 413–14).

101. Egon Caesar Count Corti, *Mensch und Herrscher*, p. 173.

102. Friedrich Engel-Janosi, *Der Freiherr von Hübner 1811–1892*, pp. 210–11.

103. Di Nolfo, *Europa*, pp. 265–66.

104. For detailed treatment of this point, see Di Nolfo, *Europa*, pp. 263–75; Umberto Marcelli, *Cavour diplomatico*, pp. 184–93.

105. Unckel, p. 207.

106. Walewski, p. 506. See also Schroeder, *Austria, Great Britain*, pp. 360–63.

107. See the protocol in De Clerq, 7: 33–34.

108. In this sense a telegram of Buol's of 10 March 1856 to Vienna (HHSA, PA XII 220 f. 58): "In order to hasten its conclusion we will limit ourselves in the peace treaty to laying down the principles."

109. Clarendon to Palmerston, 6 [?] March 1856 (Martin, 3: 465–66).

110. Geffcken, p. 244.

111. Buol/Hübner to Francis Joseph, Paris, 9 March 1856 (AGKK I, 3: 486): "Count Walewski, without giving any reason, proposes the union of Wallachia and Moldavia. Lord Clarendon agrees with this proposition, basing it on the will of the Moldavian-Wallachian nation. Count Walewski says that he forgot to mention this reason, drawn from the will of the nation, that he adopts it and advances it as the starting-point for his proposition."

112. A. J. P. Taylor, *The Struggle for Mastery in Europe 1848–1918*, p. 81 n. 1.

113. Di Nolfo, *Europa*, pp. 498–99.

114. The diplomatic bag from London was in Paris within twenty-four hours, as relevant sources hitherto published demonstrate (see for example Di Nolfo, *Europa*, p. 501 No. 35, p. 504 No. 36; Cavour, 7: 225 No. 228, 229 No. 292, 268–69 No. 334, 271 No. 337, 367 No. 455, 371 No. 447, 377 No. 455).

115. Cavour to d'Azeglio, 8 March 1856 (Cavour, 7: 285). See also Cavour to d'Azeglio, Paris, 9 March 1856 (*ibid.*, p. 290).

116. See no. 109.

117. D'Azeglio to Cavour, London, 2 March 1856 (Cavour, 7: 250); Cavour to d'Azeglio, 7 March 1856 (*ibid.*, p. 275).

118. Buol/Hübner to Francis Joseph, Paris, 9 March 1856 (AGKK I, 3: 487).

119. Telegram Werner to Buol, Vienna, 9 March 1856 (HHSA, PA XII 219 f. 26).

120. Granville to Canning, London, 22 March 1856 (Fitzmaurice, 1: 172).

121. Protocol of the sessions in De Clerq, 7: 30–31, 36–37. See also Schroeder, *Austria, Great Britain*, pp. 359–60, 363–64.

122. Buol/Hübner to Francis Joseph, Paris, 13 March 1856 (AGKK I, 3: 511–17); Buol to Francis Joseph, Paris, 13 March 1856 (*ibid.*, pp. 518–19).

123. Telegram Werner to Buol, Vienna, 16 March 1856 (HHSA, PA XII 219 f. 123–24). See also AGKK I, 3: 525–26.

124. De Clerq, 7: 40–41.

125. The Conference of Constantinople, which was supposed to settle the fourth point without Russia's participation, and the general problems arising for the Ottoman Empire from the fourth point, will be treated below in a special section (pp. 158–64).

126. Buol/Hübner to Francis Joseph, Paris, 19 and 25 March 1856 (AGKK I, 3: 534, 549); Buol to Francis Joseph, Paris, 26 March 1856 (*ibid.*, p. 552). See also Alexandre de Jomini, *Étude diplomatique sur la guerre de Crimée (1852 à 1856)*, 2: 410–11.

127. Prokesch-Osten to Buol, Constantinople, 24 March 1856 (AGKK I, 3: 546–47). See also Roderic H. Davison, "Ottoman Diplomacy at the Congress of Paris (1856) and the Question of Reforms"; Curtiss, *Russia's Crimean War,* pp. 514–16.

128. Buol/Hübner to Francis Joseph, Paris, 25 March 1856 (AGKK I, 3: 549).

129. See Protocol No. 14 of the session of 25 March 1856 (De Clerq, 7: 45–46).

130. German translation in *Aktenstücke zur orientalischen Frage,* ed. J. von Jasmund, 2: 479–81.

131. For many details about the Paris Congress, see the contemporary account of Édouard Gourdon, *Histoire du Congrès de Paris,* pp. 478–527. See also Pierre Rain's essay commemorating the centenary of the Quai d'Orsay, "Le Centenaire du Quai d'Orsay et le Congrès de Paris."

132. Schweizer to Rüdt, Paris, 16 and 24 February 1856 (GLA, Abt. 48, No. 2051 f. 117, 144–47); Cavour to Cibrario, 17 February 1856 (Cavour, 7: 184–86).

133. Buol/Hübner to Francis Joseph, Paris, 24 February 1856 (AGKK I, 3: 411).

134. Buol/Hübner to Francis Joseph, Paris, 28 February 1856 (*ibid.*, p. 445).

135. Buol/Hübner to Francis Joseph, Paris, 16 March 1856 (*ibid.*, pp. 527–28).

136. Buol/Hübner to Francis Joseph, Paris, 24 February 1856 (*Le Relazioni diplomatiche fra l'Austria e il regno di Sardegna,* ed. Franco Valsecchi, 67: 311; hereinafter cited as *Relazioni.* AGKK I, 3: 413).

137. See Di Nolfo, *Europa,* pp. 275–78, 441–42; Marcelli, pp. 247–49.

138. See the corresponding sections in Protocols No. 7 (De Clerq, 7: 35), No. 8 (*ibid.*, p. 36), No. 9 (*ibid.*, pp. 38–39), No. 12 (*ibid.*, p. 43).

139. Nesselrode to Orlov, 29 February 1856 ("K istorii Parižskogo mira," pp. 24–25).

140. See above p. 66.

141. Brunnov to Nesselrode, 19 February 1856 ("K istorii Parižskogo mira," p. 19); Orlov to Nesselrode, 2 March 1856 (*ibid.*, p. 31).

142. Because of disagreements between Walewski and Clarendon about the admission of Prussia (see below pp. 157–58) the expedient was adopted of publicly declaring the tenth session, of 18 March, the tenth and eleventh session. See Buol/Hübner to Francis Joseph, Paris, 23 March 1856 (AGKK I, 3: 537–38).

143. Temperley, "Paris," p. 406 n. 50. The discussion in the twelfth session concerning the preamble of the treaty, for example, which is recorded in the protocol in only four lines, in fact lasted many hours. See the report mentioned in the preceding note.

144. Buol/Hübner to Francis Joseph, Paris, 9 March 1856 (AGKK I, 3: 486).

145. Buol/Hübner to Francis Joseph, Paris, 9 April 1856 (*ibid.*, pp. 589, 590).

146. De Clerq, 7: 83.

147. Buol/Hübner to Francis Joseph, Paris, 14 April 1856 (AGKK I, 3: 602 No. 355).

148. See Harold Temperley and Lillian M. Penson, *A Century of Diplomatic Blue Books 1814–1914*, p. 237. In 1871, indeed, documents concerning the Paris Peace Treaty of 1856 were published (*Correspondence Respecting the Treaty of March 30, 1856*, London, 1871). They related, however, not to correspondence originating in the year 1856 (concerning the peace negotiations), but in the years 1870 to 1871 (concerning the abrogation of the Black Sea clause).

149. Raoul Genet, *Traité de diplomatie et de droit diplomatique*, 3: 2–8; Marcel Sibert, "Quelques aspects de l'organisation de la technique des conférences internationales," pp. 394–401; Marcel Sibert, *Traité de droit international public*, 2: 98–102. See also Winfried Baumgart, *Vom Europäischen Konzert zum Völkerbund*, pp. 8–10.

150. *Le Congrès de Vienne et les traités de 1815*, ed. M. Capefigue, p. 1743.

151. Metternich to Hübner, Vienna, 6 April 1858 (Maurice Bourquin, *Histoire de la Sainte Alliance*, pp. 477–78).

152. "L'Europe s'est remaniée elle-même dans son territoire, soit dans ses institutions, soit dans ses dynasties."

153. Buol to Francis Joseph, Paris, 24 February 1856 (AGKK I, 3: 413–16; extract in *Relazioni*, 67: 310.

154. Buol/Hübner to Francis Joseph, Paris, 9 March 1856 (AGKK, I, 3: 487).

155. Napoleon to Walewski, 5 March 1856 (Françoise de Bernardy, "Le Congrès de Paris [février-avril 1856]," p. 217). See also above n. 106. The passage quoted here is not given in Walewski, p. 506.

156. Buol to Francis Joseph, Paris, 13 March 1856 (AGKK I, 3: 520).

157. Werner to Buol (*ibid.*, p. 569 No. 329).

158. See above n. 76.

159. Orlov to Nesselrode, 2 March 1856 ("K istorii Parizhskogo mira," pp. 27–30).

160. Nesselrode to Orlov, 15 March and 17 April 1856 (*ibid.*, p. 43 and pp. 51–52). Already at the beginning of April the delegates as a whole had agreed to make a corresponding annulment in the form of a protocol to be communicated to the French government. Evidently Napoleon changed his mind in the meantime, for he let the delegates know that he had given up his original intention. (Buol to Francis Joseph, Paris, 9 April 1856, AGKK I, 3: 592 No. 341.)

161. *Ibid.*, p. 476 No. 273.

162. Manteuffel to Leopold von Gerlach, Paris, [mid-] April 1856 (Manteuffel, 3: 235). Napoleon may have been alerted to the question of Cracow by Czartoryski. See the undated (between 11 and 26 March 1856) notes of Czartoryski in Ennio Di Nolfo, *Adam J. Czartoryski e il congresso di Parigi*, p. 179 No. 20.

163. Clarendon to Palmerston, Paris, 19 March 1856 (Di Nolfo, *Europa*, pp. 500–1); Clarendon to Palmerston, Paris, 20 March 1856 (Fonti, 98: 250–51); Cavour to d'Azeglio, 20 March 1856 (Cavour, 7: 355).

164. See n. 162; further Manteuffel to King Leopold, Berlin, 15 February 1856 (Manteuffel, 3: 214); autograph note Prince William to Manteuffel,

Berlin, 14 March 1856 (*ibid.*, p. 224); autograph note Frederick William to Manteuffel, Charlottenburg, 28 March 1856 (*ibid.*, p. 226).

165. The negotiations led on 14 March and 11 April 1857 to treaties in which Denmark renounced the levy of the Sound Dues.

166. Telegram Werner to Buol, Vienna, 9 April 1856 (AGKK I, 3: 586 No. 339); telegram Buol to the Foreign Ministry, Paris, 10 April 1856 (*ibid.*, p. 592 No. 342). See also d'Azeglio to Cavour, London, 23 February 1856 (Cavour, 7: 205–6); Marcelli, pp. 212–14.

167. Schweizer to Rüdt, Paris, 10 April 1856 (GLA, Abt. 48, No. 2051 f. 277): "contrary to the expectation of many interested parties, there was no discussion either of Cuba or of Central America or even of the Italian question." See also Baumgart, "Probleme," p. 372.

168. Palmerston to Clarendon, London, 21 March 1856 (Di Nolfo, *Europa*, p. 502).

169. Clarendon to Palmerston, Paris, 19 March 1856 (*ibid.*, p. 501). The following quotations from Clarendon's letter to Palmerston, Paris, 31 March 1856 (*ibid.*, p. 504).

170. Rain, p. 74.

171. See the Countess of Damrémont to Thouvenel, [beginning of] April 1856 (L. Thouvenel, *Pages de l'histoire du Second Empire*, p. 260).

172. Buol to Francis Joseph, Paris, 2 April 1856 (AGKK I, 3: 566; extract in *Relazioni*, 67: 315).

173. Czartoryski to Szulczewski, Paris, 19 February 1856 (Di Nolfo, *Czartoryski*, p. 169).

174. Clarendon to Palmerston, Paris, 7 April 1856 (Di Nolfo, *Europa*, p. 507).

175. Buol to Francis Joseph, Paris, 9 April 1856 (AGKK I, 3: 591; extract in *Relazioni*, 67: 320–21).

176. Paris, 13 April 1856 (Fonti, 98: 268–70).

177. Manteuffel to Leopold von Gerlach, Paris, [mid-] April 1856 (Manteuffel, 3: 234–36).

178. Clarendon to Queen Victoria, Paris, 18 April 1856 (Fonti, 98: 272–73).

179. See below pp. 170–73.

180. For the exact titles see Bibliography.

181. Text: Adolf Beer, *Die orientalische Politik Österreichs seit 1774*, pp. 821–22 No. XVI.

182. Russell to Palmerston, London, 24 November 1854 (Fonti, 88: 309); Clarendon to Hudson, London, 29 November 1854 (*ibid.*, p. 310); Hudson to Clarendon, Turin, 15 December 1854 [2 reports] (*ibid.*, pp. 321–28).

183. The conditions were to be laid down in a secret article appended to the projected military convention. They read (Fonti, 88: 325): "I. The two western powers pledge themselves to make every effort to make Austria revoke the sequestration of the property of Sardinian subjects, affected by the decree of 13 February 1853. II. The High Contracting Parties will take into consideration the condition of Italy at the time peace is reestablished."

184. Aberdeen to Queen Victoria (for the British Cabinet's decision), London, 27 December 1854 (*ibid.*, p. 341); Cowley to Clarendon (for the French standpoint), Paris, 18 December 1854 (*ibid.*, pp. 342–44).

185. Clarendon to Hudson, London, 28 December 1854 (*ibid.*, p. 354).

186. D'Azeglio to Clarendon, London, 15 June 1855 (Fonti, 98: 116–18).
187. Clarendon to d'Azeglio, London, 19 June 1855 (*ibid.,* pp. 120–21).
188. Cavour to M. d'Azeglio, Paris, 8 December 1855 (Camillo [Benso] Cavour, *Lettere edite ed inedite,* 2: 376 No. 390).
189. Cavour to Walewski, Turin, 21 January 1856 (*ibid.,* pp. 382–89 No. 401). See also Hudson to Clarendon, Turin, 23 January 1856 (Fonti, 98: 209); Hudson to Cowley, Turin, 8 January 1856 (Di Nolfo, *Europa,* pp. 475–76).
190. Villamarina to Cibrario, Paris, 5 January 1856 (Di Nolfo, *Europa,* p. 478).
191. Walewski to Gramont, Paris, 5 February 1856 (*ibid.,* pp. 479–80).
192. Gramont to Walewski, Turin, 2 February 1856 (*ibid.,* p. 485).
193. D'Azeglio to Cavour, London, 4 February 1856 (Cavour, 7: 167).
194. Clarendon to Palmerston, 3 February 1856 (Di Nolfo, *Europa,* p. 482).
195. See d'Azeglio to Cavour (about conversation with Palmerston), London, 4 February 1856 (Cavour, 7: 164–68); Gramont to Walewski, Turin, 6 February 1856 (Di Nolfo, *Europa,* p. 487).
196. Persigny to Walewski, London, 12 February 1856 (Di Nolfo, *Europa,* pp. 488–89).
197. Buol/Hübner to Francis Joseph, Paris, 24 February 1856 (AGKK I, 3: 413; extract in *Relazioni,* 67: 311); Clarendon to Palmerston, Paris, 21 February 1856 (Di Nolfo, *Europa,* pp. 496–97); Cavour to Cibrario, 24 February 1856 (Cavour, 7: 208–9).
198. Palmerston to Clarendon, London, 3 February 1856 (Fonti, 98: 220); Palmerston to Clarendon, London, 23 February 1856 (*ibid.,* p. 240); Clarendon to Cowley, 24 February 1856 (*ibid.,* p. 242).
199. Buol/Hübner to Francis Joseph, Paris, 26 February 1856 (AGKK I, 3: 440; *Relazioni,* 67: 312 No. IV). See also Angelo Martini, "La S. Sede, la questione d'Oriente e il congresso di Parigi (1856)," who, however, offers no new information about this question. That the Curia did in fact "protest" in advance, as Geffcken asserts (p. 275), cannot as yet be proved. The word "protest" in a report of Clarendon's of 13 April 1856 (Fonti, 98: 268) on which Geffcken apparently relies, is used in the sense of "will (orally) remonstrate," and is not to be understood as a formal protest.
200. Cavour to King Victor Emmanuel, Paris, 22 February 1856 (Cavour, 7: 193–95).
201. D'Azeglio to Cavour, London, 7 February 1856 (*ibid.,* p. 173).
202. Cavour to Cibrario, 19 February 1856 (*ibid.,* p. 189).
203. Cavour's notes for Napoleon, 27 February 1856 (*ibid.,* pp. 220–21).
204. Clarendon to Palmerston, Paris, 15 April 1856 (Di Nolfo, *Europa,* p. 509 No. 42).
205. W. de la Rive, *Le Comte de Cavour,* pp. 345–46.
206. Cavour to d'Azeglio, Paris, 31 March 1856 (Cavour, 7: 400).
207. D'Azeglio to Cavour, London, 28 February 1856 (*ibid.,* pp. 221–23).
208. Palmerston to Clarendon, 7 March 1856 (Di Nolfo, *Europa,* p. 499).
209. D'Azeglio to Cavour, London, 7 March 1856 (Cavour, 7: 271–74).
210. Cavour proposed to Palmerston: "I will marry the Prince of Carignan to the Duchess of Parma. I will make him king, while declaring the Duke of Parma [the minor son of the Duchess] to be the heir presumptive. The Prince is not

very potent, the Duchess is thirty-eight years old; so it is not likely that this marriage will produce any children. The choice of the Prince of Carignan would be exceedingly popular in the Principalities" (Cavour to d'Azeglio, Paris, 29 February 1856, Cavour, 7: 233).

211. Palmerston to Clarendon, London, 30 March 1856 (Fonti, 98: 261–62).

212. Napoleon exhibited interest in the plan. His reaction is typical of his attitude in the Italian matter during the congress: "How can it be managed?" (Clarendon to Palmerston, Paris, 7 April 1856, Di Nolfo, *Europa*, p. 507).

213. Clarendon to Palmerston, Paris, 13 March 1856 (Fonti, 98: 246).

214. Clarendon to Palmerston, Paris, 19 March 1856 (*ibid.*, pp. 248–49); Clarendon to Palmerston, Paris, 19 March 1856 (Di Nolfo, *Europa*, pp. 500–1); Clarendon to Palmerston (confidential), Paris, 20 March 1856 (Fonti, 98: 249–52); Clarendon to Palmerston (confidential), Paris, 24 March 1856 (*ibid.*, pp. 256–57).

215. Clarendon to Palmerston, Paris, 27 March 1856 (Di Nolfo, *Europa*, p. 498).

216. Enclosure two to Nigra's letter to d'Azeglio, [beginning of] April 1856 (Cavour, 7: 418–19).

217. Clarendon to Palmerston (confidential), Paris, 3 April 1856 (Fonti, 98: 260n.). See also Clarendon to Palmerston, Paris, 5 April 1856 (*ibid.*, p. 264 No. 178).

218. See section on international law, pp. 168–73.

219. De Clerq, 7: 77.

220. *Ibid.*, pp. 79–80; further Clarendon to Palmerston, Paris, 8 April 1856 (Di Nolfo, *Europa*, pp. 508–9); Cavour to Cibrario, 9 April 1856 (Cavour, 7: 436–41).

221. Buol to Francis Joseph, Paris, 9 April 1856 (AGKK I, 3: 591–92; extract [not marked as such] in *Relazioni*, 67: 320–21); further Buol/Hübner to Francis Joseph, Paris, 9 April 1856 (AGKK I, 3: 586–90; extract in *Relazioni*, 67: 316–20).

222. Paris, 31 March 1856 (Di Nolfo, *Europa*, p. 504).

223. See Baumgart, "Probleme," pp. 388–91.

224. Confidential, Paris, 8 April 1856 (Fonti, 98: 265–66).

225. Paris, 13 April 1856 (*ibid.*, pp. 268–70).

226. Clarendon said, in accordance with his Liberal point of view, from lack of "moral courage, when the Pope is in question."

227. Cavour to Cibrario, 9 April 1856 (Cavour, 7: 440). See also Cavour's notes for Napoleon, 5 April 1856 (*ibid.*, p. 421): "it is to be feared that more bad than good will result from it for Italy. On one side, we will obtain no practical result; on the other, by a vague wish the Congress will have consecrated, in a sense, the occupation of Romagna by Austria." Cavour to de Launay, 5 April 1856 (*ibid.*, p. 425): "But there is scarcely anything to be hoped . . . except the more or less explicit expression of a wish, destined to remain sterile."

228. 29 March 1856 (*ibid.*, p. 395).

229. *Europa*, p. 445.

230. However, it already was this to a high degree before 1856 or even 1854.

231. Cavour to Cibrario, 9 April 1856 (Cavour, 7: 441).

232. See for example Clarendon to Hudson, London, 23 March 1854 (Fonti,

88: 267): "Austria cannot get over her fears and suspicions of Piedmont. . . . We should much regret that any insurrectionary movement took place in Italy to disturb the attention and divide the forces of Austria. We could give no encouragement whatever to it . . . although at the close of the war we shall anxiously endeavour to secure better government and a different order of things in Italy." See also Clarendon to Cowley, London, 5 December 1854 (*ibid.,* p. 346); Clarendon to Hudson, London, 28 December 1854 (*ibid.,* p. 352).

233. Peter Rassow, *Der Konflikt König Friedrich Wilhelms IV. mit dem Prinzen von Preussen im Jahre 1854,* especially p. 759.

234. A certain analogy to this state of things is found in the eastern crisis of 1840, in which France had consciously excluded herself from the concert.

235. The previous comprehensive accounts of Prussian policy at the end of the Crimean War (Kurt Borries, *Preussen im Krimkrieg (1853–1856),* pp. 314–37; Franz Eckhart, *Die deutsche Frage und der Krimkrieg,* pp. 202–15) take Prussian or German affairs as their point of reference, corresponding to their line of inquiry.

236. AGKK I, 3: 105.

237. Despatch (draft) Buol to Hübner/Colloredo, Vienna, 17 December 1855 (HHSA, PA IX 51 f. 362). Manteuffel to Hatzfeldt, Berlin, 12 January 1856 (Manteuffel, 3: 196).

238. Autograph note from Frederick William to E. von Manteuffel, Berlin, 22 January 1856 (*ibid.,* p. 203).

239. Buol to Francis Joseph, Paris, 19 March 1856 (AGKK I, 3: 536).

240. See Borries, p. 321.

241. Manteuffel to Hatzfeldt, Berlin, 26 January 1856 (Manteuffel, 3: 205).

242. *Ibid.,* pp. 213–14.

243. De Launay to Cibrario, Berlin, 16 February 1856 (Cavour, 7: 182–83).

244. Despatch Buol to Hübner/Colloredo, Vienna, 30 January 1856 (AGKK I, 3: 317).

245. Despatch (draft) Buol to Hübner/Colloredo, Vienna, 18 January 1856 (*ibid.,* p. 264).

246. Colloredo to Buol, London, 24 January 1856 (HHSA, PA VIII 42 f. 78–81).

247. Hübner to Buol, Paris, 25 January 1856 (AGKK I, 3: 302–3).

248. Hübner to Buol, Paris, 6 February 1856 (*ibid.,* pp. 341–43).

249. *Aktenstücke,* 2: 326–28.

250. Resolution of the German Diet of 2 February 1856 (*ibid.,* pp. 328–29). Bismarck managed it that before the words "with reference to" the further word "especially" was inserted.

251. Francis Joseph to Buol, n.d. [arrival 29 February 1856] (AGKK I, 3: 428).

252. Buol/Hübner to Francis Joseph, Paris, 19 March 1856 (AGKK I, 3: 535).

253. An extensive discussion of the legal questions related to this controversy is found in Geffcken, pp. 247–57. His conclusion that it remained unclear what legal relation Prussia as a signatory had in fact to the content of the peace treaty—whether simply that of an acceding power *without* the right to protest against alterations of the treaty or that of an equal signatory *with* the

right of protest—is historically without significance since Prussia participated in the execution of the treaty (for example the Bucharest Commission) and played an important role in the abrogation of Black Sea neutralization in 1870.

254. It read (De Clerq, 7: 35; italics mine): "The Congress, considering *that it is a European interest* that Prussia, a signatory of the Convention concluded at London on 13 July 1841, *participate in the new arrangements to be taken,* decides that an extract of today's protocol be sent to Berlin, by the intermediary of Count Walewski, as spokesman for the Congress, to invite the Prussian government to send plenipotentiaries to Paris."

255. *Ibid.,* pp. 39–40.

256. Cavour to d'Azeglio, Paris, 23 March 1856 (Cavour, 7: 368–69); Cavour to Cibrario, Paris, 25 March 1856 (*ibid.,* pp. 375–76).

257. Buol to Hübner, Paris, 25 March 1856 (AGKK I, 3: 549).

258. Geffcken, p. 256.

259. Frederick William to Alexander, Charlottenburg, 6 January 1856 (Borries, pp. 385–86).

260. Cited *ibid.,* p. 337.

261. "K istorii Parižskogo mira," p. 52.

262. Leopold von Ranke, "Friedrich Wilhelm IV.," p. 775.

263. Koller to Buol (confidential), Buyukdere, 13 September 1855 (AGKK I, 3: 52–53). See also Paul W. Schroeder, *Austria, Great Britain, and the Crimean War,* pp. 343–46, 351–53.

264. If one leaves aside the first, unsuccessful nationalist and revolutionary movement in the Ottoman Empire, in Serbia, 1804 to 1813.

265. See Baumgart, "Probleme," pp. 249–51; Winfried Baumgart, "Politik und Religion in Syrien im 19. Jahrhundert"; Baumgart, *Vom Europäischen Konzert zum Völkerbund,* pp. 23–27.

266. Prokesch-Osten to Buol, Constantinople, 10 January 1856 (AGKK I, 3: 226–28).

267. *Ibid.,* pp. 292–95. See also *ibid.,* pp. 290–92.

268. Text (copy) HHSA, PA XII 56 f. 173–76.

269. Prokesch-Osten to Buol, Constantinople, 30 January 1856 (AGKK I, 3: 323–27).

270. [Anton Franz Count] Prokesch-Osten, *Ein Beitrag zur Geschichte der orientalischen Frage,* p. 10.

271. AGKK I, 3: 327.

272. See Prokesch-Osten to Buol (with enclosures), Constantinople, 4 February (HHSA, PA XII 56 f. 198–207); Thouvenel to Walewski, Pera, 11 February 1856 (*Acte și documente relative la istoria renascerei Romaniei,* 2: 921–22).

273. Text: *Recueil d'actes internationaux de l'Empire Ottoman,* ed. Gabriel Effendi Noradounghian, 3: 83–88 No. 685.

274. See above pp. 128, 130, and Davison, "Ottoman Diplomacy."

275. In the original text the articles are not numbered. The articles mentioned in the following were numbered according to the Archives' copy (see n. 267).

276. For the implementation see A. Diomedes Kyriakos, *Geschichte der orientalischen Kirchen von 1453–1898,* pp. 19–26, 30–33.

277. Prokesch-Osten to Buol, Constantinople, 10 March 1856 (AGKK I, 3: 497 No. 284).

278. Prokesch-Osten to Buol, Constantinople, 11 February 1856 (*ibid.*, p. 372).

279. A pioneer work on this subject is Roderic H. Davison's book, *Reform in the Ottoman Empire 1856–1876*. See on this point Baumgart, "Probleme," pp. 249–51; Baumgart, "Politik und Religion," p. 104; Baumgart, *Vom europäischen Konzert zum Völkerbund*, pp. 23–27.

280. See Baumgart, "Politik und Religion."

281. Buol/Hübner to Francis Joseph, Paris, 9 April 1856 (AGKK I, 3: 588). Italics mine.

282. In the draft of the declaration, as it had been communicated to Clarendon some days before, it read more correctly "liberty for religious sects" (Evelyn Ashley, *The Life of Henry John Temple, Viscount Palmerston: 1846–1865*, 2: 109n.; also *British Documents on the Origins of the War 1898–1914*, ed. G. P. Gooch and Harold Temperley, 8: 205).

283. De Clerq, 7: 78–79.

284. 15: 290–91.

285. The product seems to be the draft declaration printed in Ashley, 2: 109 in the note. Italics in the following quote are my own.

286. De Clerq, 7: 91–93.

287. Text in Francis Piggott, *The Declaration of Paris 1856*, pp. 240–41. Text of the declaration by the French government, identical except for some unimportant details, issued 29 March 1854 (*ibid.*, p. 241).

288. Clarendon to Palmerston, Paris, 6 April 1856 (*British Documents*, 8: 204–5). For the position of the Cabinet, *ibid.*, pp. 205–6.

289. Piggott, pp. 142–49.

290. In the Crimean War, following British custom, in addition to unconditional contraband (weapons, etc.), only the following were recognized as contraband of "doubtful character": ships' timber, naval stores, ships' machinery, coal.

291. "Hostile infection": wares without contraband character; they are liable to seizure, if the same ship also carries contraband belonging to the same owner.

292. Contraband goods, which were being sent to a neutral port, could be confiscated, if the ultimate hostile destination were established.

293. In the official protocol (De Clerq, 7: 84) it is erroneously called Article 7.

294. Temperley, "Paris," pp. 412–13; following him, Gavin Burns Henderson, *Crimean War Diplomacy and Other Historical Essays*, pp. 146–50; see further Maureen M. Robson, "Liberals and 'Vital Interests'," pp. 49–50; Baumgart, *Vom Europäischen Konzert zum Völkerbund*, pp. 14–16.

295. AGKK I, 3: 604.

296. Paris, 14 April 1856 (*ibid.*, p. 603).

297. Paris, 6 April 1856 (*British Documents*, 8: 205); Paris, 7 April 1856 (Di Nolfo, *Europa*, p. 507).

298. Clarendon to Palmerston, Paris, 31 March 1856 (*ibid.*, p. 504). See also

Geffcken, p. 279.

299. Pierre Dubois, Georg von Poděbrad, Erasmus, Grotius, Duke of Sully, Eméric Crucé, William Penn, Abbé de Saint Pierre, Jeremy Bentham, Immanuel Kant. See Fritz Dickmann's collection of essays about the problem of peacekeeping, especially on early modern history (*Friedensrecht und Friedenssicherung*).

300. In Articles 5–7 (text: Georges Frédéric de Martens, ed. *Recueil des principaux traités,* 6: 347–57).

301. In this connection is to be seen the arbitration of conflicts between members of the German Confederation laid down by the Final Act of Vienna. In addition to many treaties between the United States and South American states, the Peace Treaty of Ghent of 28 December 1814 between the United States and Great Britain is to be mentioned: in Articles 4–7, four Mixed Commissions were established to decide about the Bay of Fundy and about different boundary stipulations.

302. AGKK I, 3: 603.

303. Cavour to Cibrario, 17 April 1856 (Cavour, 7: 475).

304. New Series, vol. 8, Nos. 71, 72 (May and June 1856).

305. Detailed discussions in the form of handbooks: Alfred H. Fried, *Handbuch der Friedensbewegung,* 2; Jacob Ter Meulen, *Der Gedanke der internationalen Organisation in seiner Entwicklung,* II, 1.

306. *Die Idee und der praktische Nutzen einer Weltakademie des Völker-Rechts.* In his book, *Die Wissenschaft des Weltfriedens im Grundrisse,* Kaufmann suggests the institution of a new learned discipline, which would occupy itself with the question of a lasting peace—thus a branch of learning, that is today fashionable once again under the title "peace research."

307. Fried, 2: 73.

308. Cavour to d'Azeglio, 11 April 1856 (Cavour, 7: 452).

309. See his "State Report" of 26 April 1856 to Manteuffel (Bismarck, 2: 138–45), in which among other things he says: "According to Viennese policy Germany is too small for us both. German dualism has, over the past thousand years occasionally and routinely in every century since Charles V, regulated its reciprocal relationships by a radical civil war, and in this century too nothing else will put the time right."

310. Manteuffel, 3: 234.

311. Émile de Girardin, *L'Équilibre européen,* pp. 42–47. See also Robson, pp. 50–51.

312. In this it is said, among other things, that it will not be presumed that a government will submit itself in advance to the decision of a court of arbitration, if what is concerned is a dispute which "affects the national honor of a state, its higher interests." In Article 2 of the agreement the signatories of the treaty pledged themselves to appeal to the good offices or mediation of uninvolved powers before recourse to armed force "insofar as circumstances will permit it." In both cases, extensive agreement with the wording of the Paris Resolution is unmistakable. Materials on the first Hague Peace Conference in Georges Frédéric de Martens, ed., *Nouveau recueil général de traités,* series 2, vol. 26.

III. Results

IMPLEMENTING THE PEACE TREATY

IN EVALUATING THE PARIS PEACE TREATY, two aspects stand out: first, the significance for the narrower sphere of the Near East;[1] second, the effects of the war and the peace, the most marked break in European diplomacy between 1815 and 1914, on international relations.

In the Paris Treaty, the allies sought to safeguard Ottoman integrity against the Russian threat in three different ways, indicated in the Four Points.

The Ottoman Empire

First Ottoman independence and territorial integrity were guaranteed by the European powers, jointly and individually (Article 7). The empire legally entered the European community in which she already played a role in fact through treaties with the European powers. In return the Porte received the task of revitalizing the empire through a comprehensive reform program (Article 9). These provisions invalidated the Russian claim, advanced since Catherine II (Kuchuk Kainarji), to a protectorate over the empire's Orthodox subjects or over the empire in general (Unkiar-Skelessi). At the same time, Britain's decades-long effort through Stratford de Redcliffe to have the need for reform recognized and tested by Europe in the absence of foreign dangers was expressed in a treaty.

The fate of Ottoman reforms in the nineteenth-century Tanzimat period demands comprehensive investigation in its own right. Superficial judgments are often made, which one-sidedly emphasize their mostly negative results, without considering their course, as yet unknown in many details. The economic decline, or rather stagnation in European terms, cannot be glossed over. The empire's territorial extent remained undiminished, but there are unmistakable centrifugal tendencies, above all in the outlying areas. The Danubian principalities passed stage after stage on the way to independence, irresistibly preparing to separate from the empire. In the Lebanon latent tension between Druses and Maronites led in 1860 to bloody confrontations, great power intervention, and, under pressure, greater autonomy. Only with difficulty could Yemen be held; and Tunisia recognized Ottoman suzerainty merely to escape French colonization. After a prelude in 1858, there were battles in 1862 between the Serbs and the garrisons of the many Ottoman fortresses, such as Belgrade.[2] Based on the decision of an ambassadorial conference in Constantinople, the Ottomans had to evacuate the precincts of some of the fortresses and gave up two entirely. By 1867, with great power support, Serbia had forced complete withdrawal of Ottoman troops; only in Belgrade did the Ottoman flag fly beside the Serbian. Meanwhile Michael Obrenovich attempted to fuse the different Balkan ethnic groups into an anti-Ottoman league, as was done briefly in 1912; he failed, because Balkan nationalism was not just anti-Ottoman, it was also exclusive and fanatically independent. Montenegro, always refractory and always pro-Russian,[3] obtained a boundary rectification in 1858 thanks to great power intervention. Faced with the independence movements between the Paris peace and the next great eastern crisis, in 1875 to 1878, the Ottomans could maintain their rights of suzerainty only in Crete's insurrection in 1866 to 1868, aimed at union with Greece.

The 1856 reform decree was rendered largely ineffective in subsequent years by the poison of nationalism—reinforced in the Balkans with Pan-Slavism. After the Christian subjects had attained formal equality, they associated social emancipation with greater political autonomy (for example, Rumania, Serbia, Bulgaria) and union with ethnic brethren across the frontier (for example, Crete). Nationalism also worked disintegratingly on the hitherto ruling class. It joined with a traditionalism hostile to reform.

Essentially the reforms were the work of a thin layer of Europeanized bureaucrats. Their critics were the orthodox Moslems, above all the leaders, the ulema, who felt it a dishonor when the Law of Islam (şari'a, şeriat) was desecrated by "heathen" Europeans. Other enemies were army officers who felt themselves pushed aside by the new class of bureaucrats; and they were recruited from the Young Ottoman movement (Yeni Osmanlılar)—the earliest manifestation of Turkish nationalism—who, to be sure, demanded a constitution (based on Islamic tradition) but opposed the secularization of Islamic culture regarded as necessary by Ali Pasha and his associates and reproached the bureaucrats with impotence in the face of constant European intervention.

The ideal of Ottomanism, a unifying imperial consciousness, could not be implemented, despite progress towards genuine equality for non-Moslems by way of the legal equality decreed in the Hatt-ı Hümayun. One may fault the reformers around Ali Pasha and Fuad Pasha for lack of realism; but the effort had to be made, if the empire were not to be given up from the start. Perhaps the results would have been greater if the European powers had not disturbed the process by continual intervention during a transition which *also* exhibited abuses (Bulgarian Massacres). But in the end the confrontation between Europe and the Ottoman Empire was irresolvable: two cultures had developed impressively in completely different directions.

The Neutralization of the Black Sea

Despite having renounced her role as protector of the Orthodox at Paris, Russia redeemed her position in the Balkans through Pan-Slavism, although to be sure this can be only partially identified with the official policy; so too, fifteen years later, she rebounded from the loss suffered through neutralization of the Black Sea.

In 1856 the British, who championed the idea most eagerly, must have seen neutralization of the Black Sea as the most effective possible method for suppressing military power on a sea which threatened to become a Russian lake. That was how Palmerston understood it, although he admitted privately that he could not believe it would last long—at most ten years.[4] Disraeli also took this point of view before the Commons in 1871, when it was a question of how to respond to unilateral Russian repudiation of Articles 11, 13, and 14.

As for Napoleon, he had not even signed the treaty before he let the Russians glimpse revision. Unlike Britain, he was not interested in this war aim in itself, but only as it helped his larger program. He may never have used the expression ascribed to him: "Particular treaties are not eternal"[5] (supposedly directed at Russia early in 1856 to persuade her to make peace quickly), but it fits with his ideas. His confidant Morny did use it to the Russians in autumn 1855 as an explicit argument for unconditional Russian acceptance.[6] Walewski had been instructed in the peace negotiations to suppress all exacerbating British proposals (inclusion of the Sea of Azov and the river mouths, demolition of forts on the east Black Sea coast). Napoleon was obliged to give such evidence of conciliation in order to promote a Franco-Russian rapprochement, which would serve his general revisionist program. After the Paris Treaty, Russia emerged as the second great power (after France) with a revisionist foreign policy. Common foreign policy assumptions made common action seem natural.

Cooperation between France and Russia as the losers at two international congresses parallels German-Russian collaboration after Versailles 1919. The Franco-Russian secret agreement of 1859 corresponds to the Rapallo Treaty of 1922. The fate of neutralization after 1856 corresponds to the fate of German demilitarization after 1919.

In fact scholarship has hunted for analogies in other peace treaties to characterize the harshness of the neutralization and has most often equated it with the demilitarization of the Rhineland.[7] In both instances, the sovereign rights of a defeated great power were limited. Both clauses sprang from a victor's need for security (in 1856 Britain, in 1919 France) when facing the loser's perceived striving for hegemony.

However, in judging the penalty imposed on Russia in 1856, one should not forget that the architects of the treaty had always doubted its durability and also that neutralization brought Russia certain advantages, at least in the short run. In Russia the worth of a Black Sea fleet had been variously assessed since its forced construction early in the nineteenth century and especially since 1841. As long as the fleet could not enter the Mediterranean, its cost might seem disproportionate to its military value. Besides relieving the Russian state budget, a further advantage after 1856 was that no non-Russian, especially no Ottoman warships, might sail in the Black Sea either; this provided an effective shield against Ottoman intervention in Russia's conquest of the Caucasus tribes and the land bridge to Persia.[8] But by 1859 or at latest 1866, after this opposition had been broken, this function no longer existed.

From that time, and indeed to a lesser degree since 1856, abolition of Black Sea neutralization dominated Russian foreign policy. The cession of Bessarabian territory, which had seemed the greatest insult in the weeks after the Austrian ultimatum and during the peace negotiations because it was so unexpected, came from a nonbelligerent power, and did not seem related to the military situation, receded in comparison with the neutralization of the Black Sea; it played only an incidental role in Gorchakov's revision claims, and then mostly in connection with neutralization.

In the fifteen years after 1856, France, Austria, and Prussia repeatedly exploited Russia's desire for revision to win her friendship for their own purposes. And Russia tried to make capital for her plans from existing great power disputes.

According to hitherto available sources, the abolition of neutralization was first offered by Napoleon during the alliance negotiations of 1858 and 1859.[9] There was no agreement because their views about announcing it differed: Napoleon wanted to see it sanctioned by a general congress, while Gorchakov demanded that France immediately repudiate the relevant articles. At any rate, Russia ascertained that neutralization had become negotiable. An offer from Austria during an 1860 Warsaw meeting of sovereigns was equally unproductive because this time Gorchakov demanded general European assent.[10] In the summer of 1866, during the Austro-Prussian War, Bismarck hinted at his readiness to support Russian wishes for eventual revision.[11] Encouraged by this innuendo and others,[12] Gorchakov drafted a circular for the Russian embassies in the European capitals, which announced Russian repudiation of the neutralization provisions. The plan was shelved as inopportune by a Crown Council, in which the war minister and the minister of finance opposed Gorchakov's step. The surprisingly short duration of the Austro-Prussian War may have been the deciding factor. Since Rechberg had wished to begin his tenure of office with a conciliatory gesture to Petersburg, Beust at the beginning of 1867 followed suit. The Cretan insurrection seemed to offer a suitable occasion for comprehensive revision of the Eastern Question.[13] But after the western powers, particularly Britain, energetically declined, Gorchakov withdrew the invitation. The outbreak of the Franco-Prussian War provided the next great opportunity.

Some days after Sedan, Gorchakov informed Prince Reuss, the Prussian representative in Petersburg, that Russia had looked on quietly for fourteen years while the Paris Treaty had been "violated and weakened" by the powers. At the right time, Russia would break silence to "overthrow" the clauses damaging her.[14] On 27 October, Tsar Alexander announced his decision to repudiate Articles 11, 13, and 14 of the Paris Peace Treaty. In a circular of 31 October, Gorchakov communicated Russian intentions to the signatory powers.[15]

Since then, Russian procedure in the autumn of 1870 has been seen as the test case for a government's appeal to the *clausula rebus sic stantibus* to justify renunciation of a treaty. In reality Gorchakov did not appeal expressly to the *clausula,* although doubtless his circular was implicitly based on it, since the circumstances he used implied such a reservation. Gorchakov referred especially to violations of the treaty concerning the Danubian principalities, which the powers had accepted unopposed. As result, Russia could not feel bound by stipulations directly harmful to her.

For Bismarck, as is evident from the German documents, the Russian action was an unwelcome surprise both in form and in timing.[16] He immediately proposed a conference when war psychosis briefly dominated British public opinion[17] and the British special representative to headquarters at Versailles, Odo Russell, threatened war, although without authorization. When the war fever declined as quickly as it had risen, and Prime Minister Gladstone assumed a conciliatory attitude, Bismarck stalled on resolving the problem—a fact not previously noticed, but one that can be proven from the documents. In view of the continuing siege of Paris, he was not displeased that European diplomacy and public opinion were at least partly distracted from the Franco-Prussian War.

The British government's main concern was to read Russia a lesson on international law and to make her recognize the legal principle that a treaty could only be altered by agreement of all the signatories. Ideally this meant withdrawal of the circular. To do this would, however, have humiliated Gorchakov by making him admit that his procedure was unjustifiable. A way out was offered by Bismarck's conference proposal: on the one hand it would let Gorchakov save face, on the other it would let Britain maintain the fiction that international treaties could only be revised by general agreement, that is, it would recognize the principle *pacta sunt servanda*. Britain posed a further rhetorical demand, that the conference open without prejudice as to results. In this way the Gorchakov circular, as W. E. Mosse put it, was "neatly and effectively by-passed" without a formal retraction.[18]

In fact the conference, which began in London on 17 January 1871 and ended with the Black Sea Treaty of 13 March 1871,[19] only sanctioned the Russian action by maintaining the fiction mentioned (Article 1) and considering the demands for compensation surprisingly produced by the Ottoman Empire and Austria. Bismarck succeeded in postponing and finally preventing participation of the French representative, Jules Favre, because he feared that France would lay the problem of the Franco-Prussian peace before this international forum. Austria posed high demands for compensation (establishment of a port on the Ottoman Black Sea coast for warships of nonriparian states, an increased number of ships stationed at the mouth of the Danube, continuation of the European Danube Commission, dominated by Austria, and improvement of the Danube's navigability); but only those relative to the Danube Commission were met (Articles 4–7). The principle of closure of the Straits, in force since 1856, was fundamentally modified in the Porte's favor mainly at Austrian insistence, for the Sultan was now allowed (Article 2) to let warships of "friendly and allied powers" pass the Straits even in peacetime.

The London Conference gave Gorchakov an unequivocal triumph. After his original painful surprise, Bismarck used the resurgence of the Eastern Question to prevent internationalization of the Franco-Prussian War. Britain achieved a moral victory in that the repudiation emerged as an international decision, not as a unilateral Russian action. Palmerston's successors opposed Russia's basic demand as little as the British government of 1936 opposed Hitler's reoccupation of the Rhineland. The principle of *clausula rebus sic stantibus* was recognized even if they worked on the assumption of "circumstances in fact changed"—a situation that despite the opposing British verbal declaration marked a decline in international morality.

One further observation which the historian can draw from the fate of this basic clause of the Paris Treaty is that the least promising treaty provisions are those imposed on an enemy who has been defeated but not destroyed, those involving a fundamental loss of power, and those signed in bad faith right from the start.

The Danubian Principalities

The infractions of the treaty relative to the Danubian principalities, which Gorchakov used as the basis for his action, could not be denied. In contradiction to the Paris Treaty and the subsequent conventions concluded in Paris, the population of the principalities had continually confronted the powers with accomplished facts—always with French support—which were then recognized after the fact.

The abolition of Russia's protectorate over the Danubian principalities and the removal of Russia from the Danube delta and the left bank was supposed to complete on land what had been attained with neutralization on the Black Sea: the restriction of Russian influence on the Porte through the creation of buffer zones under collective guarantee of the European powers. It was far more difficult to regulate land zones than sea zones. It involved the future of five million human beings, and each of the powers had a different opinion.

The crucial question, union or separation of the principalities, had not been solved during the negotiations. The attempt to resolve it occupied the signatory powers for ten years, until Napoleon finally attained his original goal, union under a foreign prince. The further history of the Rumanian state, independent in fact after 1866, and recognized as such in 1878 at the Berlin Congress, is a separate theme. But the history of the Danubian principalities during the ten years after the Paris Congress is complicated enough, since it involves the origin of a state, and only monographic treatment is adequate to the subject. Anglo-Saxon historians undertook this work as early as the 1930s, using the relevant documents, and Rumanian historians have worked for decades,[20] so here only a very abbreviated summary is appropriate.

In the second half of 1856, European diplomats were occupied with conflicts over the Bessarabian boundary and over the Serpents Island some forty-five kilometers east of the Danube delta.

In the first case the dispute concerned two places, both named Bolgrad, one on Lake Yalpukh, connected with the Danube, the other a few kilometers north. During the negotiations, the Russians intentionally played false, as now appears from Orlov's report,[21] for they mentioned only a single place, the more northerly, to their unsuspecting colleagues; later, they "discovered" the second one and declared that they meant the more southerly. Napoleon had promised the Russians in Paris that he would assign all of Bolgrad to them, as the center of the Bulgarian colony. Britain and Austria maintained that the Russian claim compromised the principle of removing Russia from the Danube.

In comparison with this trivial matter, the significance of Serpents Island was absolutely zero. It was a small, uninhabited rock in the sea that served solely to carry a lighthouse. On the map laid before the conference, the island was not marked. Russia claimed it after she "discovered" it. At least half a dozen proposals, some fantastic, were made and rejected.[22] As usual, Palmerston sent the fleet to the Black Sea, violating the treaty just signed. After some tedious haggling, Russia essentially gave way. In a protocol of 6 January 1857, she renounced claims to Serpents Island and the southerly Bolgrad in return for compensation elsewhere in the Bessarabian boundary area.[23] The petty dispute over insignificant objects had the major consequence of straining the Anglo-French alliance and leading to further disintegration of international relations.

The more important conflict over the Danubian principalities had larger results. According to the Paris Treaty, the population would be consulted about the future constitution through their own popular assemblies (divans ad hoc) representing the country under great power supervision. The previous hospodars were replaced in 1856 by provisional rulers or kaimakams. In Moldavia in July 1857, rigged elections were held, which voted to continue separation of the two principalities. Thouvenel in Constantinople demanded that the elections be annulled; when the Porte disagreed, he broke diplomatic relations. Meanwhile Britain, in contrast to her attitude at Paris, had spoken out along with the Porte and Austria for separation. In August a meeting of monarchs was held at Osborne[24] on the Isle of Wight: Napoleon promised to accept a mere "administrative union" of the two provinces, while the British would press the Porte for new elections. In the new elections in September, both provinces supported union. In May 1858 an ambassadorial conference met in Paris:[25] France, assisted by Russia, proposed a "central committee" for the two principalities. The conflict now opened over a common flag, a common system of money, militia, and post; it symbolized a widening cleavage between the powers over the Eastern Question. A compromise was worked out on 19 August: two different flags with the same jack, two militias as part of a single army, two hospodarships for which the same person could be chosen by the divans in Bucharest and Jassy; but it was overthrown at the beginning of 1859, when the population in two separate elections simultaneously chose the boyar Alexander Cuza as hospodar for both provinces.

The same scenario was repeated many times: conferences in Paris, leading to a compromise elaborated with difficulty, and immediately overturned by the people. Cavour, as cosignatory of the Paris Treaty, intervened regularly; he negotiated in 1858 to 1859 with Hungarian revolutionaries (General Klapka) to kindle insurrections in Hungary behind the Austrian front; he delivered French weapons to Cuza to incite Cuza to a raid into Bukovina. During the North Italian War the

Porte was obliged to recognize Cuza as ruler over both provinces. The ambassadorial conference in Paris finally sanctioned the new situation.

Immediately the difficulties emerged: Cuza had to rule with the Central Committee, which did not sit in either capital but in Focshani, as well as with two ministries and two assemblies. In 1861 the Porte issued a firman stating that the ministries and assemblies should be united and could work in Bucharest. However, the settlement applied only for Cuza's term of office. After that each province could again choose its own hospodar.

This did not help. In fact, social tensions caused more bitterness. Cuza opposed the great landlords (boyars) and tried to depend on the peasantry by abolishing serfdom and making landowners of half a million peasant families. In May 1864 he stage-managed a coup d'etat modelled after the Paris events of 2 December 1851, dissolved the assemblies, and promulgated a constitution. Just two years later, he himself fell victim to a conspiracy. Since experience showed that a native prince could not control corruption, the assemblies chose Count Philip of Flanders, on the suggestion of the provisional government, and then, when he declined, turned to Prince Charles of Hohenzollern-Sigmaringen, in agreement with Napoleon. The Sultan, unable in 1866 to count on his most important supporter, Austria, was obliged to grant the prince investiture whether he wanted to or not. This was a decisive step toward full independence. The Paris Treaty's validity had been significantly undermined, as Gorchakov noted with some satisfaction.

Ottoman suzerainty was now scarcely more than a formality. Full independence was recognized twelve years later at the Berlin Congress, when Russia also won back from Rumania the strips of Bessarabian territory ceded in 1856, and gave back part of the Dobruja. Thus Rumania, herself a multinational state—only two-thirds of the inhabitants were Rumanians—completely cut her ties with a multinational empire. From now on she had an irredentist problem like other newly independent Balkan states, a problem which would dominate her foreign policy in coming decades.

Rumania's national evolution was possible only because the Paris Treaty and subsequent conventions were continuously evaded. Without support from at least one great power, the national movement would not have been strong enough in itself to win independence. This interdependence, noticeable already in the case of Greece, determined Rumania's emergence as well. Here too the national forces proved unable to deal with the country's social and economic problems. The country had a very weak economic base: the boyars were one of the most corrupt and incompetent ruling elites of Europe.

Escape from the Ottoman Empire did not solve the country's problems; it intensified them. Nonetheless Rumania was able to maintain independence until 1941 to 1944 and has become alive to it again in recent years.

Navigation of the Danube and the Aland Convention

Compared with the Ottoman Empire's progressive disintegration, the fate of the neutralization of the Black Sea, and the emergence of an independent Rumania, all the other direct consequences of the treaty are secondary for European politics. The less important stipulations survived longest.

In any case, the requirements about freedom of shipping on the Danube (Articles 15–19) did not work exactly as their authors, especially Austria, intended.[26] According to the peace treaty, the European Danube Commission was to operate for just two years, but in practice it became permanent, and the permanent Riverain Commission, which drafted shipping regulations in 1857, soon became ineffective because the western powers did not recognize its prohibition, included at Austrian insistence, on participation by nonriparian states in the carrying trade within a country. The shipping regulations issued by the Paris Conference of 1865 to 1866, the London Black Sea Conference of 1871, and the Berlin Treaty of 1878 confirmed and extended the powers of the European Danube Commission. With an interruption during the First World War, the commission continued to function until the Second World War, changing its name to the International Danube Commission after 1921. After the Second World War, its status became uncertain. But the principle of freedom of navigation on the Danube remains valid.

The Aland Islands Convention also (Article 33 of the main treaty and separate convention) is still part of international law, as noted,[27] despite many modifications.[28] Again, the Russians attempted to nullify it. In 1907 in a secret Russo-German protocol, Germany agreed not to oppose its abolition.[29] Since Russia rebuilt the fortifications during the First World War, she was obliged at Brest-Litovsk to pledge their removal. In 1921, sponsored by the Council of the League of Nations, a convention between Germany, France, Britain, Italy, and all the Baltic states (except Russia) prescribed demilitarization and neutralization for the islands. Although here too the current legal situation is unsatisfactory, Finland at least pledged demilitarization (but not pacification) in the 1947 peace treaty.

Deteriorating Relations between the Powers

Scholars cannot dispute that the Crimean War and the Paris peace increased diplomatic instability in Europe. Nonetheless one should not overrate *the direct and indirect effects of the war*. Especially in English historical writing the second half of the nineteenth century has often been contrasted too sharply with the first half, with the Crimean War as the decisive break between them. Decades ago, Gladstone's biographer, J. Morley, called the Crimean War a "sanguinary prelude to a vast subversion of the whole system of European states."[30] And recently, A. J. P. Taylor, whose penchant for shocking formulas often vitiates the seriousness of his judgments, has written that the Crimean War introduced a period of "European anarchy."[31] Even so cautious a historian as Ludwig Dehio has described the years after the Crimean War as characterized by "increasing fragmentation and the highest fluidity."[32]

Such a judgment assumes erroneously that the decades after the Vienna Congress exemplified "tranquil ideological solidarity" (Dehio). Such a thesis needs revision. We must understand that nineteenth-century European states down to the Crimean War were constantly in flux not merely at home but abroad as well. The five great powers were at rest for perhaps five years after the Vienna Congress; thereafter the dynamic of international relations, never inactive, sometimes turned highly explosive. Certainly "ideological alignments" characterize this period,[33] that is, ideological opposition between the liberal West and the conservative East. Both groups, however, were highly flexible in foreign policy—the one based on a conservative principle of intervention, not attributable to the Paris Declaration of the Holy Alliance, but more correctly to the Troppau Protocol; the other working on a liberal principle of intervention, most clearly expressed in the Quadruple Alliance of 1834 created by Palmerston and Talleyrand. The consequent instability was accelerated to menacing proportions since the boundaries between the two groups were not rigidly fixed, nor were they homogeneous within their own spheres. Cross-connections appeared over and over again, and solidarity was constantly undermined by strong national egoism and a powerful policy of national interests.

Precisely in this second aspect, the concept of the Holy Alliance should only be applied with the greatest caution since it becomes increasingly illusory, the further one gets from 1820. For Metternich, Navarino signified the collapse of his lifework. At Münchengrätz, indeed, the Holy Alliance was revived but it was tepid. The status quo of the Ottoman Empire agreed upon here was infringed in 1853 by Russia, not Austria. Moreover, Holy Alliance solidarity no longer existed in other important questions. Since 1848 the rivalry between the two German powers had made it a fiction and only the pressure of

Russian paramountcy maintained it abroad. If historians still insist on conjuring up its ghost after 1827—and there are good grounds for so doing—it seems just as reasonable to speak of it after the Crimean War. The Three Emperors' League of 1872 rested on the same principle as the Troppau Protocol, namely the calculation that only the solidarity of the three eastern powers could counteract the revolution and republicanism. Beyond this, there was no common ground either after 1827 or after 1872, only increasingly divergent interests. Bismarck's goal of preserving Austria and Russia from confrontation over the Eastern Question corresponded to Metternich's similarly directed efforts in the three decades after the Vienna Congress. Conflict between the two powers in the Balkans must lead to world war. In this sense, strange as it may sound, Buol and the Prussians too acted in the spirit of the Holy Alliance during the Crimean War in trying to stay aloof from the maritime powers' war with Russia.

We must free ourselves from another common notion: from the Europe-centered picture applied to nineteenth-century history. The Crimean War demonstrates that the opposition between eastern and western Europe was not the only one running through the first half of the nineteenth century; there was another transcending it, that is, the *world confrontation between Russia and Britain.* Britain was busily extending her empire in Asia, South Africa, and Canada. Russia's push towards Constantinople seemed to threaten her imperial lines of communication at a sensitive spot. But Russia was also a world power, a fact too easily forgotten. She ruled the northern Pacific and tried to round out her position in "Russian America." She possessed Alaska and her bases on the western North American coast reached as far as California.

However, Russia's position as a world power was most deeply injured not by loss of her position in the Pacific but by the Crimean War in continental Europe. The *weakening of Russia* is the central and most significant result of the Crimean War—a weakening apparent down to the end of the Second World War. The Paris peace obliged Russia to give up her role as arbiter in both the Ottoman Empire *and* central Europe. She was thrown back on herself. The war exposed the flaws in her autocratic system: the sterile social structure and, related to this, the inferior military establishment compared with the West, the backward economy, and the lack of industry. The shock of the Crimean War made the necessity of total reform unarguable. The abolition of serfdom was the centerpiece; however, it was not an end in itself, but was subordinate to army reform. The army was still the most important pillar of the autocracy as embodied under Alexander II. Releasing social forces, to the extent that that could strengthen the army, became the dominant goal of Russian domestic policy after 1856.

With this domestic transformation, foreign policy receded in importance. Nesselrode in his political testament underscored the need to give up the primacy of foreign policy in favor of the primacy of domestic policy.[34] *Dominance of domestic policy*—this implied aloofness from all international questions, renunciation of intervention in European affairs, unless direct Russian interests were at stake, avoidance of ties going beyond existing treaties. The rapprochement with France, whose utility for the peace negotiations Nesselrode did not question, must not develop into an ordinary alliance. This would only encourage Napoleon to implement his revolutionary territorial plans. France could be hushed with the hope that Russia would not join any hostile European coalition organized by Britain. As before, Russian foreign policy must rest on the "monarchical and anti-Polish" solidarity of the three eastern powers, including Austria. Thus the aging chancellor attempted to bequeath a basic principle of the Holy Alliance to his new imperial master as the sum of political wisdom won during four decades.

Gorchakov, who became Nesselrode's successor directly after the termination of the peace negotiations, shared his predecessor's insight but did not draw exactly the same conclusions. "Russia is sulking, they say. Russia is not sulking, Russia is withdrawing within herself," he said in one of his first circulars to the Russian missions abroad.[35]

"Strategic retreat" and "abstention" are recurring slogans in his despatches during the following years and symbolize his guiding ideas. A previously unnoticed memorandum from March 1856, unsigned but either from Gorchakov himself or from a like-minded confidant, presents a cleverly veiled critique of Nesselrode and Nicholas I's foreign policy;[36] numerous marginal notes show that it was approved by Alexander II. The memorandum noted as a favorable moral result of the war the fact that Russia was now less feared in Europe. This fear of Russia had made the tsarist government universally hated and had unified the enemy coalition. Russia would have to step out of the limelight and demonstrate her disinterestedness. The previous system had burdened Russia one-sidedly with duties. Consequently she assumed moral responsibility for the failures and cowardice of other governments.

Concerning Austria there were harsh words: she had been Russia's evil genius and had held Russia to the principle of solidarity to Russia's detriment. The voices that now called for alliance with France expressed the yearning for revenge for Austrian "treachery." But the alliance with France should not be actively sought; time would bring it automatically. Generally speaking, in view of the current political situation, only alliances directed to strictly limited goals should be accepted. Russia must keep complete freedom of action and should not feel committed to any power, not even Prussia: they had indeed helped Russia by their wartime attitude, but they had done it less from sympathy to Russia than from antagonism to Austria.

In short, Gorchakov's assumption of the direction of foreign affairs meant *a new orientation of Russian foreign policy*: the role of "European policeman" was given up and the new guidelines inaugurated systematic renunciation of intervention in foreign affairs.[37] Especially revealing in Gorchakov's self-recommendation to the Tsar was the view of alliances with other powers: they should no longer defend general principles, like solidarity and legitimacy, but should aim at attainment of concrete political goals,[38] primarily revision of the Paris Treaty.

Gorchakov shared this view of political alliances with two other contemporary statesmen, Bismarck and Cavour. This generation modified European politics in subsequent decades in that diplomatic arrangements and alliances now generally pursued revisionist or aggressive goals. The Franco-Russian secret agreement of March 1859 was concluded by Gorchakov and Alexander in the expectation of achieving repudiation of the neutralization clause. Beyond this, Plombières and the Prusso-Italian alliance of 8 April 1866 are telling examples of the offensive character, intentionally short life, and specifically defined goals of political alliances. Here indeed there was a new "realism" in international relations. But it does not break definitively with the alliance system between 1815 and 1854. For the latter did not always exhibit a defensive or restorative character but, as noted, sometimes contained aggressive and egotistical elements, although it is hard to pinpoint them.

Moreover the *Franco-Russian rapprochement* itself, initiated openly at the Paris Congress, should not be overrated. Napoleon adopted it to accomplish a short-term and a long-term goal. First, Britain should be forced to consider peace in the autumn of 1855 through the threat of a Franco-Russian understanding, and once peace negotiations had begun, she should be deprived of the possibility of returning to war. This immediate political goal was accomplished.

For the future Napoleon assigned Russia a place in a Franco-Anglo-Russian triple alliance, which would be the most manageable device for reconstructing Europe. Austria should be forced out of the Crimean coalition, because she was too weak and too unreservedly conservative. A territorial regrouping in cooperation with Austria, Napoleon considered a total delusion after the failure, thanks to Austria's tough opposition, of the exchange plan of North Italy for the Danubian principalities.[39]

Henceforward, he dreamed of a new Tilsit, with Britain included. He revealed this grandiose plan to the new Russian ambassador in

Paris, Count Kiselev, during the crisis over Bolgrad: "Couldn't we reach an understanding as a trio? We will dominate Europe!"[40] But Napoleon's thoughts circled relentlessly around Europe. His mistake was not reckoning with the Russo-British world confrontation. He didn't comprehend its deep roots; he expected that the British peace negotiators, like himself, would act towards the Russians as "the altruist [and] the gentleman."[41] However, even during the peace negotiations, Britain demonstrated her immutable enmity to Russia. And correspondingly, irreconcilable hostility to Britain became a constant in Russian policy. With some justification, Nesselrode saw Anglo-Russian antagonism as the principal cause of the Crimean War. He acquiesced in a rapprochement with France only because it might moderate Britain's high peace conditions and sow disunity in the enemy camp. The tragic result of the Seymour conversations, the Crimean War, had taught him a lesson: "England is and remains our principal and implacable enemy."[42] Gorchakov adopted this as an irreversible fact: "In the Black Sea and in the Baltic, on the coasts of the Caspian Sea and in the Pacific—everywhere Britain is the unwavering enemy of our interests, everywhere she opposes us in the most aggressive fashion."[43] Napoleon's hopes for a triple alliance dominating Europe would founder on the Anglo-Russian world conflict confirmed by the Crimean War. The Franco-Russian rapprochement itself received a heavy blow right after the treaty was signed. At Buol's insistence, with Clarendon's concurrence and Napoleon's obvious reluctance, an Anglo-Franco-Austrian convention was signed on 15 April in Paris, which guaranteed more firmly the commitment expressed in Article 7 of the peace treaty to maintain the integrity of the Ottoman Empire.[44] According to this, any infringement of the treaty should be regarded as a casus belli. The convention was directed uniquely against Russia.

The idea of such a *triple treaty* derived from Buol's reflections in December 1854. At the Vienna Conference in the spring of 1855, it had been readily adopted by Lord John Russell and Drouyn de l'Huys.[45] The Franco-Austrian memorandum of 14 November 1855 provided for conclusion of a triple treaty to guarantee Ottoman integrity as an extension of the general peace treaty. During the peace negotiations, Napoleon very unwillingly let himself be reminded of the agreement made the year before, but, the promise once given, he did not wish to withdraw. He did however refuse the additional article proposed by Austria, which described more precisely the military measures to be taken by the three powers if a casus belli arose.[46]

The convention was not intended to be secret as has often been maintained; already at the beginning of May it was laid before the House of Commons. On the British side, its principal significance seemed to be its political utility against Russia. Clarendon's inquiry to Walewski as to how he had explained it to his "Russian friends" or whether he had excused himself to them suggests such an interpretation. Walewski communicated the convention to Orlov on 30 April, but tried to restrict its meaning by referring to the 14 November 1855 agreement, which, however unfortunate it might now seem, could not be circumvented.[47]

In Petersburg, Napoleon's attitude left a painful impression. Gorchakov interpreted the convention as a warning that Russia must use caution in her newfound relations with France. He considered it an advantage since it could be held before Napoleon as a reminder in case he wished to draw Russia into his "adventuresome plans."[48] Alexander noted in the margin of Orlov's report from Paris: "This action of France towards us is *not very loyal* and should serve us as a measure of the *degree of confidence* which Louis Napoleon can inspire in us."[49] In his farewell audience with Orlov, Napoleon once more asserted his love for Russia, "with tears in his eyes," but Alexander commented with the same skepticism: "All this would be just fine, if it were sincere."[50]

Alexander II's explicit distrust of Napoleon III lurked behind bilateral efforts in the next years to move closer together, and must serve as a yardstick for the Franco-Russian entente after the Crimean War, which has generally been overrated by historians as to intimacy and effectiveness.[51] Certainly Alexander went a long way with Napoleon on revolutionizing Italy, that is, upsetting the order of 1815. And his impulsive foreign minister exceeded him in stressing the value of an alliance with France, when he spoke repeatedly of the "organic relationship" between the two empires and the "natural sympathies" between the two peoples. His motive was an almost pathological hatred of Austria, and especially of Buol personally. Up to a point, Alexander shared this spirit of revenge.[52]

It must not be forgotten that foreign policy was determined personally by Alexander II just as it had been by Nicholas I. However, after Alexander had repaid Austria in 1859 in the same coin for her attitude towards Russia during the Crimean War, he became terrified of the results of Napoleon's policy. The idea of legitimacy was still strongly rooted in him, so Napoleon could no longer count on further Russian support for his reconstruction plans. Alexander was firmly convinced that Napoleon's hand lay behind the rebellion in Sicily in 1860. Even indirect cooperation with the revolution, "[which] overthrows all the princes of order and of legitimacy, who are the basis of every regular government," must undermine his own empire too.[53] Moreover, France's unilateral intervention in Syria at the same time violated the agreement reached in Stuttgart in 1857 to consult in case of complications in the Eastern Question. Alexander called it an "infamy": "After that are you going to reach an understanding with such a government!"[54]

The policy of entente with Napoleon ended in 1863 with the Polish Revolt, the fifth[55] revolutionary nationalist upsurge supported materially or morally by Napoleon since the Paris Congress. It cast a harsh light on Russia's problems as a multinational empire, as had occurred earlier with Austria and the Ottoman Empire.

The Franco-Russian entente after the Crimean War, never a formal alliance, cannot be compared with Franco-Russian cooperation after Bismarck. In Russia's eyes it was designed to separate Britain and France, to isolate Austria, and to help her reestablish the influence in the Balkans lost in 1856. Only the second goal was completely fulfilled. But even Russia's hostility towards Austria must not be overestimated. It is questionable whether Russia could have saved Austria from forced retreat from Italy, even if the Holy Alliance had continued. During the 1848 to 1849 revolution, Russia did not intervene in Italy, but only in Hungary, out of clear self-interest.

No other experience in the nineteenth century had such important consequences for *Austria's foreign policy* as the Crimean War. Austrian isolation after 1856 was total. The convention of 15 April 1856 could not save her. Buol and Francis Joseph, who alone matter for Austria's foreign policy, certainly did not overrate the convention's importance, despite scholarly assertions.[56] In reports from Paris it was described as "an infallible means of obviating the difficulties and of conjuring away the dangers of the new situation," as a "cornerstone" of the new policy inaugurated with the December Treaty, and as an act that would erect before enemies of the "new European system" a "strong dam" and would protect Austria from danger.[57] But these formulations all came from Hübner, who cherished enormous illusions about the solidity of the Austro-French alliance because he assumed that Napoleon in his own best interest would shy away from revolution and would have to act conservatively at Austria's side. Buol, on the contrary, even before the Crimean War, regarded Napoleon with deep mistrust.[58] In an important memorandum, of September 1857, "Reflections on the Policies of the French Second Empire," he described the basic ingredient of Napoleon's diplomacy as the attempt "to spy out the favorable moment for redrafting the map of Europe."[59] Napoleon would have to keep European politics in flux, in order to seize the occasion "when he would be able, *without straining his program,* to deliver a body blow to the social organism." In Paris Napoleon, superficially the protector of Ottoman integrity, spoke to him of the "poor sick man" "as of a man whom they must hasten to bury." Today there might be disturbances in the Danubian principalities, tomorrow a revolution in the Serail, the day after an uproar somewhere in Italy; he was waiting to step forward as the umpire and to propose a solution, as in the Neufchâtel question. Buol considered an honest entente between the two empires impossible, since their political principles contrasted "like fire and water." Cooperation with France to maintain order and respect existing rights could only occur if Austria were to belie her past.

This perception of Napoleon's real motives did not prevent Buol from miscalculating in 1859. But the mistakes of 1859 appear on a different page. The Crimean War policy did indeed lead to Austrian isolation in Europe; but this more or less predictable result was far less drastic than the revolutionary consequences that would certainly have flowed from Austria's entry into the war on *either* side. *One* ethnic revolution had already shaken the Hapsburg empire to its foundations, without leading to collapse. Austrian entry into the war would have transformed the Anglo-Russian confrontation into a world war with incalculable consequences for the political map of Europe and the social structure of each individual European country. The collapse of the Hapsburg empire would then have been virtually inevitable. A revolution would have endangered its existence, but a world war would have been fatal. In the end, it was world war, not revolution, that brought its fall.

Napoleon is generally regarded as the real victor of the Crimean War: he was apparently at the peak of his power at the Paris Congress. This judgment is accurate in many respects. Napoleon triumphed over the Holy Alliance, the guardian of the 1815 order. He had isolated Russia and persuaded her to join him; he had impressed Germany, dragged Austria in his wake, and let Prussia seek an alliance with him; he had even done what the first Napoleon had never succeeded in doing, forced Britain to follow him.[60] The months between Sevastopol and Paris could be considered the richest in his entire reign.[61]

But there is another legitimate way of looking at things, namely comparing the results with his original intentions and expectations and measuring the degree to which they were fulfilled. His grandiose program of remodelling the European map stalled at the Paris Congress. This was how Napoleon himself judged the congress. "The war in the East could have brought the anticipated revolution . . . , if Austria's indecision and the slow course of the military operations had not transformed what looked like the beginning of the great political revolution into a mere tournament," he wrote Walewski on 24 December 1858.[62] Since he had not achieved the great political revolution in

Paris in 1856, Napoleon remained a troublemaker. As a shrewd contemporary put it, he could not keep the peace because of his position, his character, and his habits.[63] He would fall through war.

The same view is even more justifiable with regard to *Britain*. The Paris peace fell far below British wishes, even if they are not identified with Palmerston's ideas. It was forced on Britain by her ally. The peace negotiations and the peace treaty disappointed and embittered a large section of public opinion. Clarendon put it accurately when he wrote Stratford on 8 February 1856: "The French have really in the most reckless and wilful manner destroyed our chances of a good peace by their open and avowed determination not to continue the war."[64] When Stratford learned of the conclusion of the treaty, he replied that he would sooner have cut off his right hand than sign such a treaty.[65] The unnerving trench warfare at the negotiating table with Walewski, whom Clarendon termed a "regular third Russian Plenipotentiary,"[66] made him seriously doubt the staying power of the French alliance. In fact, during the Bolgrad crisis, it hung on a silken thread.

Beginning the following year, Britain was less and less involved in continental affairs. First she had to suppress the mutiny in India; thereafter she dedicated herself increasingly to constructing her world empire and developing her admirably rich economic resources.

The wish to withdraw from European complications had been powerfully stimulated by the shock of the Crimean War. In the eyes of the Englander who looked overseas, the fate of a Balkan principality like Moldavia, "a little barbarous province at the end of Europe,"[67] must seem more and more insignificant, the more time elapsed after that war, "one of the most curious and unnecessary wars in history."[68] After Palmerston's departure, Britain passed fully for at least five years into a phase of "splendid isolation," which Gladstone, who in the spring of 1855 had resigned to protest his government's rejection of the Austrian peace proposals, came to symbolize.

There is profound meaning in the phrase uttered by one of the participants in the congress concerning the treaty: "When you read this treaty, you wonder, who was the loser, who was the victor?"[69]

The Crimean War ended before the issue was decided; the Paris peace brought chagrin and disappointment. The two giant organisms of the British and the Russian world empires had clashed only lightly. The empire in the center of Europe, Austria, had been able to prevent the fatal step from a peripheral siege war on a peninsula in the Black Sea to a world war. In the perspective of a world war, the four short wars of the decade and a half after 1856 appear "mere tournaments." The "great political revolution," which would start precisely in those regions where the Crimean War had been kindled, in the Balkans, was still two whole generations away. The world could have been thankful for that. Sixty consecutive years of peace have not been known in our century. To a high degree, the European Concert continued to fulfill its original peacekeeping function even after 1854–1856.

NOTES

Full citations appear in the bibliography.

III. Results

1. The author believes that it is precisely in this area of the execution of the Paris Peace Treaty that the most, and the most difficult, scholarly work remains to be done. He intends to write at length in this field at a later date. Meanwhile, see W. E. Mosse, *The Rise and Fall of the Crimean System 1855–71,* and Gaston de Monicault, *La Question d'Orient.*

2. Concerning Serbia, the Paris Treaty stipulated that like Moldavia and Wallachia the principality should be placed under the collective guarantee of the contracting parties while maintaining its traditional relationship with the Porte (Article 28) and that the Ottoman right of garrison would be recognized, but armed intervention on their part must not occur without previous arrangement with the signatories (Article 29). For the situation in Syria, see the more recent literature cited in Winfried Baumgart, "Politik und Religion in Syrien im 19. Jahrhundert."

3. The Prince received a pension from Russia; the Greek clergy had severed its relations with Constantinople and associated itself with the Moscow Patriarchate.

4. According to information given by the foreign secretary, Granville, in the House of Commons on 14 February 1871 (*Hansard Parliamentary Debates,* 3rd series, 204: 248).

5. De Launay to Cibrario, Berlin, 11 April 1856 ([Camillo Benso] Cavour, *Cavour e i'Inghilterra,* 7: 454).

6. See above pp. 60–61.

7. Analogies are to be found in the peace of Tilsit (drastic army reduction) and to a certain extent in the peace of Utrecht as well (razing of Dunkirk).

8. Joachim Hoffmann recently alluded to this ("Die Politik der Mächte in der Endphase der Kaukasuskriege," p. 257).

9. See Mosse, *Crimean System,* pp. 120–21. As yet unexploited documents are to be found among the materials in "K istorii franko-russkogo soglašenija 1859 g.," ed. F. Rotštejn.

10. As yet unexploited documents in HHSA PA X 49 (fascicle "Entrevue de Varsovie").

11. Telegram Bismarck to E. von Manteuffel, Berlin, 9 August 1866 ([Prince Otto von] Bismarck, *Die gesammelten Werke,* 6: 114–15 No. 543); telegram Bis-

marck to E. von Manteuffel, Berlin, 18 August 1866 (*ibid.*, pp. 131–32 No. 571); telegram E. von Manteuffel to Bismarck, Alexandria, 24 August 1866 (*Die auswärtige Politik Preussens 1858–1871,* ed. Herbert Michaelis, 8: 41 No. 3); Alexander II to King William I, Peterhof, 24 August 1866 (*ibid.*, pp. 42–43 No. 5).

12. See Chester W. Clark, "Prince Gorchakov and the Black Sea Question, 1866," on all this.

13. Kurt Rheindorf, *Die Schwarze-Meer-(Pontus-) Frage vom Pariser Frieden von 1856 bis zum Abschluss der Londoner Konferenz von 1871,* pp. 54–56. On the Cretan insurrection of 1866 see I. G. Senkevič, *Rossija i Kritskoe Vosstanie 1866–1869 gg.*

14. Reuss to Bismarck, Petersburg, 9 September 1870 (Rheindorf, pp. 148–49).

15. On this whole question see Rheindorf, pp. 75–131, 141–67; Mosse, *Crimean System,* pp. 158–83; further Winfried Baumgart, "Probleme der Krimkriegsforschung," pp. 396–97; the newest treatments are Lev Michajlovič Šneerson, *Franko-prusskaja vojna i Rossija,* pp. 193–218; Barbara Jelavich, *The Ottoman Empire, the Great Powers, and the Straits Question, 1870–1887,* pp. 25–84.

16. The documents are now in PA Bonn, I.A.B.q. 69 vols. 5–13.

17. See W. E. Mosse, "Public Opinion and Foreign Policy."

18. Mosse, *Crimean System,* p. 182.

19. Protocols and text of the treaty in *Recueil d'acts internationaux de l'Empire Ottoman,* ed. Gabriel Effendi Noradounghian, 3: 301–37 (Nos. 802–4).

20. See Baumgart, "Probleme," pp. 258–64.

21. See Part II, n. 52.

22. Documents not yet exploited on this subject in HHSA, PA IX 53–57, PA X 43–44, PA XII 58–60.

23. Text: *Recueil des traités de la France,* ed. [Alexandre Jean Henri] de Clerq, 7: 207.

24. See recently A. Oţetea "L'accord d'Osborne (9 août 1857)."

25. Extensive reporting on this in HHSA, PA IX 58–61. For the following sketch of developments in Rumania, see recently, E. E. Čertan, "Otnošenie velikich deržav k konfliktu meždu Aleksandrom Kuzoj i Zakonodatel'nym sobraniem v načale 1863 goda."

26. Documents not yet exploited on this subject in HHSA, PA X (for 1856 et seq. *passim*) and in BGSA, MA 1921 A.V. Vol. V Nos. 63769–70, 63772, 63788, 63790–91. A monograph is lacking.

27. See above p. 167.

28. More recent monograph with emphasis on the twentieth century by James Barros, *The Aland Islands Question.*

29. *Die Grosse Politik der Europäischen Kabinette 1871–1914,* XXIII, 2: 484–85 (enclosure to No. 8095).

30. John Morley, *The Life of William Ewart Gladstone,* 1: 550–51.

31. A. J. P. Taylor, *The Struggle for Mastery in Europe 1848–1918,* p. 61.

32. Ludwig Dehio, *Gleichgewicht oder Hegemonie,* p. 176. The conclusions that Paul W. Schroeder draws in his work *Austria, Great Britain, and the Crimean War,* pp. 392–427, point in part in a different direction.

33. Heinz Gollwitzer, "Ideologische Blockbildung als Bestandteil internationaler Politik im 19. Jahrhundert."

34. [Karl Vasil'evič, Carl Robert von] Nesselrode, *Lettres et papiers du chancelier Comte de Nesselrode 1760–1856*, 11: 112–16.

35. On 2 September 1856 (S. S. Tatiščev, *Imperator Aleksandr II*, 1: 212). See also the recent general account by Nina Stepanovna Kinjapina, *Vnešnjaja politika Rossii vtoroi poloviny XIX v.*, especially pp. 1–14.

36. "K istorii Parižskogo mira 1856 gg.," ed. M. Ja. Bessmertnaja, pp. 45–51.

37. Bray to King Max, Petersburg, 2 August 1856 (*Russland 1852–1871*, ed. Barbara Jelavich, p. 58n.).

38. "The political system as it has taken shape in Europe makes useless and unreasonable any alliance not concluded for some specific goal" ("K istorii Parižskogo mira," p. 49).

39. Concerning a conversation with Napoleon on 19 March 1856, in which Italian affairs were discussed, Clarendon reported to Palmerston (*Le Relazioni diplomatiche fra la Gran Bretagna e il regno di Sardegna*, series III: 1848–1860, ed. Federico Curato, 98: 249; hereinafter cited as Fonti): "I don't like Austria, His Majesty said with some warmth, I detest her policy but I don't wish to quarrel with her."

40. Kiselev to Gorchakov, 6 November 1856 (*Recueil des traités et conventions conclus par la Russie avec les puissances étrangères*, 15: 298–99. Hereinafter cited as F. de Martens).

41. Clarendon to Stratford de Redcliffe, 22 March 1856 (Stanley Lane-Poole, *The Life of the Right Honourable Stratford Canning Viscount Stratford de Redcliffe*, 2: 435).

42. Principal instruction, Nesselrode to Orlov, 11 February 1856 ("K istorii Parižskogo mira," p. 14).

43. Gorchakov in a report on the year 1856, cited in V. N. Vinogradov, *Rossija i ob-edinenie Rumynskich knjažestv*, p. 89.

44. Text: Noradounghian, 3: 88–89 No. 686; for its background, see Mosse, *Crimean System*, pp. 34–52.

45. See Bernhard Unckel, *Österreich und der Krimkrieg*, p. 210, 229–30; Mosse, *Crimean System*, p. 34; Ennio Di Nolfo, *Europa e Italia nel 1855–1856*, p. 458.

46. Text: *Akten zur Geschichte des Krimkriegs*, ed. Winfried Baumgart, I, 3: 599–600; hereinafter cited as AGKK.

47. Orlov to Nesselrode, 30 April and 1 May 1856 ("K istorii Parižskogo mira," pp. 52–56).

48. Gorchakov to Orlov, 4 May 1856 (*ibid.*, p. 57).

49. F. de Martens, 15: 293. Italics original.

50. *Ibid.*, p. 294

51. See on this whole subject Ernst Schüle, *Russland und Frankreich vom Ausgang des Krimkrieges bis zum italienischen Krieg 1856–1859* (using French documents). Also important are Christian Friese, *Russland und Preussen vom Krimkrieg bis zum polnischen Aufstand* (using Prussian documents); Kinjapina, pp. 14–40.

52. See Alexander to Barjatinskij, Petersburg, 14 December 1858 (*The Politics of Autocracy*, ed. Alfred J. Rieber, p. 126): "Wisdom tells us . . . to be ready to enter the lists if our interests oblige us, but certainly not to rescue Austria as in 1849." Alexander to Barjatinskij, Petersburg, 1 April 1859 (*ibid.*, p. 128): "As for

us we will try . . . to remain neutral spectators for as long as possible while observing towards Austria the role that she adopted towards us during the last war."

53. Alexander to Barjatinskij, Carskoe Selo, 23 July 1860 (*ibid.*, p. 138).

54. *Ibid.*; further Alexander to Barjatinskij, Carskoe Selo, 12 September 1860 (*ibid.*, p. 140).

55. Danubian principalities, Italy, Serbia, Greece.

56. Unckel, pp. 277–78; Harold Temperley, "The Treaty of Paris of 1856 and its Execution," p. 528.

57. Buol/Hübner to Francis Joseph, Paris, 28 February 1856 (AGKK I, 3: 446); Buol/Hübner to Francis Joseph, Paris, 16 April 1856 (*ibid.*, pp. 606–7).

58. Paul W. Schroeder was so kind as to remind me that it is clear from Buol's diary that Buol clung to the hope as late as the summer of 1856 of being able to salvage the Austro-French entente after the Crimean War.

59. "La France et l'Autriche en 1857," ed. Charles W. Hallberg, pp. 353–60.

60. See also L. von Gerlach's diary entry of 4 January 1856 (Leopold von Gerlach, *Denkwürdigkeiten aus dem Leben Leopold von Gerlachs*, 2: 379).

61. See Di Nolfo, *Europa*, p. 248: "The Emperor enjoyed a rather happy period, perhaps the happiest in all the years of his reign."

62. Franco Valsecchi, *L'unificazione italiana e la politica europea dalla guerra di Crimea alla guerra di Lombardia 1854–1859*, p. 338.

63. King William of Württemberg. See Bismarck to Leopold von Gerlach, Frankfurt, 21 December 1855 (Bismarck, XIV, 1: 425).

64. Lane-Poole, 2: 434.

65. *Ibid.*, p. 436.

66. Clarendon to Hammond, Paris, 13 March 1856 (Fonti, 98: 247). See also Hübner's diary entry of 28 February 1856 ([Joseph Alexander von] Hübner, Count Hübner, *Neuf ans de souvenirs d'un ambassadeur d'Autriche à Paris sous le Second Empire 1851–1859*, 1: 398).

67. Cited by M. S. Anderson, *The Eastern Question 1774–1923*, p. 152.

68. Vernon John Puryear, *England, Russia and the Straits Question 1844–1856*, p. xiii.

69. Baron Bourqueney in conversation with Beust (Friedrich Ferdinand, Count Beust, *Aus drei Viertel-Jahrhunderten*, 1: 203).

Bibliography

Unpublished Documents

Politisches Archiv, Bonn I.A.B.q. 69 vols. 5–13 Turkey (November 1869–March 1871).

Generallandesarchiv, Karlsruhe Abt. 48, Nos. 2050–51: Diplomatic correspondence. France I A 2. Correspondence of the envoy Freiherr von Schweizer with the minister, Freiherr Rüdt von Collenberg Bödigheim (1855–1856).

Nos. 2503–04: Diplomatic correspondence. Austria. Correspondence of the envoy Freiherr von Andlaw with the minister of state, Freiherr Rüdt . . . (1855–1856).

No. 2507: Diplomatic correspondence. Austria. Correspondence of Freiherr Rüdt . . . with the minister of state, Freiherr von Meysenbug (1857).

No. 2653: Diplomatic correspondence. Prussia. Correspondence of the envoy Freiherr von Meysenbug with the minister, Freiherr Rüdt . . . (1856).

Bayerisches Hauptstaatsarchiv, Abteilung Geheimes Staatsarchiv, Munich MA I 597–98: Papers of the Royal Bavarian minister of state for internal and external affairs. Concerning the Eastern Question (1855–1856).

MA 1921 A.V. Vol. V:

No. 63769: Records of the Danube Commission.

No. 63770: Memorandum by the Sardinian minister Paleocapa concerning the question of the Danube delta.

No. 63772: Statistics concerning the Danube and its tributaries and communications concerning navigation in general.

No. 63788: Note on the work of the European Danube Commission.

No. 63790: Implementation of the agreements concerning navigation of the Danube. . . .

No. 63791: Conclusion of the agreement concerning navigation of the Danube. . . .

Österreichisches Staatsarchiv, Abt. Haus-, Hof- und Staatsarchiv, Vienna PA VIII: England, cartons 38, 42. Reports, Instructions, Miscellaneous Despatches (1853, 1856).

PA IX: France, cartons 48–57. Reports, Instructions, Miscellaneous Despatches (1854–1857).

PA X: Russia, cartons 42–44, 49. Reports, Instructions, Miscellaneous Despatches (1855–1856, 1860).

PA XII: Turkey, cartons 55–60. Reports, Instructions, Miscellaneous Despatches (1855–1856).
    carton 218—Vienna Conferences 1853–1856.
    carton 219–20—Paris Conferences 1856.
PA XL: Interna, carton 49. Reports to and letters from the Emperor (1855–1856).
    carton 277a—Private letters and notes from the Emperor to Buol (1852–1859).

Published Documents and Secondary Literature

Acte și documente relative la istoria renascerei Romaniei. Vol. II. Ed. Ghenadic Petrescu, Dimitrie A. Sturdza, Dimitrie C. Sturdza. Bucharest, 1889.

Akten zur Geschichte des Krimkriegs. Serie I. Österreichische Akten zur Geschichte des Krimkriegs. Ed. Winfried Baumgart. Vol. III: 10. September 1855 bis 24. Mai 1856. Ed. Winfried Baumgart. Munich, 1979. (Cited AGKK.)

Aktenstücke zur orientalischen Frage. Nebst chronologischer Uebersicht. Ed. J. von Jasmund. Vol. II. Berlin, 1856.

Alstyne: see under Van Alstyne.

Anderson, M. S. *The Eastern Question 1774–1923. A Study in International Relations.* London, 1966.

Anderson, Olive. *A Liberal State at War. English Politics and Economics during the Crimean War.* London, 1967.

————. "Some Further Light on the Inner History of the Declaration of Paris." *Law Quarterly Review* 76 (1960): 379–85.

Argyll, George Douglas Eighth Duke of. *Autobiography and Memoirs.* Ed. The Dowager Duchess of Argyll. Vols. I–II. London, 1906.

Ashley, Evelyn. *The Life of Henry John Temple, Viscount Palmerston: 1846–1865. With Selections from His Speeches and Correspondence.* Vol. II. London, 1876.

Auswärtige Politik Preussens, Die, 1858–1871. Dritte Abteilung: Die auswärtige Politik Preussens und des Norddeutschen Bundes vom Prager Frieden bis zur Gründung des Reiches und zum Friedensschluss mit Frankreich. Vol. VIII: August 1866 to May 1867. Ed. Herbert Michaelis. Oldenburg, 1934.

Balfour, Frances. *The Life of George, Fourth Earl of Aberdeen.* Vol. II. London, [1922].

Bapst, Germain. *Le Maréchal Canrobert. Souvenirs d'un siècle.* Vol. III: "Paris et la Cour pendant le Congrès. La Naissance du Prince Impérial. La Guerre d'Italie." Paris, 1904.

Barros, James. *The Aland Islands Question. Its Settlement by the League of Nations.* New Haven, 1968.

Baumgart, Winfried. "Die Aktenedition zur Geschichte des Krimkriegs. Eine Zwischenbilanz auf Grund der österreichischen Akten." *Festschrift für Gotthold Rhode,* forthcoming.

————. "Brest-Litovsk und Versailles. Ein Vergleich zweier Friedensschlüsse." *Historische Zeitschrift* 210 (1970): 583–619. Reprinted in *Versailles-St.*

Germain-Trianon. Umbruch in Europa vor fünfzig Jahren, ed. Karl Bosl, pp. 49–76. Munich, 1971.

————. "Eisenbahnen und Kriegführung in der Geschichte." *Technikgeschichte* 38 (1971): 191–219.

————. "Die grossen Friedensschlüsse der Neuzeit (1435–1945). Ein Forschungsüberblick." *Geschichte in Wissenschaft und Unterricht* 29 (1978): 778–806.

————. "Das 'Kaspi-Unternehmen'—Grössenwahn Ludendorffs oder Routineplanung des deutschen Generalstabs? Ein kritischer Rückblick auf die deutsche militärische Intervention im Kaukasus am Ende des Ersten Weltkriegs" 2 parts. *Jahrbücher für Geschichte Osteuropas* N.F. 18 (1970): 47–126; 231–78.

————. "Ein Kriegsrat Napoleons III. französisch-englische Militärbesprechungen im Januar 1856." *Festschrift für Eberhard Kessel,* forthcoming.

————. "Der Krimkrieg in der angelsächsischen und russischen militärgeschichtlichen Literatur der sechziger Jahre." *Militärgeschichtliche Mitteilungen* 2 (1970): 181–94.

————. "Österreich und Preussen im Krimkrieg 1853–1856. Neue Forschungsergebnisse auf Grund der österreichischen Akten." *Neue Forschungen zur brandenburgisch-preussischen Geschichte* 2, forthcoming.

————. "Politik und Religion in Syrien im 19. Jahrhundert. Bericht zu einigen neuen Büchern." *Zeitschrift für Missionswissenschaft und Religionswissenschaft* 55 (1971): 104–8.

————. "Probleme der Krimkriegsforschung. Eine Studie über die Literatur des letzten Jahrzehnts (1961–1970)." *Jahrbücher für Geschichte Osteuropas* N.F. 19 (1971): 49–109; 243–64; 371–400.

————. *Vom Europäischen Konzert zum Völkerbund. Friedensschlüsse und Friedenssicherung von Wien bis Versailles.* Erträge der Forschung 25. Darmstadt, 1974.

Bayley, C. C. *Mercenaries for the Crimea. The German, Swiss, and Italian Legions in British Service, 1854–1856.* Montreal, 1977.

Beer, Adolf. *Die orientalische Politik Österreichs seit 1774.* Prague, 1883.

Bernardy, Françoise de. "Le Congrès de Paris (février-avril 1856)." *Revue des deux mondes* (March–April 1956): 207–23.

Bestužev, I. V. "Iz istorii Krymskoj vojny 1853–1856 gg." *Istoričeskij archiv* 1 (1959): 204–8.

————. "Krymskaja vojna i revoljucionnaja situacija." In *Revoljucionnaja situacija v Rossii v 1859–1861 gg.,* pp. 189–213. Moscow, 1963.

Beust, Friedrich Ferdinand, Count. *Aus drei Viertel-Jahrhunderten. Erinnerungen und Aufzeichnungen.* Vol. 1: 1809–1866. Stuttgart, 1887.

Bismarck, [Prince Otto von]. *Die gesammelten Werke.* Vol. II: "Politische Schriften (1855 I 1–1859 III 1)." Ed. Herman von Petersdorff. Berlin, 1924. Vol. VI: "Politische Schriften (1866 VI 16–1867 VII 9)." Ed. Friedrich Thimme. Berlin, 1929. Vol. XIV, 1: "Briefe (1822 IV 27–1862 IV 19)." Ed. Wolfgang Windelband and Werner Frauendienst. Berlin, 1933.

Blackwell, William L. *The Beginnings of Russian Industrialization 1800–1860.* Princeton, N.J., 1968.

Böhm, Wilhelm. *Konservative Umbaupläne im alten Österreich. Gestaltungsprobleme des Völkerreiches.* Vienna, 1967.

Borries, Kurt. *Preussen im Krimkrieg (1853–1856).* Stuttgart, 1930.

Bourquin, Maurice. *Histoire de la Sainte Alliance.* Geneva, 1954.

Brandt, Harm-Hinrich. *Der österreichische Neoabsolutismus: Staatsfinanzen und Politik 1848–1860.* Vols. I–II. Schriftenreihe der Historischen Kommission bei der Bayerischen Akademie der Wissenschaften 15. Göttingen, 1978.

British Documents on the Origins of the War 1898–1914. Ed. G. P. Gooch and Harold Temperley. Vol. VIII: "Arbitration, Neutrality and Security." London, 1932.

Case, Lynn M. *French Opinion on War and Diplomacy during the Second Empire.* Philadelphia, 1954.

Castel de Saint Pierre, Charles Irénée Abbé de. *Projet pour rendre la paix perpétuelle en Europe.* [Various eds.] Vols. I–III. Utrecht, [1712–1717].

Cavour, [Camillo Benso]. *Cavour e l'Inghilterra. Carteggio con V. E. d'Azeglio.* Vol. I: "Il congresso di Parigi." Bologna, 1933. Reprint 1961. (*Carteggi di Cavour,* VII.)

————. *Lettere edite ed inedite.* Ed. Luigi Chiala. Vol. II. Turin, 1884.

Čertan, E. E. "Otnošenie velikich deržav k konfliktu meždu Aleksandrom Kuzoj i Zakonodatel'nym sobraniem v năcale 1863 goda." In *Russko-rumynskie i sovetsko-rumynskie otnošenija. Sbornik statej i soobščenij,* pp. 42–56. Kišinev, 1969.

Charles-Roux, François. *Alexandre II, Gortchakoff et Napoléon III.* Paris, 1913.

Clark, Chester W. "Prince Gorchakov and the Black Sea Question, 1866. A Russian Bomb that did not Explode." *American Historical Review* 48 (1942–43): 52–60.

Clerq, De: see under *Recueil des traités de la France.*

Conacher, J. B. *The Aberdeen Coalition 1852–1855. A Study in Mid-Nineteenth-Century Party Politics.* Cambridge, 1968.

Congrès, Le, de Vienne et les traités de 1815. Précédé et suivi des actes diplomatiques qui s'y rattachent. 2 parts. Ed. and introd. M. Capefigue [Comte d'Angeberg, Leonard Jakób Chodźko]. Paris, [1863].

Conversations with Napoleon III. A Collection of Documents, mostly Unpublished and almost entirely Diplomatic. Ed. Sir Victor Wellesley and Robert Sencourt. London, 1934.

Corespondenţa lui Coronini din Principate. Acte şi Rapoarte din Iunie 1854–Martie 1857. Ed. Ion I. Nistor. Czernowitz, 1938.

Corti, Egon Caesar Count. *Mensch und Herrscher. Wege und Schicksale Kaiser Franz Josephs I. zwischen Thronbesteigung und Berliner Kongress.* Graz, 1952.

Craig, Gordon A. *War, Politics, and Diplomacy. Selected Essays.* London, 1966.

Curtiss, John Shelton. *The Russian Army under Nicholas I, 1825–1855.* Durham, N.C., 1965.

————. *Russia's Crimean War.* Durham, N.C., 1979.

Daniels, Emil. *Geschichte der Kriegskunst im Rahmen der politischen Geschichte,* Part 5. Berlin, 1928. (Hans Delbrück, *Geschichte der Kriegskunst im Rahmen der politischen Geschichte,* con. Emil Daniels, 5).

Davison, Roderic H. "Ottomon Diplomacy at the Congress of Paris (1856) and the Question of Reforms." *Türk Tarih Kurumu,* VII. *Türk Tarih Kongresi, Kongreye sunulan bildiriler* 2 (1973): 580–86.

———. *Reform in the Ottoman Empire 1856–1876.* Princeton, N.J., 1963.

De Clerq: see under *Recueil des traités de la France.*

Dehio, Ludwig. *Gleichgewicht oder Hegemonie. Betrachtungen über ein Grundproblem der neueren Staatengeschichte.* Krefeld, n.d.

Delord, Taxile. *Histoire du Second Empire 1848–1869.* Vol. I. Paris, 1869.

Dickmann, Fritz. *Friedensrecht und Friedenssicherung. Studien zum Friedensproblem in der neueren Geschichte.* Göttingen, 1971.

Di Nolfo, Ennio. *Adam J. Czartoryski e il congresso di Parigi. (Questione polacca e politica europea nel 1855–56.)* Università degli studi di Padova. Collana di studi sull'Europa orientale 3. Padua, 1964.

———. *Europa e Italia nel 1855–1856.* Istituto per la storia del Risorgimento italiano. Biblioteca scientifica. Series II: memorie 25. Rome, 1967.

Documents, British: see under *British Documents.*

Echard, William E. "Napoleon III and the Concert of Europe: Conference Diplomacy and the Congress Idea to 1863." Ph.D. dissertation, University of Pennsylvania, 1960.

Eckhart, Franz. *Die deutsche Frage und der Krimkrieg.* Osteuropäische Forschungen, N.F. 9. Berlin, 1931.

Ekmečić, Milorad. "Mit o revoluciji i Austrijska politika prema Bosni, Hercegovini i Crnoj Gori u vrijeme Krimskog rata 1853–1856." *Godišnjak. Društva istoričara Bosne i Hercegovine* 13 (1962): 95–165.

Engel-Janosi, Friedrich. *Der Freiherr von Hübner 1811–1892. Eine Gestalt aus dem Österreich Kaiser Franz Josephs.* Innsbruck, 1933.

Ernest II, Duke of Saxe-Coburg-Gotha. *Aus meinem Leben und aus meiner Zeit.* Vol. II. Berlin, 1888.

Euler, Heinrich. *Napoleon III in seiner Zeit.* Vol. II, forthcoming.

Fadner, Frank. *Seventy Years of Pan-Slavism in Russia. Karamzin to Danilevskiĭ.* [Washington], 1962.

Fitzmaurice, Edmond. *The Life of Granville George Leveson Gower, Second Earl Granville K. G. 1815–1891.* Vol. I. London, 1905.

Fonti: see under *Relazioni.*

"France, La, et l'Autriche en 1857. Un memorandum du comte Buol." Ed. Charles W. Hallberg. *Revue d'histoire diplomatique* 53 (1939): 353–60.

Freyer, Hans. *Soziologie als Wirklichkeitswissenschaft. Logische Grundlegung des Systems der Soziologie.* Leipzig, 1930.

Fried, Alfred H. *Handbuch der Friedensbewegung.* Part II: "Geschichte, Umfang und Organisation der Friedensbewegung." Berlin, 1913.

Friedjung, Heinrich. *Der Krimkrieg und die österreichische Politik.* Stuttgart, 1911.

Friese, Christian. *Russland und Preussen vom Krimkrieg bis zum polnischen Aufstand.* Osteuropäische Forschungen, N.F. 11. Berlin, 1931.

Geffcken, F. Heinrich. *Zur Geschichte des orientalischen Krieges 1853–1856.* Berlin, 1881.

Genet, Raoul. *Traité de diplomatie et de droit diplomatique.* Vol. III. "Les Actes diplomatiques. Congrès et conférences. Technique-histoire-résultats. Les Traités et conventions. L'Arbitrage et la conciliation." Publications de la revue générale de droit international public 6. Paris, 1932.

Gerlach, Ernst Ludwig von. *Von der Revolution zum Norddeutschen Bund. Politik* und Ideengut der preussischen Hochkonservativen 1848–1866. Aus dem Nachlass von Ernst Ludwig von Gerlach. Ed. and intro. Hellmut Diwald. Part I: "Tagebuch 1848–1866." Deutsche Geschichtsquellen des 19. und 20. Jahrhunderts 46, 1. Göttingen, 1970.

Gerlach, Leopold von. Denkwürdigkeiten aus dem Leben Leopold von Gerlachs, Generals der Infanterie und General-Adjutanten König Friedrich Wilhelms IV. Ed. according to his notes by his daughter. Vol. II. Berlin, 1892.

Geuss, Herbert. Bismarck und Napoleon III. Ein Beitrag zur Geschichte der preussisch-französischen Beziehungen 1851–1871. Kölner Historische Abhandlungen 1. Graz, 1959.

Girardin, Émile de. L'Equilibre européen. Paris, 1859.

Gladstone, W. E. Gleanings of Past Years, 1843–78. Vol. I: "1875–8. The Throne, and the Prince Consort; the Cabinet, and Constitution." London, 1879.

Golder, Frank A. "Russian-American Relations during the Crimean War." American Historical Review 31 (1925–26): 462–76.

Gollwitzer, Heinz. Europabild und Europagedanke. Beiträge zur deutschen Geistesgeschichte des 18. und 19. Jahrhunderts. Munich, 1964.

———. "Ideologische Blockbildung als Bestandteil internationaler Politik im 19. Jahrhundert." Historische Zeitschrift 201 (1965): 306–33.

Gooch, Brison D. The New Bonapartist Generals in the Crimean War. Distrust and Decision-making in the Anglo-French Alliance. The Hague, 1959.

Gorce: see under La Gorce.

Goriainow, Serge. Le Bosphore et les Dardanelles. Étude historique sur la question des détroits. D'après la correspondance diplomatique déposée aux Archives centrales de Saint-Pétersbourg et à celles de l'Empire. Paris, 1910.

Gourdon, Édouard. Histoire du Congrès de Paris... Avec une introduction par M. J[oseph] Cohen. Paris, 1857.

Greville, [Charles Cavendish Fulke]. The Greville Memoirs 1814–1860. Ed. Lytton Strachey and Roger Fulford. Vol. VII (1854–1860). London, 1938.

Grosse, Die, Politik der Europäischen Kabinette 1871–1914. Sammlung der diplomatischen Akten des Auswärtigen Amtes. Sponsored by the Foreign Ministry. Ed. Johannes Lepsius, Albrecht Mendelssohn Bartholdy, Friedrich Thimme. Vol. II: "Der Berliner Kongress und seine Vorgeschichte." Berlin, 1922. Vol. XXIII: "Die Zweite Haager Friedenskonferenz. Nordsee- und Ostsee-Abkommen." Part two. Berlin, 1925.

Hallendorff, Carl. Konung Oscar I's politik under Krimkriget. Kungl. Vitterhets historie och antiquitets akademiens handlingar 41, 2. Stockholm, 1930.

———. Oscar I, Napoleon och Nikolaus. Ur diplomaternas privatbrev under Krimkriget. Stockholm, 1918.

Hansard Parliamentary Debates, 3rd series, vol. 140. London, 1856. Vol. 204. London, 1871.

Hantsch, Hugo. Die Geschichte Österreichs. Vol. II. Graz, 1968.

Hausmann, Paulus Andreas. "Friedenspräliminarien in der Völkerrechtsgeschichte." Zeitschrift für ausländisches öffentliches Recht und Völkerrecht 25 (1965): 657–92.

Haym, Rudolf. Die deutsche Nationalversammlung von den Septemberereignissen bis zur Kaiserwahl. Ein weiterer Parteibericht. Berlin, 1849.

Heindl, Waltraut. Graf Buol-Schauenstein in St. Petersburg und London (1848–

1852). Zur Genesis des Antagonismus zwischen Österreich und Russland. Studien zur Geschichte der Österreichisch-Ungarischen Monarchie 9. Vienna, 1970.

Henderson, Gavin Burns. *Crimean War Diplomacy and Other Historical Essays.* Glasgow University Publications 68. Glasgow, 1947.

Hoffmann, Joachim. "Die Politik der Mächte in der Endphase der Kaukasus-kriege." *Jahrbücher für Geschichte Osteuropas* N.F. 17 (1969): 215–58.

Hoffmann, Peter. *Die diplomatischen Beziehungen zwischen Württemberg und Bayern im Krimkrieg und bis zum Beginn der italienischen Krise (1853–1858).* Veröffentlichungen der Kommission für geschichtliche Landeskunde in Baden-Württemberg. Reihe B. Forschungen 23. Stuttgart, 1963.

Hölzle, Erwin. *Russland und Amerika. Aufbruch und Begegnung zweier Weltmächte.* Munich, 1953.

Hösch, Edgar. "Neuere Literatur (1940–1960) über den Krimkrieg." *Jahrbücher für Geschichte Osteuropas* N.F. 9 (1961): 399–434.

Hübner, [Joseph Alexander von], Count Hübner. *Neuf ans de souvenirs d'un ambassadeur d'Autriche à Paris sous le Second Empire 1851–1859.* Ed. Alexander Count Hübner. Vol. I. Paris, 1905.

"Imperator Aleksandr Nikolaevič v èpochu vojny 1855 goda." Ed. M. I. Bogdanovič. *Russkaja starina* 37 (1883): 117–30; 39 (1883): 195–220; 299–330; 597–608.

Isser, Natalie. *The Second Empire and the Press. A Study of Government-Inspired Brochures on French Foreign Policy in their Propaganda Milieu.* The Hague, 1974.

"Istorii: k istorii franko-russkogo soglašenija 1859 g." Ed. F. Rotštejn. *Krasnyj Archiv* 88 (1938): 182–255.

"Istorii: k istorii Parižskogo mira 1856 g." Ed. M. Ja. Bessmertnaja. *Krasnyj Archiv* 75 (1936): 10–61.

Jelavich, Barbara. *The Ottoman Empire, the Great Powers, and the Straits Question, 1870–1887.* Bloomington, Indiana, 1973.

Jomini, Alexandre de. *Étude diplomatique sur la guerre de Crimée (1852 à 1856). Par un ancien diplomate.* Vol. II. St. Petersburg, 1878.

Kaehler, Siegfried A. "Realpolitik zur Zeit des Krimkrieges. Eine Säkularbetrachtung." In *Studien zur deutschen Geschichte des 19. und 20. Jahrhunderts. Aufsätze und Vorträge,* ed. Walter Bussmann, pp. 128–70. Göttingen, 1961.

Kann, Robert A. *The Multinational Empire. Nationalism and National Reform in the Habsburg Monarchy, 1848–1918.* Vols. I–II. New York, 1950 (Reprint 1964).

Kaufmann, P[eter]. *Die Idee und der praktische Nutzen einer Weltakademie des Völker-Rechts, erörtert und zur Vergleichung gestellt mit dem Amphiktyonen-Verein der Griechen sowie mit der christlichen Staaten-Republik Königs Heinrich des Vierten von Frankreich. Ein Beitrag zur sittlichen Organisation der Menschheit.* Bonn, 1855.

⸻. *Die Wissenschaft des Weltfriedens im Grundrisse. Versuch einer wissenschaftlichen Darlegung der Wege und Mittel, durch welche der allgemeine beständige Frieden der Völker und Staaten herbeigeführt und erhalten wird.* Bonn, 1866.

Kinjapina, N. S. *Vnešnjaja politika Rossii vtoroj poloviny XIX v.* Moscow, 1974.

Kolb, Eberhard. "Kriegführung und Politik 1870/71." In *Reichsgründung 1870/71. Tatsachen, Kontroversen, Interpretationen,* ed. Theodor Schieder and Ernst Deuerlein, pp. 95–118. Stuttgart, 1970.

Konferenzen und Verträge. Vertrags-Ploetz. Ein Handbuch geschichtlich bedeutsamer

Zusammenkünfte und Vereinbarungen. Part II, vol. III: "Neuere Zeit 1492–1914." Ed. Helmuth K. G. Rönnefarth. Würzburg, 1958.

Kübeck von Kübau, Carl Friedrich. *Aus dem Nachlass des Freiherrn Carl Friedrich Kübeck von Kübau. Tagebücher, Briefe, Aktenstücke (1841–1855).* Ed. and intro. Friedrich Walter. Veröffentlichungen der Kommission für neuere Geschichte Österreichs 45. Graz, 1960.

Kyriakos, A. Diomedes. *Geschichte der orientalischen Kirchen von 1453–1898.* Leipzig, 1902.

La Gorce, Pierre de. *Histoire du Second Empire.* Vol. I. Paris, 1902.

Lamer, Reinhard J. *Der englische Parlamentarismus in der deutschen politischen Theorie im Zeitalter Bismarcks (1857–1890). Ein Beitrag zur Vorgeschichte des deutschen Parlamentarismus.* Historische Studien 387. Lübeck, 1963.

Lane-Poole, Stanley. *The Life of the Right Honourable Stratford Canning Viscount Stratford de Redcliffe. From his Memoirs and Private and Official Papers.* Vol. II. London, 1888.

La Rive, W. de. *Le Comte de Cavour. Récits et souvenirs.* Paris, 1862.

Mackintosh, John P. *The British Cabinet.* London, 1968.

Malkin, H. W. "The Inner History of the Declaration of Paris." *The British Year Book of International Law* 8(1927): 1–44.

Manteuffel, Otto Freiherr von. *Preussens auswärtige Politik 1850 bis 1858. Unveröffentlichte Dokumente aus dem Nachlasse des Ministerpräsidenten Otto Frhrn. von Manteuffel.* Ed. Heinrich von Poschinger. Vol. III: "Von der Beendigung der orientalischen Krisis bis zum Beginn der neuen Aera (1854–1858)." Berlin, 1902.

Marcelli, Umberto. *Cavour diplomatico. (Dal congresso di Parigi a Villafranca.)* Biblioteca di storia e di antichità 1. Bologna, 1961.

Martens, F. de: see under *Recueil des traités et conventions.*

Martens, Georges Frédéric de, ed. *Recueil des principaux traités....* Vol. VI. Göttingen, 1800. *Nouveau recueil général de traités....* Series 1, vol. XV. Göttingen, 1857. *Nouveau recueil général de traités....* Series 2, vol. XXVI. Göttingen, 1902.

Martin, Theodore. *The Life of His Royal Highness the Prince Consort.* Vol. III. London, 1878.

Martini, Angelo. "La S. Sede, la questione d'Oriente e il congresso di Parigi (1856)." In *La Civiltà Cattolica* 110, 1(1959): 165–79.

Matter, Paul. *Cavour et l'unité italienne.* 3 vols. Paris, 1922–1927.

Maxwell, Herbert. *The Life and Letters of George William Frederick Fourth Earl of Clarendon.* Vol. II. London, 1913.

Metternich, [Klemens Wenzel Nepomuk Lothar von]. *Briefe des Staatskanzlers Fürsten Metternich-Winneburg an den österreichischen Minister des Allerhöchsten Hauses und des Äussern, Grafen Buol-Schauenstein aus den Jahren 1852–1859.* Ed. Carl J. Burckhardt. Munich, 1934.

Meyendorff, Peter von. *Ein russischer Diplomat an den Höfen von Berlin und Wien. Politischer und privater Briefwechsel 1826–1863.* Ed. and intro. Otto Hoetzsch. Vol. III. Berlin, 1923.

Monicault, Gaston de. *La Question d'Orient. Le traité de Paris et ses suites (1856–1871).* Paris, 1898.

Morley, John. *The Life of William Ewart Gladstone.* Vol. I: 1809–1859. New York, 1903.

Morny, [Charles Auguste Louis Joseph] Duke of. *Une ambassade en Russie. 1856. Extrait des mémoires du Duc de Morny.* Paris, 1892.

Mosse, W. E. "Public Opinion and Foreign Policy. The British Public and the War-Scare of November 1870." *Historical Journal* 6(1963): 38–58.

————. *The Rise and Fall of the Crimean System 1855–71. The Story of a Peace Settlement.* London, 1963.

Napoleon III. *Discours, messages, lettres et proclamations de S. M. Napoléon III, Empereur des Français.* First Series. 1849–1861. Paris, 1861.

Nesselrode, [Karl Vasil'evič, Carl Robert von]. *Lettres et papiers du chancelier Comte de Nesselrode 1760–1856. Extraits de ses archives.* Ed. Comte A. de Nesselrode. Vol. XI: 1854–1856. Paris, [1912].

Neue Quellen zur Geschichte Preussens im 19. Jahrhundert. Ed. Hans-Joachim Schoeps. Berlin, 1968.

Noradounghian: see under *Recueil d'actes.*

Nouveau recueil général: see under Martens, G. F. de.

Omodeo, Adolfo. *L'opera politica del Conte di Cavour.* Part 1: 1848–1857. Vols. I–II. Documenti di storia italiana. N.S. Florence, 1940.

Oncken, Hermann. *Die Rheinpolitik Kaiser Napoleons III. von 1863 bis 1870 und der Ursprung des Krieges von 1870/71. Nach den Staatsakten von Österreich, Preussen und den süddeutschen Mittelstaaten.* Vol. I: 1863–1866. Berlin, 1926.

Oţetea, A. "L'accord d'Osborne (9 août 1857)." *Revue roumaine d'histoire* 3(1964): 677–96.

Piggott, Francis. *The Declaration of Paris 1856. A Study (Documented).* "Law of the Sea" Series of Historical and Legal Works 4. London, 1919.

Pintner, Walter McK. "Inflation in Russia during the Crimean War Period." *American Slavic and East European Review* 18 (1959): 81–87.

Politics, The, of Autocracy. Letters of Alexander II to Prince A. I. Bariatinskii 1857–1864. Ed. with an historical essay by Alfred J. Rieber. Études sur l'histoire, l'économie et la sociologie des pays slaves 12. Paris, 1966.

Prokesch-Osten, [Anton Franz Count]. "Ein Beitrag zur Geschichte der orientalischen Frage. Aus dem Nachlass des Grafen [Anton Franz] Prokesch-Osten, k. k. österr. Feldzeugmeisters und Botschafters." Ed. Anton Count Prokesch-Osten. Part 2: "Erinnerungen aus Konstantinopel. Aus dem Nachlass. . . ." *Deutsche Revue* 4, 1(1879): 6–19; 4, 2(1880): 61–74.

Puryear, Vernon John. *England, Russia and the Straits Question 1844–1856.* Berkeley, Calif., 1931. Reprint. Hamden, Conn., 1965.

Rain, Pierre. "Le Centenaire du Quai d'Orsay et le Congrès de Paris." *Revue d'histoire diplomatique* 70(1956): 61–75.

Ranke, Leopold von. "Friedrich Wilhelm IV." In *Allgemeine Deutsche Biographie,* vol. VII, pp. 729–76. Leipzig, 1878.

Rassow, Peter. *Der Konflikt König Friedrich Wilhelms IV. mit dem Prinzen von Preussen im Jahre 1854. Eine preussische Staatskrise.* Akademie der Wissenschaften und der Literatur. Abhandlungen der Geistes- und Sozialwissenschaftlichen Klasse, 1960, No. 9. Wiesbaden, 1961.

"Razgovor imperatora Napoleona III s gen.-ad. Totlebenom v 1857 g." Ed.

N. K. Šilder. *Russkaja starina* 16(1885): 717–19.

Recueil d'actes internationaux de l'Empire Ottoman. Traités, conventions. . . . Ed. Gabriel Effendi Noradounghian. Vol. III: 1856–1878. Paris, 1902.

Recueil des principaux traités: see under Martens, G. F. de.

Recueil des traités et conventions conclus par la Russie avec les puissances étrangères. Ed. F. de Martens. Vol. XV: "Traités avec la France 1822–1906." St. Petersburg, 1909.

Recueil des traités de la France. Ed. [Alexandre Jean Henri] de Clerq. Vol. VI: 1850–1855. Paris, 1866. Vol. VII: 1856–1859. Paris, 1866.

Relazioni, Le, diplomatiche fra l'Austria e il regno di Sardegna. Series III: 1848–1860. Vol. IV: 1853–1857. Ed. Franco Valsecchi. Fonti per la Storia d'Italia [67], Documenti per la storia delle relazioni diplomatiche fra le grandi potenze europee e gli stati italiani, 1814–1860, part two, documenti esteri. Rome, 1963.

Relazioni, Le, diplomatiche fra la Gran Bretagna e il regno di Sardegna. Series III: 1848–1860. Vol. IV: 1852–January 1855; vol. V: January 1855–1856. Ed. Federico Curato. Rome, 1968, 1969. (Fonti . . . [88, 98], Documenti. . . .)

Rheindorf, Kurt. *Die Schwarze-Meer- (Pontus-) Frage vom Pariser Frieden von 1856 bis zum Abschluss der Londoner Konferenz von 1871. Ein Beitrag zu den orientalischen Fragen und zur Politik der Grossmächte im Zeitalter Bismarcks*. Berlin, 1925.

Ritter, Gerhard. "Bismarck und die Rhein-Politik Napoleons III." *Rheinische Vierteljahrsblätter* 15/16 (1950–51): 339–70.

Ritter, Monika. "Frankreichs Griechenland-Politik während des Krimkrieges (Im Spiegel der französischen und bayerischen Gesandtschaftsberichte 1853–1857)." Ph.D. thesis, Munich, 1966.

Rive: see under La Rive.

Robson, Maureen M. "Liberals and 'Vital Interests'. The Debate on International Arbitration, 1815–72." *Bulletin of the Institute of Historical Research* 32 (1959): 38–55.

Rohl, Eva-Renate. "Metternich und England. Studien zum Urteil des Staatskanzlers über eine konstitutionelle Monarchie." Ph.D. thesis, Vienna, 1968.

Russell, John. *The Later Correspondence of Lord John Russell 1840–1878*. Ed. G. P. Gooch. Vol. II. London, 1925.

Russland 1852–1871. Aus den Berichten der bayerischen Gesandtschaft in St. Petersburg. Ed. Barbara Jelavich. Veröffentlichungen des Ost-Europa-Institutes Munich 19. Wiesbaden, 1963.

Saab, Ann Pottinger. *The Origins of the Crimean Alliance*. Charlottesville, 1977.

Schelting, Alexander von. *Russland und Europa im russischen Geschichtsdenken*. Bern, 1948.

Schieder, Theodor. "Bismarck und Europa. Ein Beitrag zum Bismarck-Problem." In *Deutschland und Europa. Historische Studien zur Völker- und Staatenordnung des Abendlandes*. (Festschrift für Hans Rothfels), pp. 15–40. Düsseldorf, 1951.

Schneider, Jutta-Martina. "Christian Friedrich von Stockmar. Ein geistesgeschichtlicher Beitrag zum Liberalismus im 19. Jahrhundert." Ph.D. thesis, Erlangen/Nürnberg, 1968.

Schoeps, Hans-Joachim. *Der Weg ins deutsche Kaiserreich*. Berlin, 1970.

Schroeder, Paul W. "Austria and the Danubian Principalities, 1853–1856." *Central European History* 2 (1969): 216–36.

———. *Austria, Great Britain, and the Crimean War. The Destruction of the European Concert.* Ithaca, 1972.

Schüle, Ernst. *Russland und Frankreich vom Ausgang des Krimkrieges bis zum italienischen Krieg 1856–1859.* Osteuropäische Forschungen, N.F. 19. Cologne, 1935.

Senkevič, I. G. *Rossija i Kritskoe vosstanie 1866–1869 gg.* Moscow, 1970.

Sibert, Marcel. "Quelques aspects de l'organisation de la technique des conférences internationales." *Recueil des cours* 48 (1934): 387–458.

———. *Traité de droit international public. Le droit de la paix.* Vol. II. Paris, 1951.

Simpson, F. A. *Louis Napoleon and the Recovery of France.* 3rd ed. 1951. Reprint. London, 1965.

Sirtema de Grovestins, [Charles-Frédéric]. *Le Congrès de Vienne en 1814 et 1815, et le Congrès de Paris en 1856.* Paris, 1856.

Šneerson, Lev Michajlovič. *Franko-prusskaja vojna i Rossija. Iz istorii russko-prusskich i russko-francuzskich otnošenij v 1867–1871 gg.* Minsk, 1976.

Southgate, Donald. *'The Most English Minister. . . .' The Policies and Politics of Palmerston.* London, 1966.

Srbik, Heinrich Ritter von. *Deutsche Einheit. Idee und Wirklichkeit vom Heiligen Reich bis Königgrätz.* Vol. II. Munich, 1935.

Stein, Lorenz. *Österreich und der Frieden.* Vienna, 1856.

Straube, Harald, "Sachsens Rolle im Krimkrieg." Ph.D. thesis, Erlangen, 1952.

Strumilin, S. G. *Očerki ėkonomičeskoj istorii Rossii.* Moscow, 1960.

Tarle, Evgenij Viktorovič. *Krymskaja vojna.* Vol. II, 4th ed. Ed. N. M. Družinin. Sočinenija v dvenadcati tomach 9. Moscow, 1959.

Tatiščev, S. S. *Imperator Aleksandr II: Ego žizn' i carstvovanie.* Vol. I. St. Petersburg, 1911.

Taylor, A. J. P. *The Hapsburg Monarchy 1809–1918. A History of the Austrian Empire and Austria-Hungary.* London, 1948. Reprint. New York, 1965.

———. *The Struggle for Mastery in Europe 1848–1918.* Oxford History of Modern Europe. Oxford, 1954.

Temperley, Harold. "Austria, England, and the Ultimatum to Russia 16 Dec. 1855." In *Wirtschaft und Kultur. Festschrift zum 70. Geburtstag von Alfons Dopsch,* pp. 626–37. Baden, 1938.

———. "The Treaty of Paris of 1856 and its Execution." *Journal of Modern History* 4 (1932): 387–414; 523–43.

———, and Penson, Lillian M. *A Century of Diplomatic Blue Books 1814–1914.* Cambridge, 1938.

"Temps, Au, de la Guerre de Crimée. Correspondance inédite du Comte de Morny et de la Princesse de Lieven." Ed. Geneviève Gille. *Revue dex deux mondes* (January–February 1966): 328–45; 545–59.

Ter Meulen, Jacob. *Der Gedanke der internationalen Organisation in seiner Entwicklung.* Vol. II: 1789–1889. First Part: 1789–1870. The Hague, 1929. Reprint. 1968.

Thouvenel, L. *Pages de l'histoire du Second Empire. D'après les papiers de M. [Édouard Antoine] Thouvenel.* Paris, 1903.

———. *Trois années de la question d'Orient. 1856–1859. D'après les papiers inédits de*

M. [*Edouard Antoine*] *Thouvenel.* Paris, 1897.

Treitschke, Heinrich von. *Deutsche Geschichte im Neunzehnten Jahrhundert.* Part I: "Bis zum zweiten Pariser Frieden." New ed. Leipzig, 1927.

Unckel, Bernhard. *Österreich und der Krimkrieg. Studien zur Politik der Donaumonarchie in den Jahren 1852–1856.* Historische Studien 410. Lübeck, 1969.

Valsecchi, Franco. *Il Risorgimento e l'Europa. L'alleanza di Crimea.* Biblioteca storica . . . Studi e ricerche 6. Milan, 1948.

————. *L'unificazione italiana e la politica europea dalla guerra di Crimea alla guerra di Lombardia 1854–1859.* Documenti di storia e di pensiero politico. Milan, [1939].

————. "Das Zeitalter Napoleons III. und Bismarcks 1854–1878." In *Historia Mundi,* vol. X: "Das 19. und 20. Jahrhundert," pp. 53–92. Bern, 1961.

Van Alstyne, Richard W. "Anglo-American Relations, 1853–1857. British Statesmen on the Clayton-Bulwer Treaty and American Expansion." *American Historical Review* 42 (1936–37): 491–500.

Victoria. *The Letters of Queen Victoria. A Selection from Her Majesty's Correspondence between the Years 1837 and 1861.* . . . Ed. Arthur Christopher Benson and Viscount Esher. Vol. III: 1854–1861. London, 1908.

Vinogradov, V. N. *Rossija i ob-edinenie Rumynskich knjažestv.* Moscow, 1961.

[Walewski, Alexandre-Florian-Joseph Colonna, Count]. "Les Papiers inédits du Comte Walewski. Souvenirs et correspondance (1855–1868)." Part IV. Ed. G. Raindre. *Revue de France* 5, 1 (1925): 485–510.

Wellesley, Henry Richard Charles. *The Paris Embassy during the Second Empire. Selections from the Papers of Henry Richard Charles Wellesley 1st Earl Cowley, Ambassador at Paris 1852–1867.* Ed. F. A. Wellesley. London, 1928.

Wörterbuch des Völkerrechts. Ed. Karl Strupp. 2nd ed., rev. and enlarged, by Hans-Jürgen Schlochauer. Vol. I. Berlin, 1960.

Zablockij-Desjatovskij, A. P. *Graf P. D. Kiselev i ego vremja. Materialy dlja istorii imperatorov Aleksandra I, Nikolaja I i Aleksandra II.* Vol. III. St. Petersburg, 1882.

Zajončkovskij, A. M. *Vostočnaja vojna 1853–1856 gg. v svjazi s sovremennoj ej političeskoj obstanovkoj.* Vol. II: "Priloženija." St. Petersburg, 1912.

Zajončkovskij, P. A. *Voennye reformy 1860–1870 godov v Rossii.* [Moscow], 1952.

Zechlin, Egmont. "Friedensbestrebungen und Revolutionierungsversuche." In *Aus Politik und Zeitgeschichte. Beilage zur Wochenzeitung "Das Parlament."* Vol. 20/61 (17 May 1961) pp. 269–88; vol. 24/61 (14 June 1961) pp. 326–37; vol. 25/61 (21 June 1961) pp. 341–67; vol. 20/63 (15 May 1963) pp. 3–54; vol. 22/63 (29 May 1963) pp. 3–47.

Index